The Forgotten Scrolls

The Real Book of Enoch

Rev. Mother Mary Kateryn H.P., D.D.

The Forgotten Scrolls: The Real Book of Enoch

Rev. Mother Mary Kateryn H.P., D.D.

First Printing 2025

Author Contact:

Rev. Mother Mary Kateryn H.P., D.D.
The Order of Sen-Taur
P O Box 1041
Eldorado, TX 76936

www.sen-taur.com

ISBN: 979-8-9913960-5-9

This book is dedicated to all the seekers of

Sophia —Wisdom—

who come after me,

unafraid to step beyond the mainstream,

to think deeper,

to question boldly,

and to uncover the truths long buried in the

forgotten scrolls.

TABLE OF CONTENTS

PREFACE

The Book of Enoch has been buried, dismissed, rediscovered, and debated for centuries. It confronts modern assumptions about early Jewish cosmology, celestial hierarchies, and prophetic tradition. Long excluded from religious canons, its influence still echoes. It shaped early Christian doctrine, esoteric systems, and modern interpretations of ancient knowledge.

This is not a reprint. It is a fully reconstructed and deliberately defiant translation. Prioritizing the Aramaic and Greek from the Dead Sea Scrolls where available, then the Ethiopic Ge'ez, Latin, and finally Lazarus Goldschmidt's 1892 Hebrew edition when nothing earlier survives, this edition restores the oldest voices possible.

Each verse has been rigorously compared across sources to preserve both its clarity and its depth. While past translations, including the work of R. H. Charles, have shaped mainstream understanding, this version breaks from tradition. It is independent, unfiltered, and faithful to the original manuscripts, not to later theology.

Every verse is written in modern English for directness and precision. Instead of traditional footnotes, appendices hold the deeper commentary. The formatting itself reveals manuscript differences, linguistic clarity, and historical context without diluting the reader's experience.

For too long, The Book of Enoch has been treated as a marginal curiosity. This edition challenges that view. It restores Enoch's place as a foundational source, not just for theology, but for ancient astronomy, metaphysics, and even theories of lost civilizations. Whether approached as sacred scripture, suppressed history, or something stranger, this is a text that refuses to be forgotten.

INTRODUCTION

The Book of Enoch is a mysterious and powerful text—filled with visions of celestial beings, divine justice, and revelations of the end of days. Attributed to Enoch, great-grandfather of Noah, it was excluded from most biblical canons, yet survived in the Ethiopian Orthodox tradition. Its rediscovery among the Dead Sea Scrolls confirmed its ancient origin and enduring significance.

This edition is not a reprint. It is a new and fully reconstructed translation, based on direct comparison of the surviving Aramaic from the Dead Sea Scrolls, the oldest available Greek, Ge'ez, and Latin manuscripts, in that exact order of priority.

While past translations shaped modern interpretations of the text, many introduced distortions, whether through theological smoothing or assumptions about missing content. This edition has been independently reviewed and revised for clarity, accuracy, and authenticity. Every verse has been preserved with care, maintaining the depth of the original while making it readable for a modern audience.

Appendix entries offer insight into manuscript variations, historical context, and translation choices, while avoiding unnecessary complexity. Where helpful, they also connect key historical references and texts that support or parallel the themes of The Book of Enoch, grounding it in a broader ancient tradition. This edition is designed to be accessible while staying faithful to the raw, ancient voice it carries.

The Book of Enoch is not a Christian text. It predates the Christian canon entirely. It stands as a work with deep roots in Jewish mysticism, cosmic justice, and prophetic legacy. More than a relic, it remains a vital piece of spiritual literature.

Although the Ge'ez version is the only "complete" surviving manuscript, it is not the earliest form of the text. The Dead Sea Scrolls Aramaic dates from 150–300 BCE and points to an even older oral tradition. Greek fragments of 1 *Enoch*, including those from Oxyrhynchus (~200 CE), Gizeh (~300 CE), and Syncellus (~800 CE), predate the Ge'ez (~1400 CE) by centuries.

While only portions survive in Aramaic, the existing fragments are indisputable evidence of pre-Christian Jewish literature. Their widespread dissemination across time and culture confirms the significance of the text. The Greek preserves an older, less theologically redacted form, while the Ge'ez shows signs of later editing. This translation evaluates these textual differences carefully to restore the most authentic reading possible.

- Chapters 19, 20, 21 – Gizeh 2
- Up to Chapter 72 – Gizeh 1 (Codex Panopolitanus)
- Chapter 72 - 108 Lazarus Goldschmidt's 1892 Hebrew Edition
- Chapter 77 – POxy 2069, Gizeh 1
- Chapters 85, 86, 87 – POxy 2069
- Chapter 89 – Vaticanus 1809 (V1809) V42-49
- Chapter 97 – Syncellus (Byzantine Chronicle)
- Chapters 97–107 – CB 185 (Codex Bodleianus 185)
- Chapter 99, 106 – Latin (BL), CB185
- Chapter 103 – 7QEnoch (DSS), CB185

This translation preserves each verse without additions, omissions, or bias. Appendix summaries of each chapter provide modern insight while maintaining historical accuracy. **Bold italics** mark Aramaic DSS. **Bold** marks Greek and Ge'ez comparisons, and Greek alone, while Ge'ez alone remains unbolded. Goldschmidt's 1892 Hebrew is in *unbolded italics*. **Bold italics** are also used for Hebrew-Greek comparisons. (Parentheses) mark minor additions, and greyed text indicates author reconstructions. [Brackets] indicate scribal interpolations.

CHAPTER 1

¹ Enoch to the chosen ones...

² ... his parables, and he said ... and from the words of the Watchers and the holy ones, all of them ... to this generation and to a distant generation, I speak ...

³ ... the Holy One shall go forth, the Great One from ...

⁴ ... the Great One shall appear in power, in His strength ...

⁵ ... the ends of the earth shall tremble, and all the ends ...

⁶ ... and they ...

⁷ And the earth shall be split apart with a great rupture, and all that is upon the earth shall perish, and judgment shall come upon all.

⁸ Peace will be made with the righteous, and the chosen will be protected. Mercy will rest upon them, and they will all belong to 'äməlak. They will prosper and be blessed, and guidance will be given to them. The light of 'äməlak will shine upon them, and peace will be established with them.

⁹ Behold! A multitude of q'doshim comes to execute judgment upon all, to destroy the ungodly, and to convict all flesh for their ungodly deeds and the harsh words that sinners have spoken against the Divine.

CHAPTER 2

¹ And you ... consider your flesh ...

² Look at the earth and consider its works ... and all that is seen ...

³ Therefore, look at the signs ... and in the signs of the sky ... the clouds pour rain.

CHAPTER 3

¹ Look at all the trees ... how they wither ... and yet they remain ... until two or three years pass.

CHAPTER 4

¹ Look, therefore, at the signs ... the heat and the frost ... and they provide shade and shelter ... and to walk upon the dust ... and upon their hands you will not forget ...

CHAPTER 5

¹ ... all the trees ... among them are green and covered ... to glory and praise ... and consider all works ... He is forever ... all these works ...

² The years ... and all of them act in defiance.

³ And observe how the seas and rivers, together, fulfill their tasks.

⁴ But you—your years shall pass, and your deeds ... yet you will transgress against it, mighty and harsh, on the day of your death ... and their hearts will not be at peace because of this.

⁵ Then your days will be cursed ... and the years of your destruction shall be many in curses ... and mercy ...

⁶ ... your names shall be ... forever for all ... and to all ...

⁷ And for the righteous shall be light, joy, and peace, And faith they shall inherit, the land. And for you all, the cursed ones, will be given damnation.

⁸ And mercy shall be given to them, to the righteous, wisdom. And all of them, these ones, shall live. And they shall not sin by wickedness, nor by injustice, nor by arrogance. Forever, they shall walk because of them, wisdom.

⁹ They shall not sin at all. And they shall not be harmed. All the work of their life, and they shall not die in anger nor in wrath, forever. But they shall complete the work of their life in fulfillment. And they shall rejoice in their life in peace. And their years of joy shall be increased in gladness and in peace forever, into all the work of their life.

CHAPTER 6

¹ And it came to be, when they multiplied, the children of men, in those days, an event took place. Children were born to them, beautiful and lovely ones.

² And they saw, and behold, mal'əkt the children of heaven, and they lusted after them. And they said to one another: 'Come, let us choose for ourselves wives from the daughters of men, and let us bear for ourselves offspring.

³ And he said to them, Samyāzā, who was their leader, 'their messengers, I fear that perhaps you will lack courage to accomplish this deed. But if not, I alone will pay the price for this great sin.'

⁴ And they said to him, all of them... [...]... let us all swear an oath together and bind ourselves by a curse.'

⁵ All of them, together, and they bound [...] by a curse...

⁶ In the days of [...], they descended upon [...]. And they bound themselves there with a curse.

⁷ Semjaza, Ramṭa'el, Kokabel, Ramiel, Daniel, Baraqiel, Asael, Matariel, Ananel, Shamsiel, Sahariel, Turiel, Yamiel.

⁸ These were the chiefs and the great ones, the ten... [...]..

CHAPTER 7

¹ They were the chiefs, and the great ones. The ten [...] women from all whom they chose, and they taught them sorcery, and [...]

² And they became pregnant from them, and they bore... [...]. And they were born upon the earth... [...]

³ The labor of all the sons of men, and to... [...]. And they were eating... [...].

⁴ They conspired to kill men, and... [...].

⁵ Against all the winged ones and the creatures of the earth... [...], and the ones of the sea... [...]. And to consume their flesh... [...].

⁶ Then something happened to the earth... [...].

CHAPTER 8

¹ Azazel taught people how to make swords, shields, and weapons of iron. He revealed the working of metals, gold, and silver, how to craft ornaments and bracelets, and the use of antimony for the eyes.

² And they were reckless... [...].

³ Semjaza, the leader, spells, magic, divinations, and enchantments. Divination, stars, and Zikiel... [...]. Shamsiel, the leader, divination, and the sun... [...]. To reveal mysteries to their women.

⁴ And in response to the deeds... from the earth... it rose up before... [...].

CHAPTER 9

¹ And then, looking down, Michael, and Uriel, and Raphael, and Gabriel, these from heaven, they saw much blood being poured out upon the earth.

² And they spoke among themselves, a loud voice upon the earth, up to the gates of heaven.

³ They make an appeal, the souls of men, saying, 'Bring forth our justice,' to the highest.

⁴ And they said to the Kyriō, 'You are Lord of Lords, and God of Gods, and King of the Ages. The throne of your glory into all generations of the age.

⁵ You have made all things, and all power is with You. All wisdom and might are before You. And You see all things, and nothing is hidden or concealed from You.

⁶ You see, what he has done? Azazel, how he taught all lawlessness upon the earth? And he revealed the mysteries of the age, which are practiced in the heavens, and he taught the sons of men.

⁷ And Semjaza, to whom You have given the authority to lead, who was with him, together with his companions.

⁸ And they went to the children of men, their allies, and they made them swear with them, with their wives, the women, and they defiled, and they revealed, to them, those who sinned.

⁹ The women gave birth to Titans, and they increased, and all the earth was filled with blood and injustice.

¹⁰ And now, behold, they cry out, the souls of those who have died, and they plead up to the gates of heaven. And their wailing ascended, and it could not be stopped, and it went forth before the face of the lawlessness that was being done upon the earth.

¹¹ And you, you know all which has been done and which exists, and you know what is to come upon them. And there is nothing that has been told to us, or how long the judgment shall be passed upon them because of these things.

CHAPTER 10

¹ And then, the Exalted, the Great, and the Holy One spoke, and He sent Uriel (*the Light of God upon the Earth*) to the son of Lamech, and He said to him.

² He said in the name of The Most High, 'Go to your leader and tell him his fate. The end is not yet, for it will be destroyed, the earth, completely. Hide yourself. And the waters, they shall not come upon it forever. The earth, entirely, and it shall be destroyed because of him. The destruction.'

³ And then, He instructed him so that he may escape, and his offspring shall remain for all generations of the age(s).

⁴ And 'əgzī said to Raphael, 'Bind Azazel by his hands and his feet and throw him into the darkness. Open the wilderness in Dudael and cast him there.

⁵ And place upon him rough and jagged stones, and cover him with darkness. Let him dwell there for the age, and cover his face so that he does not see the light.

13

⁶ And on the great day, when the appointed time has come, he will be cast into the fire.

⁷ And heal the earth that the mala'əkt have corrupted, and let the life of the earth be restored, so that it may be healed. And do not let all the children of men perish because of the secrets that the egrēgoroi have revealed and taught to their offspring.

⁸ And all the earth was devastated by the teachings and works of Azazel, and upon him was written all sin.

⁹ And the Most High said to Gabriel, 'Proceed against the rebellious ones and the corrupters, and against the offspring of fornication. Destroy the offspring of fornication and the offspring of the mighty ones from among men. Remove them and cast them out among themselves, so that through slaughter they may perish. Because Noah may be preserved alone.

¹⁰ And all of them will beg you, but it shall not be. For their fathers, because of them, because they shall perish from eternal life. And so they shall live, one by one, their five hundred years.

¹¹ And the Most High said to Michael, 'Proceed and declare to Semjaza, and to all those with him, those who joined with women, so that they may be defiled with them, with all impurity that is among them.'

¹² Therefore, all their offspring will fight, and they shall see their destruction. For their beloved ones, bind them for humanity, for generations, under the depths of the earth. Until the day of their judgment and their end. Until the judgment of eternity is fulfilled, for the age.

¹³ And at that time, they shall be taken away into the abyss of fire, into torment, and into the house of correction. They shall be bound for eternity, the age.

¹⁴ And then, he shall be burned up and destroyed. From that time onward, with them, bound together, they shall be imprisoned until the completion of the generation of generations.

[15] Destroy them, all of them, the spirits of corruption and their offspring, the mighty ones. For they have wronged mankind.

[16] Destroy all injustice from the face of the earth, and let every evil work perish. Let the seed of righteousness and truth be revealed and firmly established for the ages. With joy, they shall take root and flourish as a blessing for the world.

[17] And then, all the righteous shall flourish and live until they give birth to thousands. And all the days of their youth and their sabbaths shall be fulfilled in peace.

[18] And in those days, he shall be preserved. All the earth shall be renewed in righteousness, and its inhabitants shall be planted. Trees shall be filled with blessings.

[19] And all trees and fruit shall be planted in their place. And vines and wine that were not planted shall produce fruit in abundance. And all seed that was not sown in its place shall yield one measure a thousandfold, and one measure of olive oil shall produce ten measures of oil.

[20] And you shall purify the earth from all uncleanness, from all injustice, from all sin, and from all impiety. And all uncleanness that has arisen upon the earth, let it be wiped away.

[21] And they shall become, all the children of men, righteous. And all of them, nations, shall obey, and they shall be blessed. And they shall multiply, and all of them, on the earth, shall worship.

[22] And the earth shall be cleansed from all deception, and from all sin, and from all punishment, and from all torment. And it shall not return as they have done, in their place. No, not for the generation of generations, and until, forever.

CHAPTER 11

[1] And in those days, it shall be revealed, I shall open the treasuries of blessings which are in the heavens, so that they shall descend upon the earth, upon their deeds, and upon their toil, for the children of men.

² And then, truth and peace shall dwell together in all the days of the world, and in all generations of the world.

CHAPTER 12

¹ And before all events, Enoch was hidden, and there was no one who was instructed from the children of men. In the presence, he was hidden, and given this. And from that, he was.

² And all his work with the holy ones and with the mighty ones, in the days of those.

³ And I, Enoch, was blessed to the Most High, Mighty, and to the King of the ages. And behold, the mighty ones caused me distress on the earth. To Enoch the scribe, and they spoke to me.

⁴ And I, Enoch, the scribe of righteousness, go forth and declare to the mighty ones of the heavens, who have left the exalted place, and with women they have defiled, and they have done as the children of men do. They have taken women for themselves, and have caused great deception upon the earth.

⁵ And there shall not be for them, upon the earth, peace nor forgiveness of sin.

⁶ Because they will witness the killing of their beloved ones and see the destruction of their sons. They shall mourn and beg, forever. And there shall not be for them mercy or peace.

CHAPTER 13

¹ And Enoch said to Azazel: Go! There shall be no peace for you. A great punishment has gone out upon you, and it shall bind you.

² And there will be no forbearance, mercy, pleading, or intercession for you, because of the violence you have taught, and because of all the deeds of defilement, oppression, and sin, which you have shown to the children of men.

³ Then I went and spoke to all of them, and they were all afraid, and fear and trembling seized them.

⁴ And they begged me to write down for them a remembrance, a plea for mercy and forgiveness, so that I might intercede for them before the Lord of the heavens.

⁵ Because they can no longer speak, nor lift their eyes to heaven, due to their shame for what they have sinned, and they have been condemned.

⁶ Then I wrote down the record of their plea and their supplications concerning their spirits and what they begged for, so that they might receive release and reprieve.

⁷ And having gone, I sat by the waters of Dan, in the land of Dan, which is on the right side of the west of Hermon. And I read aloud the record of their plea until I finished.

⁸ As I slept, behold, dreams came upon me, and visions fell upon me. And I saw visions of wrath, and a voice came saying: 'Speak to the sons of heaven and rebuke them.'

⁹ And having woken up, I went to them, and they were all gathered, sitting in mourning at Ebelsata, which is between Lebanon and Senisel, covering their faces.

¹⁰ Before them, I declared all the visions I had seen in my dreams, and I began to speak the words of righteousness, rebuking the Watchers of heaven.

CHAPTER 14

¹ The book of the words of righteousness and the rebuke of the Watchers, those who have existed from eternity, according to the command of the Holy and Great One, in this vision.

² I saw in my dreams what I now speak, in a tongue of flesh, by the spirit of my mouth, what the Great One has given to men, so that they may speak through it and understand in their hearts.

³ The One who created and gave authority to rebuke the Watchers, the sons of heaven.

⁴ I wrote down your petition, and in my vision, this was revealed: Your petition has not been accepted, and judgment is upon you.

⁵ So that you may never again ascend into heaven for all eternity, and it has been decreed that you shall be bound in the bonds of the earth for all the generations of eternity.

⁶ So that you will see the destruction of your beloved sons, and you will gain nothing from them. But they shall fall before you by the sword.

⁷ Your petition concerning them shall not be, nor concerning you. You will weep and beg, but you will not speak nor hear a word from the writing I have recorded.

⁸ And in my vision, this was shown to me: Behold, clouds were calling, and mists were speaking to me. The stars and flashes of lightning urged me, and the winds lifted me up into heaven.

⁹ And I entered until I approached a wall of a structure built with hailstones and surrounded by tongues of fire. And they began to frighten me.

¹⁰ And they lifted me up and brought me into heaven.

¹¹ And the roofs were like the movement of stars and lightning, and between them were fiery cherubim. And their heaven was water.

¹² And fire was blazing around the walls, and the doors were burning with fire.

¹³ I entered into that house, and it was hot as fire and cold as snow. No nourishment of life was in it. Fear covered me, and trembling took hold of me.

¹⁴ And I was shaking and trembling, and I fell on my face. And I was observing in my vision.

¹⁵ And behold, another door was opened before me, and the house was larger than the first, entirely built with tongues of fire.

¹⁶ And all of it was surpassing in glory, honor, and greatness, so that I was unable to describe it to you concerning its glory and its majesty.

17 And its ground was fire, but its upper part was lightning and the movements of stars. And its roof was blazing fire.

18 And I was observing, and I saw a high throne inside it, and its appearance was like crystal. And its wheel was like the shining sun, and a mountain of Cherubim.

19 And beneath the throne, great rivers of blazing fire were flowing out, and I was not able to see.

20 And the great glory was enthroned upon it, and its covering was like the appearance of the sun, brighter and whiter than all snow.

21 And no angel was able to enter this house or see His face because of the honor and the glory, and no flesh was able to see Him.

22 Blazing fire surrounded it, and a great fire stood before it, and no one could approach. Around it stood myriads upon myriads before Him, and every word of His was action.

23 And the holy ones among the angels who draw near to Him do not depart by night, nor do they ever leave Him.

24 And I remained there, fallen upon my face and trembling. And the Lord called me with His mouth and said to me, 'Come here, Enoch, and listen to my word.

25 And one of the holy ones approached me, raised me up, made me stand, and brought me to the entrance. But I lowered my face downward.

CHAPTER 15

1 And He answered and said to me, 'The true man, the man of truth, the scribe. And I heard His voice: Do not be afraid, Enoch, true man and scribe of truth. Come here and listen to my voice.

2 Go and say to those who sent you: 'You should have asked about mankind, not for mankind to ask about you.

3 Why did you abandon the high and holy heaven of eternity, and sleep with the women, and defile yourselves with the daughters of men, and take wives for yourselves? Like the sons of the earth, you acted and begot children, Tall Ones.

4 And you were holy and eternal living spirits, but you defiled yourselves in the blood of women, and you begot in the blood of flesh, and you desired in the blood of men. Just as they make flesh and blood, so too do they die and are destroyed.

5 For this reason, I gave them females so that they may sow seed in them and bear children through them, so that no work may cease upon the earth.

6 But you were living beings, not dying, for all generations of the ages.

7 Because of this, I did not make females for you. The spirits of the heavens, their dwelling is in the heavens.

8 And now, the giants who were born from spirits and flesh shall be called mighty spirits upon the earth, and their dwelling shall be within the earth.

9 Evil spirits came forth from their bodies, because they were born from above and from the holy Watchers. This was the beginning of their creation and the foundation of their origin. They shall be called evil spirits, and their dwelling shall be upon the earth.

10 The spirits of heaven, their dwelling shall be in the heavens. And the spirits of the earth, those who were born on the earth, their dwelling shall be upon the earth.

11 The spirits of the giants oppress like storm clouds, bringing destruction, falling upon the earth, fighting, and scattering violently. They are cruel spirits, making their paths but consuming nothing. They hunger and thirst, yet they are never satisfied, and they cannot rest.

12 And these spirits shall rise up against the sons of men and against the women, because they have come forth from them.

CHAPTER 16

¹ From the day of slaughter, destruction, and death, their spirits shall proceed from the soul of their flesh, causing destruction without judgment. Thus, they shall bring ruin until the appointed day of completion, the great judgment, when the great age shall be fulfilled.

² And now, to the Watchers who sent you, ask concerning them, those who were once in heaven.

³ You were in heaven, and every mystery that was not revealed to you—yet you came to know the mystery that was from God. And you made this known to the women in your stubborn hearts. And through this mystery, the women multiplied, and mankind increased in evil upon the earth.

⁴ I said to them: There is no peace.

CHAPTER 17

¹ And they took me to a certain place, where those who were there became like blazing fire. And when they wished, they appeared as men.

² And they led me into a dark place and to a mountain whose summit reached into heaven.

³ And I saw the place of the luminaries and the storehouses of the stars and of the thunder, and into the deep places of the air, where there was a bow of fire, and arrows, and their quivers, and all the lightning bolts.

⁴ And they led me to the waters and to the place where fire sets, which provides all the settings of the sun.

⁵ And we came to a river of fire, where fire flows like water, and it empties into the great sea of sunset.

⁶ And I saw the great rivers, and I arrived at the great river and the great darkness, and I departed to where all flesh moves.

[7] And I saw the storm winds of the darkness, the winter ones, and the outpouring of the abyss of all waters.

[8] I saw the mouth of the earth of all the rivers, and the mouth of the abyss.

CHAPTER 18

[1] And I saw the storehouses of all the winds, and I saw that in them he arranged all creation and the foundation of the earth. And I saw the cornerstone of the earth.

[2] And I saw the four winds supporting the earth and the firmament of heaven.

[3] And I saw the firmament of heaven, and they stand between earth and heaven.

[4] And I saw the winds of heaven turning and guiding the course of the sun and all the stars.

[5] And I saw the winds upon the earth carrying the clouds. And I saw the ends of the earth and the foundation of heaven above.

[6] And I passed by a place burning night and day, where seven mountains of precious stones stood, three toward the east and three toward the south.

[7] And those toward the east were of colored stone, and one was of pearl stone, and one was of carved stone. And those toward the south were of red stone.

[8] And the middle of them reached into the heavens, like the throne of God, made of phouka stone, and the top of the throne was of sapphire.

[9] And I saw a fire that does not cease, beyond these mountains.

[10] It is a place at the end of the great earth. There the heavens shall be completed.

[11] And I saw a great chasm into which columns of fire descended, and there was no measure, neither in height nor in depth.

¹² And beyond this chasm, I saw a place where there was no firmament of heaven above, nor was the earth established below, nor was there water beneath it, nor any bird. It was a desolate and terrifying place.

¹³ There I saw seven stars, like great burning mountains, that do not move. And when I inquired about them, they did not answer me.

¹⁴ The messenger said, 'This is the place at the end of heaven and earth. It has become a prison for the stars and the forces of heaven.'

¹⁵ And the stars that roll in the fire, these are the ones who transgressed the command at the beginning of their rising. A place outside heaven is empty, for they did not appear at their appointed times.

¹⁶ And he was enraged with them and bound them until the time of the completion of their sins, for thousands of years.

CHAPTER 19

¹ And Uriel said to me, 'Here the angels who mingled with women will stand, and their spirits, becoming diverse, will corrupt humans and lead them astray, urging them toward demons until the great judgment, in which they will be judged for destruction.'

² And their wives of the transgressing angels shall become sirens.

³ And I, Enoch, alone saw the visions, the ends of all things. And no one among men has seen as I have seen.

CHAPTER 20

¹ These are the names of the holy messengers who stand guard.

² Uriel, one of the holy messengers, who is over the world and Tartarus.

³ Raphael, one of the holy messengers, who is over the spirits of men.

⁴ Raguel, one of the holy messengers, who exacts vengeance upon the world and the luminaries.

⁵ Michael, one of the holy messengers, who is appointed over the good things of the people and over the chaos.

⁶ Sariel, one of the holy messengers, who is over the spirits who sin against the spirit.

⁷ Gabriel, one of the holy messengers, who is over Paradise, the dragons, and the Cherubim. Remeiel, one of the holy messengers, whom God appointed over those who rise again. And the names of the seven archangels are these.

CHAPTER 21

¹ And I journeyed until the unformed place, where nothing was made.

² And there I saw a terrifying sight: I saw neither a heaven above nor a firmly established earth, but a formless and dreadful place.

³ And there I saw seven of the stars of heaven, bound and cast into it, like great mountains, and burning in fire.

⁴ Then I said, 'For what reason were they bound, and why were they cast down here?

⁵ Then Uriel, one of the holy messengers who was with me, and he was their leader, said to me, 'Enoch, about what do you ask, or for what do you seek the truth?'

⁶ These are of the stars of heaven who transgressed the command of the Lord, and they were bound here until they fulfill ten thousand years, the time of their sins.

⁷ And from there, I traveled to another place, more terrifying than this, and I saw even more dreadful works: a great fire there, burning and blazing. The place had a chasm reaching the abyss, filled completely with massive pillars of fire descending. Neither measure nor breadth was I able to see, nor could I estimate it.

⁸ Then I said, 'How terrifying is this place, and how dreadful in appearance.

⁹ Then one of the holy messengers who was with me answered and said to me, 'Enoch, why are you afraid? Why are you so terrified?' And I answered, 'Because of this terrifying place and its dreadful appearance.'

¹⁰ And he said, 'This place is the prison of the messengers; here they shall be confined until eternity, forever.'

CHAPTER 22

¹ And from there, I traveled to another place, and he showed me a great and high mountain toward the west, made of solid rock.

² And four hollow places were in it, deep and very smooth. Three of them were dark, and one was bright, and a spring of water was in the middle of it. And I said, 'How smooth are these hollows, and how deep and dark in appearance?'

³ Then Raphael, one of the holy messengers who was with me, answered and said to me, 'These hollow places exist so that the spirits of the souls of the dead may be gathered into them. For this purpose, they were judged, so that all the souls of men may be gathered here.'

⁴ And these places were made to gather them until the day of their judgment, and until the appointed and determined time when the great judgment shall take place among them.

⁵ And I saw the spirits of the dead pleading, and their voices went up to heaven and made supplication.

⁶ And I asked Raphael, the messenger who was with me, and said to him, 'This spirit that is pleading, who does it belong to, and why does its voice go forth like this and plead until heaven?'

⁷ And he answered me, saying, 'This is the spirit that came out from Abel, whom Cain, his brother, killed. And Abel pleads concerning him until his offspring is destroyed from the face of the earth, and from the seed of men his lineage shall perish.

⁸ Then I asked about all the enclosures, 'Why were they separated, one from another?

⁹ And he answered me, saying, 'These three were made to separate the spirits of the dead, and thus the spirits of the righteous were set apart, where the bright spring of water is above it.'

¹⁰ And thus, it was created for sinners, when they die and are buried in the earth, and judgment was not executed upon them in their lifetime.

¹¹ Here their spirits are separated into this great torment until the great day of judgment, of scourging and afflictions of the accursed, until eternity. There was retribution for their spirits, and there they will be bound until eternity.

¹² And thus, it was separated for the spirits of those who plead, who make known about their destruction when they are killed in the days of the sinners.

¹³ Thus, it was created for the spirits of men who were not righteous but sinners, and they will be companions of the lawless. But as for their spirits, those who suffer here are punished less than they, yet they will not be judged on the day of judgment, nor shall they ever rise from here.

¹⁴ Then I blessed the Lord of Glory and said, 'Blessed are you, Kyriō, the One of Righteousness, ruling over eternity.

CHAPTER 23

¹ And from there, I traveled to another place, towards the west, until I reached the ends of the earth.

² And I saw a fire that never stopped, nor did it cease. It did not rest, nor did it stray from its course, but remained day and night together, continuing without end.

³ And I asked, saying: What is this thing that has no rest?

⁴ Then Raguel, one of the holy messengers who was with me, answered and said to me: This is the course of the fire that moves westward, the fire that drives all the luminaries of the heavens.

CHAPTER 24

¹ And he showed me mountains of fire, burning at night.

² And beyond them, I went and saw seven glorious mountains, each different from the other, whose stones were precious and beautiful. All were magnificent and splendid. Three were set toward the east upon one, and three toward the south upon one, with deep and rugged valleys, each not approaching the other.

³ And the seventh mountain was in their midst, towering above them in height. It resembled a throne-seat, and beautiful trees surrounded it.

⁴ And among them was a tree, whose fragrance I had never smelled before, nor had anyone else delighted in it, nor was anything like it. Its scent was sweeter than all perfumes, and its leaves, blossoms, and the tree itself never wither forever. Its fruit clustered like date palms.

⁵ Then I said: 'How beautiful and fragrant this tree is! Its leaves are lovely, and its blossoms are beautiful to behold.'

⁶ Then Michael, one of the holy and great messengers who was with me, answered me. He was their leader.

CHAPTER 25

¹ And he said to me: 'Enoch, why do you ask and why do you marvel at the fragrance of this tree? And why do you desire to learn the truth?'

² Then I answered him: 'I want to know about everything, but especially about this tree.'

3 And he answered me, saying: 'This high mountain, whose peak is like the throne of God, is the seat where the Great Lord, the Holy One of Glory, the King of the Age(s), sits whenever he descends to visit the earth for good.'

4 And this fragrant tree is beautiful, and no flesh has the authority to touch it until the Great Judgment, in which all will be avenged and completed until the age(s). Then it shall be given to the righteous and the holy.

5 Its fruit shall be given to the chosen for life, and it shall be transplanted to the north, to a holy place beside the house of God, the King of the Age(s).

6 Then they shall rejoice and be glad, and they shall enter into the holy place. Its fragrance shall be in their bones, and they shall live longer on the earth than their fathers lived. In their days, sorrow, illness, afflictions, and scourges shall not touch them.

7 Then I blessed the God of Glory, the King of the Age(s), who prepared such things for mankind, for the righteous. He created them and said to give them to them.

CHAPTER 26

1 And from there, I journeyed to the middle of the earth, and I saw a blessed place that was separated, but the tree there had withered and no longer grew.

2 And there I saw a holy mountain. Beneath the mountain, water flowed from the east, and its direction was toward the south.

3 And I saw another mountain toward the east, higher than the first. In the middle of them was a deep, narrow valley, and through it, water flowed beneath the mountain.

4 And toward the west of this, I saw another mountain, lower than the previous one, and it had no height. Between them was a deep and dry valley, and another deep and dry valley lay at the peaks of the three mountains.

⁵ And all the valleys were deep, made of solid rock, and no tree was planted upon them.

⁶ And I marveled at the valley, and I greatly marveled.

CHAPTER 27

¹ And I said, 'Why is this land blessed and full of trees, but this valley in the middle of them is cursed?

² This land is cursed for the accursed ones until the age. Here, all those who spoke improper words against the Lord and His glory will be gathered. Here they will be gathered, and here will be their dwelling place.

³ At the end of the ages, in the days of true judgment before the righteous, for all time, the wicked shall bless the Lord of Glory, the King of the Age.

⁴ And in the days of their judgment, they will bless in mercy, as He has apportioned to them.

⁵ Then I blessed the Lord of Glory and declared His glory, and I praised magnificently as is fitting for the Great One.

CHAPTER 28

¹ And from there, I went into the middle of Mandobara, and I saw it desolate and completely abandoned.

² And it was full of trees, growing from its own seeds, with water coming from above, not from rain.

³ Like an abundant water channel, bringing water and dew from all sides, flowing toward the north and west.

CHAPTER 29

¹ And again, I went to another place, in Babdera, and I traveled east toward this mountain.

² And there I saw trees of judgment, spreading fine aromas of frankincense and myrrh. Their trees were like nut trees.

CHAPTER 30

¹ And beyond these, I traveled far toward the east and saw another great place, a valley of water, unknown.

² And I saw trees with fragrant bark, like the mastic tree.

³ And along the edges of these valleys, I saw fragrant cinnamon. And beyond these, I traveled toward the east.

CHAPTER 31

¹ And I saw other mountains, and in them, groves of trees. Flowing from them was nectar, called Sarran, and galbanum.

² And beyond these mountains, I saw another mountain, far east at the ends of the earth. Its trees were full, like almond trees.

³ And when its fruit is crushed, its scent surpasses all others.

CHAPTER 32

¹ And I looked to the north and east and saw seven mountains, full of spikenard, mastic trees, cinnamon, and pepper trees.

² And from there, I traveled to the tops of all these mountains, far toward the east. I passed over the Red Sea and went upon the heights. From there, I passed over the angel Zotiel.

³ And I came to the Paradise of Righteousness and saw from afar many trees, and two very large, beautiful, and magnificent ones. And the Tree of Wisdom, from which they eat and learn great wisdom.

⁴ And it was as tall as a fir tree, and its leaves were like those of a carob tree. Its fruit was like grape clusters of the vine, small and beautiful. Its fragrance spread far beyond the tree.

⁵ Then I said, 'How beautiful is the tree, and how pleasing to the sight!

⁶ Then Raphael, the holy angel who was with me, answered and said, 'This is the Tree of Wisdom, from which your father, the elder, ate. And he learned wisdom, his eyes were opened, and he knew he was naked. And he departed and was expelled from the garden.

CHAPTER 33

¹ And from there I went to the boundary of the earth, and I saw there great beasts that were different from all others, and birds whose appearances, sizes, and voices were different from all.

² And beyond them, for all the beasts, I saw the boundary of the earth, where the sky ended and stretched over the vast expanse.

³ And I saw how the stars of heaven emerge and are divided according to their paths, and they move accordingly. And I wrote down all their exits, their names, their ranks, their positions, their times, and their cycles, as the angel Uriel explained them to me.

⁴ And everything was shown to me on the tablet, and I wrote and arranged their names, which were recorded on the tablet, along with their commands and their deeds.

CHAPTER 34

¹ And from there I went west, to the boundary of the earth, and there I saw a great and mighty assembly, which surrounded the entire boundary of the earth.

² And there I saw the sky, with openings in the heavens, three from each direction, through which the winds emerge. From the direction of the west, they blow forth cold, hail, frost, heat, mist, and rain.

³ And from one cavern in the heavens, it will blow. And therefore, in all of them, they shall breathe. With power and great strength, it shall be established upon the earth. And with might, it will blow.

CHAPTER 35

¹ And from there, I went in the direction of 'Arab, to the edge of the earth. And I saw there three heavenly winds stretching forth, just as I had seen in the east, in their going out and in their arrival.

CHAPTER 36

¹ And from there, I journeyed south to the ends of the earth. And there I saw three heavenly winds, gentle ones, as they emerged from the south, along with mist, rain, and wind.

² And from there, I traveled north to the ends of the heavens. And there I saw three heavenly winds, gentle ones, moving toward the north. And above them were powerful winds.

³ From one direction, powerful winds pass through the stars of the heavens and disturb the west with force, whenever they appear.

⁴ [And therefore, I saw them bless, and at all times I blessed the Lord of glory, who has made great wonders. And we praised him, because he reveals his glorious works to his angels and the souls of men, so that they may praise his deeds. And all his works shall be seen, so that they may glorify his mighty power and bless his great work forever.]

CHAPTER 37

¹ A vision that was seen, another vision of wisdom that Enoch, son of Jared, son of Mahalalel, son of Cainan, son of Enos, son of Seth, son of Adam, saw.

² And this is the beginning of the words of wisdom that I raise up, that is spoken, and I will declare them to those who dwell on the earth. Listen to what came before, and behold what comes after, the holy words which I speak before the Lord of Spirits.

³ Those who came first have passed away in power, but those who come after shall not attain understanding of wisdom.

⁴ Until now, wisdom was not given to me from before the Lord of Spirits, that I might lift it up as I have inquired. As it was decreed by the Lord of Spirits, what was given to me was a portion of the life that is eternal.

⁵ And thus, there were three parables, and I lifted them up as I spoke to those who dwell upon the dry land.

CHAPTER 38

¹ The first parable: Thus shall arise the assembly of the righteous, and the sinners shall be forsaken because of their sins, and they shall be seen upon the dry land.

² [And thus, the Righteous One shall appear before them, for the righteous and the elect, whose deeds are weighed before the Lord of Spirits. And the light shall appear for the righteous and the elect who dwell upon the earth. Woe to the dwelling place of the sinners and woe to their resting place, to those who deny the Lord of Spirits, for they shall perish, and they shall not be born.]

³ And thus, the countenances of the righteous shall be covered, but the sinners shall be rejected, and the wicked shall be removed from before the presence of the righteous and the elect.

⁴ And from that time, the mighty and the exalted ones who possess the earth shall no longer exist, and they shall no longer behold the face of the holy ones. For before the Lord of Spirits, the light shall be revealed upon the countenance of the holy, the righteous, and the elect.

⁵ And the kings and the mighty shall perish in that time, and they shall be delivered into the hands of the righteous and the holy ones.

⁶ And from that time, there shall be no mercy that is shown before the Lord of Spirits, for they shall fall away from life.

CHAPTER 39

[1] And it shall come to pass in those days that the children of the elect and the holy ones shall descend from the heights of the heavens, and their offspring shall be with the children of men.

[2] During that time, Enoch was lifted up, and the books of zeal and wrath, and the books of confusion and weeping, were revealed. And mercy shall no longer exist for them, declared the Lord of Spirits.

[3] And during that time, the clouds carried me, and the wind lifted me up from the surface of the earth and set me within the firmament of the heavens.

[4] And there, I saw another vision: the dwelling place of the righteous and the resting places of the holy ones.

[5] And there, my eyes saw their dwelling place with the angels, and their resting places with the holy ones. And they supplicate, petition, and bless on behalf of the children of men, and righteousness flows before them like water. And mercy, like dew, is poured upon the earth, for this is their portion forever and ever.

[6] And during that time, my eyes saw the dwelling place of the elect ones of righteousness and faith. Righteousness shall remain in their time, and the righteous and the elect shall be innumerable before Him, forever and ever.

[7] And I saw their dwelling place beneath the wings of the Lord of Spirits. And all the righteous and the elect shone before Him like the light of fire. Their mouths were full of blessings, and their lips praised the name of the Lord of Spirits. And righteousness shall not fail before Him, nor shall uprightness cease.

[8] There, I longed to dwell, and my soul yearned for that dwelling place. For it was my portion, since it had been established for me before the Lord of Spirits.

⁹ And in that moment, I praised and exalted the name of the Lord of Spirits with blessings and praises. For He strengthened me with blessings and praise, according to the will of the Lord of Spirits.

¹⁰ And altogether, my eyes saw in that place, and they blessed and praised the One who is exalted and blessed. And may He be blessed from the beginning and forever.

¹¹ And before Him, there was no division. He is the Eternal One, who said, 'Let the world be created.' Since that time, the world has existed, and it shall continue for all generations.

¹² They will bless You, those who do not sleep, and they will stand before Your glory. [And they will bless, glorify, and exalt, saying: 'Holy, Holy, Holy is the Lord of Spirits!' The earth will be filled with spirits.]

¹³ And there I saw with my own eyes all those who do not sleep standing before Him. And they will bless and say: 'Blessed are You, and blessed is His Name, the Lord, forever and ever!'

¹⁴ And my face was transformed until I could not endure it, and I trembled.

CHAPTER 40

¹ And I saw, after that, an innumerable host, countless multitudes, thousands upon thousands, and ten-thousands beyond measure, without number or calculation, standing before the glory of the Lord of Spirits.

² And I saw at the four sides of the Lord of Spirits, four different faces. I saw them, but from those who stood there, their names I heard—names I had not known before. And an angel who came with me revealed all their strengths to me.

³ And I heard their voices as they spoke, the four faces who glorify before the Lord of Glory.

⁴ The first word blesses the Lord of Spirits forever and ever.

⁵ And I heard another voice that blesses the righteous and the chosen ones, those who humble themselves before the Lord of Spirits.

⁶ And I heard a third voice [interceding and praying on behalf of those who sleep in the grave].

⁷ [And I heard a fourth voice, and they drove out the accusers. They did not prevail but cried before the Lord of Spirits.]

⁸ And after this, the angels of peace who do not sleep were sent. He showed me all who stand, and they were those with four faces. I saw them, and I heard their words, and they recorded them.

⁹ And they said to me: The first, who is merciful and removes wrath, is the holy Michael. The second, who is over all disease and wounds of mankind, is Raphael. The third, who is over all power and might, is the holy Gabriel. And the fourth, who is over repentance and the hope of eternal life, is Phanuel.

¹⁰ And these four angels stand before the Lord Most High, and I heard four voices in that moment when they spoke.

CHAPTER 41

¹ And after this, I saw all their hidden things of the heavens and the kingdom, how it is divided and the deeds of men, according to their measures, are weighed.

² There, I saw the dwelling place of the righteous and the resting places of the holy ones. And I saw with my own eyes there all the sinners who are expelled, those who reject the name of the Lord of Spirits. They are given no rest, and there is no escape from torment if it comes forth from the Lord of Spirits.

³ And there I saw with my own eyes a gathering of lightning flashes and great thunderings, and a collection of storm-winds that were separating as they blew upon the earth. And there was a gathering of clouds and mist, and from that place they emerged and were scattered upon the earth.

⁴ And there I saw the storehouses of the winds, and from them, they are divided. And the storehouse of hail, and the storehouse of mist, and the storehouse of clouds. And the cloud that hovers above the earth, stationed since the beginning of the world.

⁵ And I saw the storehouses of the Sun and the Moon, from which they emerge and into which they return. And their paths are wondrous in splendor, honoring one above all. Their orbits are mighty, and they do not deviate from their course, nor do they rest or cease from their movement. They keep their appointed order in faithfulness, like all things, by the command of the One who established them.

⁶ And first, the Sun goes forth and carries out its path by the command of the Lord of Spirits, and its name is called forever and ever.

⁷ And after this, the path that they fulfill and the order that they maintain, the Moon and its orbit, its course is completed within that system, by day and by night. One is exalted and is observed before the Lord of Spirits, and they are strengthened and give praise. And they do not fail, because their order does not allow them to rest.

⁸ For the Sun is radiant and abundant, and it gives its position for blessing, for punishment, and for judgment. Its path is also for the Moon, bringing light to the righteous and darkness to the sinners, by the name of the Lord who created the center of light and the center of darkness. And He divided His spirit for mankind and strengthened His spirit for the righteous, by the name of the righteousness that is His.

⁹ For no messenger is able to speak, because all the rulers see, and all their exalted ones stand before him. He remains steadfast.

CHAPTER 42

¹ Wisdom found no place where it could dwell, so it returned to its dwelling in the heavens.

² And wisdom went forth to dwell among the children of men, but it found no dwelling place. So it returned and was enthroned in the midst of the angels.

³ And transgression went forth, and she went out from her scribes, those whom she did not permit to be found. And she returned to dwell in their habitation, like rain in drought, and like dew upon the earth, in silence.

CHAPTER 43

¹ And I saw another light, lightnings and the stars of heaven. And I saw how they are all called by their names, and they listen.

² And I saw how righteousness is measured by their light, and by the vastness of their places, and by the days of their existence and their motion. Lightning is born, and their paths are set by the cycles of the angels, and their order is guarded by their understanding.

³ And I asked the angel who was with me, the one who showed me, 'What are these?'

⁴ And he said to me, 'These are what the Lord of Spirits has shown you. These are their names for the righteous, those who keep the way and guard it, for the Lord of Spirits, for eternity.'

CHAPTER 44

¹ And I saw other things concerning lightning: how it stands apart from the stars, and whether the lightning ceases or continues, and how new flashes are born with it.

CHAPTER 45

¹ [And another parable concerning those who deny His name, the dwelling place of the holy ones, and the Lord of Spirits.]

² [The heavens will be shaken, and the earth will be removed, because a portion of the sinners, those who deny the name of the Lord of Spirits, will be afflicted on the day of judgment and distress.]

³ [On that day, the throne of glory will be established, [and the Chosen One will sit in judgment. He will judge their deeds, their thoughts, and their hidden things, and nothing will be concealed. Their spirits will be firm among them. Then they will see the Chosen One who was revealed, and those who denied my holy and praised name will be judged.]

⁴ [And on that day, I will dwell among them, for the Chosen One who was revealed. And it shall be exalted to the heavens, and it shall be made great for blessing and for the light of eternity.]

⁵ And it shall be exalted for the righteous, and it shall be strengthened for the blessing and for the chosen ones who were revealed. They will dwell in their midst. But those who commit sin and wickedness will not endure among them.

⁶ Because I have seen them, and I have testified to them in peace for the righteous. And I will bless them before me, and I have brought my judgment near for the sinners, because their end is from the face of the earth.

CHAPTER 46

¹ And there I saw an ancient one, and his head was like white wool, bright and pure. And with him was another, whose face had the appearance of a man, and his face was full of grace, like one of the holy angels.

² And I asked one of the holy angels who was with me and spoke with me, and I said to him concerning this being who appeared to me: 'Who is he, and from where does he come, this one who is with the Ancient One of Days?

³ And he answered me and said to me: 'This is the offspring of humanity who has become righteous, and righteousness is with him. And all the treasures of wisdom are with him, and he is known because the Lord has appointed him and hidden him. And he has given him power over the world, in the presence of the Lord of Spirits, for a set time.'

4 And this offspring of humanity, whom I saw, will remove the kings and the mighty ones from their thrones. He will cast down the strong ones from their positions, and he will loosen the control of the powerful. He will shake the sinners and overthrow the transgressors.

5 And the kings shall be driven from their thrones, and their kingdoms will be taken from them. For they will not be exalted, nor will they be honored, nor will they be recognized, because of their deeds. And the kingdom shall be given to another.

6 And the faces of the mighty ones shall be cast down, and they shall be filled with shame and humiliation. Disgrace shall be their dwelling place, and their seats shall be in dishonor. They shall not rise again from their fall, [for they did not exalt the name of the Lord of Spirits.]

7 And the faithful ones will shine like the stars of heaven, and they will walk in the ways of the Most High. But the wicked will be judged for their oppression, and they will perish in darkness. Their rebellious deeds will be revealed, and their strength, their very bodies, and their faith were given to false gods. For they denied the name of the Lord of Spirits.

8 And they shall be cast out from their dwellings and removed from their gatherings because of this. But the righteous and the chosen ones, who are in his name, shall remain before the Lord of Spirits.

CHAPTER 47

1 And in that time, the prayers of the righteous were lifted up, and the blood of the just rose from the earth before the Lord of Spirits.

2 And in that time, the holy ones who dwell in the heights of heaven will speak with one voice. They will pray, praise, and bless the name of the Lord of Spirits because of the blood of the righteous that has been shed, and the prayers of the just that have been lifted up before him. So that justice will be done for them, and vengeance will not be delayed forever.

³ And in that moment, I saw an ancient one seated on the throne of his glory, and the Books of the Living were opened before him. And all the power of the heavens and the multitudes stood before him.

⁴ And for the holy ones, joy shall be fulfilled, for righteousness has prevailed. The prayers of the righteous have been heard, and the blood of the just has been acknowledged before the Lord of Spirits.

CHAPTER 48

¹ And in that time, I saw righteousness was opened, and it did not cease. And many drank of it. Many. The wise ones, wisdom, and all the thirsty ones were satisfied from it. And wisdom was fulfilled. And their dwelling places with the righteous, and the holy ones, and the chosen ones.

² [And in that hour, she was named 'Purity.' The offspring of humanity before the Lord of Spirits. And his name before the Head of Days.]

³ [And before the sun was created, and the signs, and before the stars of the heavens were formed, his name was proclaimed before the Lord of Spirits.]

⁴ [This one shall be a staff for the righteous and the holy ones, because they have chosen it, and they shall be supported and not fall. This one is the light of the nations, and it shall be the hope for those who are troubled in their hearts.]

⁵ [And they shall bow and worship before him—all those who suffered from oppression. And they shall bless, and praise, and sing for him, for the name of the Lord of Spirits.]

⁶ [And because of this, he was chosen and given before him, from before the world was created, until forever.]

⁷ [And wisdom was established for the holy and righteous before the Lord of Spirits, because he preserved their portion for the righteous, because they prayed and endured in this world of transgression. And all their works and their suffering, they prayed before the Lord of Spirits in his name. Because in the name of this one, they shall be delivered, and the decree was made for their lives.]

41

[8] [And in that time, the faces of the kings of the earth shall be humbled, and the mighty ones who seized power for oppression. Because of the works of their hands, on the day of their cries, outcry, and suffering, their souls shall not be delivered.]

[9] [Their deeds shall be seen by the chosen ones, and they will be despised like hair in fire, and like foam in water they shall vanish. From before the face of the righteous and from before the face of the holy ones they shall be rejected, and no bond shall be honored by them.]

[10] [And on the day of their suffering, rest shall be upon the earth. And before him, they shall fall and never rise again. There will be no one to pity them for their deeds, nor one to raise them up, because they hated the Lord of Spirits and his Messiah. And they shall bless his name, the name of the Lord of Spirits.]

CHAPTER 49

[1] For wisdom has been poured out like water, and glory shall not cease before him forever.

[2] For the Lord of Spirits is mighty in all, both in the beloved ones of righteousness and the transgressors. The transgressors are like a shadow and vapors none shall remain standing. [And one has stood before the Lord of Spirits, and his glory endures forever, and his strength for the generations of generations.]

[3] [And in him dwells wisdom, and the spirit is poured out, and the hidden knowledge is revealed. And the spirit of instruction, strength, and power dwells in those who abide in righteousness.]

[4] [In righteousness, he grants what is given and speaks, but not with force. For he is gentle before the Lord of Spirits, as he was accepted.]

CHAPTER 50

[1] And in those days, a covering shall be for the holy and the elect, and a light shall appear for them. Honor, praise, and majesty will be given to the holy ones on the day of trouble.

² A gathering shall take place over the sinners, and they shall perish. The righteous shall rise before the Lord of Spirits, and all shall see as they stand and the wicked flee because of their deeds.

³ The wicked shall have no honor before the Lord of Spirits, and they shall not stand in His presence. The Lord of Spirits shall grant understanding, for great is His mercy.

⁴ And the righteous one shall remain in his state, and before his splendor, the sinners shall not stand. They will not endure before him, and they shall fall.

⁵ And from that time, they shall no longer be taught, and it will be declared by the Lord of Spirits.

CHAPTER 51

¹ And in those days, an event will occur, and the earth will return what was stored in it, and Sheol will return what was entrusted to it, and the abyss will release what was never freed.

² And the righteous and the holy ones shall rejoice because the day has drawn near, and they shall be delivered.

³ And wisdom shall dwell in those days, and a sign shall be upon his dwelling, and all the treasures of wisdom shall come forth from his mouth, for the Lord of Spirits has given and bestowed it.

⁴ And in those days, an event shall occur, and the deserts shall burn like a furnace, and the abyss shall be torn open like churned milk. And all the angels in heaven shall tremble, and their faces shall shine with joy.

⁵ Then the exalted ones, the chosen, shall rise. And the earth shall rejoice, and the righteous shall dwell in it. They shall remain in it, and the chosen ones shall stay forever. They shall shine, and they shall find rest.

CHAPTER 52

¹ And after the vision, in that exalted place, I saw all the mighty appearances. Because of this, I was carried away by the turbulence of the wind, and they took me into the desert.

² And there I saw with my own eyes the treasures of the heavens, all that is eternal and does not perish, which had descended upon the earth. And there were mountains: a mountain of iron, a mountain of copper, a mountain of silver, a mountain of gold, a mountain of molten metal, and a mountain of clay.

³ And I asked the angel who was with me, saying: 'Explain to me what this hidden thing is, which is mighty and which I have seen.

⁴ [And he answered me, saying: 'All that you have seen is for the authority of the Anointed One. This hidden thing shall exist just as it has been established, and it shall be strong upon the earth.]

⁵ And he took me so that the angel of peace might show me and say: 'You will see and understand all that is mighty, which was planted by the Lord of Spirits.'

⁶ And these mountains that you have seen, the mountain of iron, the mountain of copper, the mountain of silver, the mountain of gold, the mountain of molten metal, and the mountain of clay, before the chosen they shall exist no more. They shall melt like wax before the fire and like water that does not flow down from above. This is the vision: these mountains shall be as nothing, beneath the earth.

⁷ And in this vision, the exalted place shall be. They shall not take delight in gold, nor in silver, nor shall they trust in riches or possessions.

⁸ And iron shall not be for war, nor shall it be worn for armor. Bronze shall not be used for strength, nor shall it bring power. Nor shall it be cut, and clay shall not be shaped.

⁹ All of these shall be destroyed, and they shall vanish from the face of the earth. Then the chosen shall appear before the presence of the Lord of Spirits.

CHAPTER 53

¹ And then I saw with my eyes a deep and wide valley, and its mouth was open. And all those who were gathered for judgment, and the sea, and the pillars, and fire, and torment, shall be brought upon them. And they shall be cast into the deep valley, which is never filled.

² And torment shall be upon them, and it shall be inflicted. And all that does not cease from suffering shall consume the sinners. And before the presence of the Lord of Spirits, the sinners shall tremble. And before the face of the earth, they shall be cast down, and they shall not escape forever and ever.

³ [For I saw the angels of punishment, who kept watch and prepared all the instruments for Satan.]

⁴ And they were shown to the Angel of Peace, who was with me, the instruments of punishment that had been prepared.

⁵ And he said to me: These have been prepared for the kings and the mighty ones who ruled the earth, so that they will be terrified.

⁶ And after this, the righteous and the chosen ones shall be preserved. They shall dwell in honor in this place, and from now on, they will not be harmed, for they are in the name of the Lord of Spirits.

⁷ And these mountains shall be before his presence like the earth, and the abyss shall be like disturbed waters. And the righteous shall be separated from among the sinners.

CHAPTER 54

¹ And I looked, and I turned to another side of the earth, and I saw there a deep valley, where fire was shaking.

45

² And they brought the kings and the mighty ones and threw them into that valley.

³ And there I saw with my own eyes their instruments, which they were making, iron chains that could not be broken.

⁴ And they were brought to the Angel of Peace, who was with me, and he lifted up the chains, the instruments prepared for the rulers, so that they might be cast down.

⁵ And he said to me: 'These will be cast down as a spectacle for Azazel, because they will be punished and thrown beneath all the heavens. The weight of their oppression will be set upon them, as the Lord of Spirits has commanded.'

⁶ And Michael, Gabriel, Raphael, and Phanuel will seize them on that great day and throw them into the burning fire that shakes. And on that day, the Lord of Spirits will repay them for their rebellion, because they acted against Him and led astray those who dwelled on the earth.

⁷ And at that time, the wrath of the Lord of Spirits will go forth, and all the storehouses of water above the heavens and the springs beneath the heavens and the earth will shake.

⁸ And all the waters above the heavens will perish, the highest waters of heaven, the first ones. And the waters beneath the earth, the second ones, will also be destroyed.

⁹ And all those who dwelled on the dry land will be destroyed, along with those who lived beneath the ends of heaven.

¹⁰ And because of this, it was destroyed, because of their rebellion and the deeds they committed upon the earth. And for this, they will suffer.

CHAPTER 55

¹ [And after this, at the appointed time of repentance, it was said: 'If they repent, I will show mercy to all who dwell upon the earth.']

² [And he swore by his great name: 'From this time forward, I will not do this again to all who dwell upon the earth. And a sign will be placed in the heavens as a pledge, and their faith shall remain as long as the heavens endure above the earth.']

³ "And from that (time), by my command, this is what I have decreed: that they shall be delivered into the hands of the angels, on the day of their trial and torment, before their eyes. And my punishment shall be heavy upon them, my punishment and my wrath," said the Lord, the Lord of Spirits.

⁴ The kings and the mighty ones who have gathered in the wasteland shall witness it. They will be astonished at the chosen one, for he will dwell upon the throne of my glory. And they shall acknowledge Azazel and all his assembly, and in the sight of all, they will do so in the name of the Lord of Spirits.

CHAPTER 56

¹ And I saw there a vision, a spectacle of the angels of punishment, who were going forth. And they held whips, scourges, instruments of torment, for suffering and affliction.

² And the angels of peace were stirred up, those who did not go forth with them. And a disturbance was brought forth. And those who moved clashed. [And they said to me.]

³ One by one, the chosen ones and the beloved ones shall be cast into the depths of the valley of confusion.

⁴ And a cry shall fill that valley from the chosen ones and the beloved ones, and their days of life and the days of their transgression shall be lost, and from now on, they shall no longer be counted.

⁵ And in those days, the rulers shall assemble, and the angels shall join them. They shall turn their heads toward the east, preparing shields and spears for war against the kings. A spirit of confusion shall fall upon them, and they shall deceive their allies. They shall go out like wild animals from their fortresses, and like starving dogs, they shall roam amidst the battlefield.

⁶ And they shall stir up war, and they shall strike against the land of the chosen ones. And the land of the chosen ones shall be shaken before them, bringing destruction. And he shall be bound.

⁷ And he bound and exiled the righteous ones, and a division shall arise among their offspring. And they shall rise up against one another, and there shall be slaughter. Their dwelling shall be shaken, and their words shall persist, but no one shall have mercy, not upon the elders, nor their brothers, nor the child, nor the father, nor the mother, until there is annihilation, ruin, and death. And their suffering shall be great, and there shall be no escape.

⁸ And in those days, Sheol shall open its mouth, and they shall be swallowed into its depths. Their destruction in Sheol shall be revealed as a testimony to the sinners, before the face of the chosen ones.

CHAPTER 57

¹ And it came to pass after this, I saw another vision: chariots that were being lifted up by the wind. And men were speaking, and they came forth with the storm, from the east and from the west, until the turmoil of the day.

² And the voice, the roar of their chariots, was heard. And then there was a great commotion, as the holy ones from heaven gave orders. And the pillars of the earth were shaken from their place. And the sound was heard from the ends of the earth to the ends of heaven, in a single day.

³ And they all fell down, and they prostrated themselves before the Lord of Spirits. And this was the fulfillment of another parable.

CHAPTER 58

¹ And I took up another, a third parable, concerning the righteous and the chosen ones.

² Blessed are you, the righteous and the chosen ones, for the splendor is yours.

³ And the righteous shall be in the light of the sun, and the chosen ones in the light of eternal life. And their days shall not end, nor shall the days of the holy ones be completed.

⁴ And they shall seek the light, and they shall find rest in righteousness with the Lord of Spirits. Peace shall be for the righteous in the presence of the Lord forever.

⁵ And after this, it shall be told to the holy ones that they shall be lifted up into the heavens. The treasures of righteousness and the portion of that which is steadfast shall rise like the sun over the earth, and the darkness shall pass away.

⁶ And the light that shall not end shall be, and the completion of days shall not come. For at first, darkness had been overturned, but the light shall endure before the Lord of Spirits. And the light of righteousness shall remain forever before the Lord of Spirits.

CHAPTER 59

¹ And in those days, I saw with my eyes the treasures of lightning, the lights, and their movement. And they flashed for blessing and for a warning, as was appointed by the Lord of Spirits.

² And there I saw the treasures of thunder, and it resounded at the height of the heavens. Their voices were heard, and the dwellings of the earth were shaken. And the voice of the thunder was for peace and for blessing, and also for a curse, according to the word of the Lord of Spirits.

³ And after that, a pillar appeared, and all their treasures of lights and lightning flashes were seen. And they flashed for blessing and for prosperity.

CHAPTER 60

¹ In the year five hundred, in the seventh month, on the fourteenth day of the month [in the life of Enoch], I saw a vision. The heavens were violently shaken, and the heavens trembled greatly. The power of the Most High caused the angels to retreat, and the outposts of heaven were thrown into great turmoil.

² And after this, I saw the [chief of the vision] sitting upon the throne of his glory, and the angels and the righteous stood around him.

³ And a great trembling seized me, and I was lifted up, and terror took hold of me. My heart quaked and was overcome. My strength failed, and I collapsed, falling on my face.

⁴ And the holy Michael, one of the holy angels, came forth. He raised me, and he also restored my spirit, for I could not endure the vision. I was overwhelmed, my strength withered, and my body trembled. And I was flung... heaven..

⁵ And the holy Michael said to me: 'Why has this vision been revealed? Until this day, the day of His mercy has lasted, and He has granted compassion. But now, wrath has been set apart for those who dwell on the earth.'

⁶ Then the day shall come, of power, of punishment, and of judgment, when the Lord of Spirits separates those who bow in righteousness from those who reject it. Those who exalt His name will be set apart. This is the day of covenant for the chosen and reckoning for the sinners.

⁷ And on that day, two monsters shall be divided: the female serpent, whose name is Leviathan, so that she may dwell in the depths of the sea, above the fountains of the waters.

⁸ And the second, his name, Behemoth, who dwells in his wilderness, in the dry land, which is not seen, and its name is Duidain. In the east of the garden where the chosen and the righteous dwell. It was planted from the beginning of that one, seventh from Adam, their first for man that was made by the Lord of Spirits.

⁹ And they were separated from that place, and another angel showed me their power, the monsters, the female and the male, and they were divided on one day. And one was carried into the depths of the sea, and the other into the dry land.

10 And he said to me, 'You, son of man, because of this, you will understand the signs which are great.'

11 And another angel, who was with me, who was mighty, spoke to me and showed me what moves and what is fixed in the heavens, in the heights above, in the midst of the earth, in the depths, in the ends of the heavens, and in the foundations of the heavens.

12 And in the turbulence of the winds, there the spirits shall be divided, some shall perish, and some shall be bound in chains. And the winds, by the power of the spirit, and their strength, shall be for the light and the moon, like the power of righteousness. And the divisions of the stars shall be by their names, and each shall be assigned its portion.

13 And there was a great tumult in their destruction, and for every portion that is divided, it was like the flashing of lightning. And their vision was as a creation, and they shall be heard.

14 For the tumult of thunder is established in its chambers with restraint, and the voice of it has been given its place. And neither the tumult nor the lightning nor a single wind shall be separated, for they remain as they were revealed.

15 Because lightning shall flash, and thunder shall give its voice. And the wind, in its time, shall rest. And the storm shall be divided in their midst, for the storehouse of their times has been set. And each of them, in its time and cycle, shall take hold, shall be transformed by the power of the spirit, and shall be driven according to its abundance as it passes over the earth.

16 And the wind of the sea, the second, is strong. And according to the power of its might, in its cycle, it shall strike. And as it is driven, it shall be seen throughout all the high places of the earth.

17 And the wind of the east has its angel, this one. And the wind of the north, the angel of it is good, this one.

18 And the wind of the south is strong because of its power. And the wind of the west is at rest, but it brings dew from it, like a mist. And its name is Dedek.

[19] And the Gimē wind shall not be joined with them in their storehouses, except the storehouse of the west wind, for its movement is in praise, in light, in darkness, in fruitfulness, and in drought. And its storehouse is light, and its angel is this one.

[20] The wind of dew has its dwelling at the ends of the heavens, and its path moves together with the storehouses of rain. And its movement is in fruitfulness and in drought. And the clouds of it, and the clouds of Gimē, are joined, and one to another, they give.

[21] And the wind of rain moves from its storehouse, and the angels come forth, open the storehouse, and bring it out. And thus, it is seen over all the dry land, and it joins with all the waters that are over the land. And thus, in all times, it is joined with the waters upon the earth.

[22] For the waters exist for those who dwell upon the dry land, as a blessing for the earth, from the exalted ones that are from the heavens. Because by this measure, the rain remains, and the angels oversee it.

[23] These all I saw, up to the Garden of the Righteous.

[24] And the angel of peace who was with me said: 'These two great monsters, which the Lord created for destruction, will be stirred up like a punishment from the Lord. And they shall be slain, along with their offspring, together with their mothers and fathers.'

[25] Thus, the punishment of the Lord of Spirits is completed upon them, so that no punishment shall remain. After this, a new condition shall exist, in His mercy and in His justice.

CHAPTER 61

[1] And I saw in that time a throne was given to him, and the angels, a great and shining host, stood before him. And they spread their wings and flew, following the path of service.

[2] And they were sent to the angel who was appointed, and those great and shining ones arose and flew. And he said to me, 'They fly so that they might measure.'

³ And the angel who was with me said: 'These faithful ones will be brought forth, and the righteous and the chosen ones will appear. They will be strengthened and glorified in the name of the Lord of Spirits, forever and ever.'

⁴ They will praise and assemble, the holy ones with the holy ones, and those who were gathered will be given faith, and they will be strengthened in the word of righteousness.

⁵ And those who were gathered will be punished, all the beloved ones who were cast into the depths of the earth. Those who were corrupted from the wilderness, those who were swallowed by the sea creatures, and those taken by the beasts will all be destroyed and judged on the day of the holy ones. For there will be no one left uncorrupted before the Lord of Spirits, and none who were defiled will be spared.

⁶ And they arose, and a command was given to those in the heights of the heavens, all of them. And power, and a voice, and a single light like fire went forth.

⁷ [And for this, before the word, they will bless, and they will exalt, and they will glorify with wisdom. And they will guard it with speech and with the spirit of life.]

⁸ The spirits will take their place in the throne of his glory, and they will sit for the holy ones. And they will rejoice, and all their works for the righteous will be honored in the heights of heaven and in their dwelling places, as their deeds are recognized.

⁹ [And therefore, they will exalt their faces so that their ways may be in righteousness. If they love the word of the name of the Lord of Spirits. And He has established them in the paths of justice and righteousness of the Exalted Lord. And they will speak to one another with one voice, and they will bless, glorify, exalt, and renew in His name, the Lord of Spirits.]

[10] And all the powers of the heavens shall tremble, and all the holy ones above, and the powers of the Lord, the Cherubim, the Seraphim, and the Ophanim, and all the angels of power, and all the angels of dominion, and the Watchers, and all the forces who are in the earth and in the waters shall be shaken on that day.

[11] [And they will rise up, and they will bless, and they will glorify, and they will renew, and they will exalt with the spirit of faith, and with the spirit of wisdom, and with reverence, and with the spirit of mercy, and with the spirit of justice, and peace, and with the spirit of righteousness. And they will speak all together with one voice: 'Blessed and may His name be blessed, the Lord of Spirits, forever and ever.']

[12] [All those who do not sleep in the heights of heaven will bless you. All the holy ones in heaven and all the chosen ones who dwell in the [Garden of Life] will bless you. All the spirits of light, who proclaim, bless, sing, exalt, and sanctify your holy name. And all flesh, which perishes from strength, will glorify and bless your name forever and ever.]

[13] [For great is the mercy of the Lord of Spirits, and He is long-suffering in wrath, and all His works and all His power, as He brings forth in abundance, are done for the righteous and the chosen in His name, the Lord of Spirits.]

CHAPTER 62

[1] [Then the Lord commanded the kings, the mighty, the exalted ones, and those who dwell on the earth, and He said: 'Open your eyes and lift your heads, if you are able to understand the Chosen One.']

[2] [And the Lord of Spirits sat upon the throne of His glory, and the spirit of righteousness was poured out upon Him. And the word from His mouth shall slay all the sinners and all the unrighteous, and from His face they shall perish.]

³ [And they shall be terrified in that day, all the kings, the mighty, the exalted ones, and those who hold power over the earth. And they shall see and be amazed because He will sit upon the throne of His glory, and the righteous shall stand before Him in righteousness. And the word of His mouth shall go forth, for there is no falsehood before Him.]

⁴ And their distress shall come, suffering like a woman in labor. And she will writhe and bring forth. Thus, it shall come forth, a child from the mouth of the womb, and she will suffer in birth.

⁵ [And their spirits shall be troubled, and their spirits will be shaken. They will be terrified, and their faces will be ashamed. And affliction shall seize them, because of the offspring of the woman who dwells near the throne of His glory.]

⁶ [They shall praise, bless, and exalt the kings and the mighty ones, all those who seized the earth, all who were not righteous and who have done evil.]

⁷ [For from the beginning, the offspring of the woman of life was hidden. The Most High guarded him before His power, and He appointed him for the righteous.]

⁸ [And they shall see the assembly of the holy ones and the elect, and all the elect shall stand before him on that day.]

⁹ [And all the kings, the mighty ones, and the exalted ones shall fall. They shall bow before him, before his face, and they shall beg for mercy. But they shall be handed over to the offspring of the woman of life, and they shall seek mercy from his hands.]

¹⁰ [They shall be terrified, for the Lord of Spirits will drive them away. They shall flee from before his face, but their faces shall be filled with shame, and darkness shall cover them.]

¹¹ They shall be handed over to the angels of punishment, so that vengeance may be taken upon those who oppressed the children and the elect.

¹² There they shall cry out, for the wrath of the Lord of Spirits is complete upon them. Their judgment is fulfilled, and their torment shall remain upon them forever.

¹³ The righteous and the elect shall be saved on that day, and from then on, the sinners and the wicked shall no longer be seen.

¹⁴ [And the Lord of Spirits shall dwell with them, and with these ones, the offspring of the woman of life, he shall dwell. And they shall be exalted, and glorified, and they shall rise forever and ever.]

¹⁵ The righteous and the elect shall arise from the earth, and their troubles shall cease. Their faces shall be lifted, and they shall be clothed with the garments of life.

¹⁶ And this shall be the garment of life, given by the Lord of Spirits. Your clothing shall not wear out, and your glory shall not fade before the Lord of Spirits.

CHAPTER 63

¹ In those days, the mighty kings who possess the earth shall tremble because of the deeds of their hands. For on the day of their anguish and affliction, they shall have no rest to find. [And they shall fall and worship before the Lord of Spirits and confess their sins before Him.]

² [And they shall bless and glorify the Lord of Spirits, and they shall say: 'Blessed is the Lord of Spirits and the Lord of kings, the Lord of the mighty, and the Lord of the rich, the Lord of glory, and the Lord of wisdom.']

³ [And splendid in every secret thing is your power from generation to generation, and your glory forever and ever. Deep are all your secrets, countless and infinite, and your righteousness is beyond comprehension.]

⁴ [Now we understand that we must glorify and bless the Lord of kings and Him who reigns over all kings.]

⁵ And they shall say, 'Who will grant us rest so that we might glorify and thank Him and bless Him and trust in the presence of His glory?'

⁶ And now we seek rest, but rest has fled from us. We are driven away, we cannot obtain it; and light has vanished from before us, and darkness will be our dwelling forever and ever.

⁷ For before Him we did not believe and did not glorify the name of the Lord of kings; nor did we glorify our Lord for all His works. But our hope was in the scepter of our kingdom and our glory.

⁸ And in the day of our affliction and trouble He does not save us, and we find no rest to trust in, for our Lord is faithful in all His works and in all His judgments, and His judgments do not depart from their paths.

⁹ And we pass away from before His presence on account of our deeds, and all our sins are reckoned in righteousness.

¹⁰ Now they will say, 'Our souls are filled with wickedness; and our wealth will not save us but descends from us in the flames of heavy Sheol.'

¹¹ And from then on, their faces shall be covered with darkness and shame before the chosen ones and the children of the living. And before his face, they shall bow down. And the sword shall remain before His face, in their midst.

¹² And then, the Lord of Spirits will say: 'This is the judgment, the decree, and the fate for the mighty ones, the kings, the exalted ones, and those who took possession of the earth' before the Lord of Spirits

CHAPTER 64

¹ And I saw all the faces in that place, the dwelling place of the righteous.

² And I heard the voice of the angel who was speaking concerning the faithless angels who descended from heaven onto the earth and what they did to the children of men. And they corrupted them and led them astray into transgression.

CHAPTER 65

¹ And at that time, Noah saw the earth, that it was destroyed, and that great destruction had taken place.

² And he lifted his steps from there and went to the ends of the earth. And he cried out to his forefather Enoch, and Noah spoke with a bitter voice, saying: 'Hear me, hear me, hear me!' three times.

³ And he said to me: Tell me, what is this that is happening on the earth? Because the earth has labored and trembled violently, and I am perishing along with it!

⁴ And after this time, a mighty disturbance came upon the earth, and a voice was heard from the heavens, and they fell before my face.

⁵ And Enoch came from his dwelling and stood before me, and he said to me: 'Why have you cried out before me with bitter lamentation and weeping?

⁶ And a command went forth from before the presence of the Lord against those who dwell in corruption, that their destruction would come because they have learned from all the beloved ones of the angels, and all the tyrants, and all the satans, and all their power was given to those who do their works, and to the conspirators, and to all who spread corruption over the earth.

⁷ And until a pure one is born from the seed of the earth, then there will be cleansing upon the earth.

⁸ Because a curse and affliction will no longer be born from the earth as in former times; those who have fallen, those who were not born, and the angel who did not remain in his place will be destroyed.

⁹ And after this, Enoch took me from my place by his hand, lifted me up, and said to me: 'Flee! For you have seen the Lord of Spirits concerning this great destruction that is upon the earth.'

¹⁰ And he said to me: 'Because of their rebellion, their judgment is fulfilled, and they will not escape before me. Because of the unrighteousness they have committed and what they have learned, the earth shall be destroyed, and those who dwell upon it.'

¹¹ Behold, their deeds are not for eternity, for they have seen the wicked and those who have been corrupted. And He has confirmed to you, my son, that the Lord of Spirits has commanded, because you are pure and upright, that you will be saved from this destruction of the wicked.

¹² And he established your name among the holy ones and protected you from those who dwell in corruption. And he established your descendants in righteousness, for kings and for great glory. And from now on, the chosen righteous ones and the holy ones shall go forth, and they will never be removed from the world.

CHAPTER 66

¹ And after this, I saw the angels of punishment who were prepared, and they went forth and opened all the power of the waters that are under the earth, so that it would become judgment and destruction for all who dwell and reside in corruption.

² And the Lord of Spirits commanded the angels who were sent out, so that they would not allow the waters to continue, and to restrain them, because those angels had been overcome by the power of the waters.

³ And I went out from before the presence of Enoch.

CHAPTER 67

¹ And in that appointed time, the word of the Lord came to me, and He said to me: 'Noah, behold, your portion has been set apart before me. A portion that is not corrupt, a portion of favor and honor.'

² And then the angels of punishment acted. They opened, and they went out to those ones—the angels—to the place appointed by my hand. And they stood, and they stood, and they began. From her, the seed of life was scattered upon her, so that she would not be destroyed by the wrath of corruption.

³ And he established your offspring before me for eternity and for the people. And he set them apart from those who dwell with you in the presence of corruption. It shall not be overturned because of the face of the earth. He shall be blessed and shall increase despite corruption, [in his name, of the Lord].

⁴ And they shall bind them for the chosen angels, those who saw them in the rebellion, within this valley. If it quakes, if I have seen this before from my lifetime, Enoch, saw it in the west, near the desert of gold, silver, iron, lead, and tin.

⁵ And I saw this valley, when it became great and boiling, and its waters were disturbed.

⁶ And this all was made from it: lead, fire, and they became molten, but what was not molten remained in that place. A stench was produced and spread, and it mixed with the waters. And this valley, when the angels who sinned were there, quaked beneath this earth.

⁷ And when these valleys burned, a pillar of fire rose, and fire went forth. The chosen angels trembled, for the fallen ones had sinned against them and against those who dwelled in corruption.

8 And now, the chosen waters bear witness to the event for the kings, the mighty ones, and those who dwelled in corruption, for the perishing of both soul and flesh, and for the existence of spirit. Their destruction is fulfilled, so that their flesh trembles, because they denied the Lord of Spirits. And they saw their own existence, when all their days came to an end, yet they did not believe in his name.

9 And as their pain was great, their flesh suffered, just as their bodies were transformed for the spirit, for the age of eternity. Because they had no place before the Lord of Spirits, who does not speak, and the land was not with them.

10 [Because their existence shall come to an end against them, because they did not believe in the destruction of their flesh. And they blasphemed [the Lord], and they shall perish.]

11 And thus, in that event, the waters twisted their bodies, and fear seized them as the waters trembled. The angels of the depths and those who were bound were twisted, for the waters of the abyss boiled and churned.

12 And they heard the Holy Michael when he raised his voice and spoke: 'This is the state in which the angels of heaven shall tremble, and it is for the kings and the mighty ones who hold onto corruption.'

13 Because these waters are for the destruction of the flesh of the angels and of the dead. And they did not see, [and they did not believe, so that the faithful waters would test them.] And now, the fire that does not cease burns forever.

CHAPTER 68

1 And after these things, he gave to me all of the signs and warnings from Enoch in the book, and the parables that were given to him. And they taught him to read and to speak the parables in the book.

² [And on that day, the Holy Michael called forth and spoke to Raphael: 'Let his power be given to the spirit, and let him announce to me concerning the tree and the state of being, if warnings exist for the angels. This one, who has power, is upheld by the tree, for it was made and remains, yet it will be rejected before her.']

³ And again, the Holy Michael called forth and spoke to Raphael: 'This is the one who cannot find mercy, whose heart is unyielding concerning her, and he does not change in his entirety from these words of existence. And it has gone forth concerning them, from those who were summoned, thus.'

⁴ [And it came to be, therefore he stood before the Lord of Spirits, and thus Holy Michael spoke to Raphael: 'And it cannot be for them in the presence of the Lord, because the Lord of Spirits is filled with wrath, for in the likeness of the Lord they shall act.']

⁵ Because of this, it shall come upon them—the existence of those who have chosen, forever, because it shall not be fulfilled, and it shall not be good. They will not be preserved; their portion, their faith, their disgrace—they are consumed. Their existence (remains) as this, for eternity.

CHAPTER 69

¹ And after this, existence shall be revealed, and they shall make it known and instruct, because these things were seen by those who dwell in corruption.

² And these are the names of the angels: The first among them is Shemihazah, followed by Arstikifa, Armen, Lekaba'ēl, Tur'ēl, Rumyāl, Dāni'ēl, Nuqa'ēl, Beraqi'ēl, and Azāz'ēl. The others are Armrəs, Baṭaryāl, Basas'ēl, Anan'ēl, Ṭurya'ēl, Simaṭīsē'ēl, Yitər'ēl, Ṭuma'ēl, Ṭar'ēl, Ruma'ēl, and Izēzē'ēl.

³ And these are their chiefs, the heads of their angels, and their names, for the rulers of one hundred, the rulers of fifty, and the rulers of ten.

⁴ His name was the first, and these are those who transgressed, all the lesser holy angels, and they inherited corruption, and they transgressed with the children of men.

⁵ And the next, his name was Asb'el. This one gave corrupt counsel and led the lesser holy angels into transgression so that they defiled their flesh with the children of men.

⁶ And the third, his name was Gader'el. This one showed all the blows of death to the children of men. And this one led Eve astray. And this one showed the ways of death to the lesser men, and the shield, and the breastplate, and the sword for killing, and all the ways of death to the children of men.

⁷ And from his hands, it went forth upon those who dwelt in corruption, from that time and until eternity.

⁸ And the fourth, his name was Penemue. This one revealed to the children of men embittered knowledge and deception, and he showed them all their skill and understanding.

⁹ [And this one taught men writing, and by ink and parchment, and because of this, many were led astray from the world, and until eternity, and until that day.]

¹⁰ [Because humanity was created, and just as with a stylus and with ink, suffering arose, and they corrupted their understanding.]

¹¹ Because man was not created to be like the angels, that they should abide (forever), righteous and pure, and death, which destroys all, does not reach them. But in their minds, they transgress, and by this power, they perish.

¹² And the fifth (of the Watchers), Kasyadea, this one revealed to the children of men all the cutting of embryos, of souls, and of spirits. And the cutting (of flesh) in the womb so that it perishes, and the severing of the breath from the body, and the cutting of that which is unlawful by the knife. And he was born of the body, whose name was Taba'eth.

¹³ And this one, the mighty one, Kesabel, the chief of the oath, who revealed it to the holy ones. Thus, he caused the exalted one to descend in glory. And his name was Beqa.

¹⁴ And this one spoke to the holy one, Michael, and revealed to them the name of the beloved one, so that they may see and remember this name and the oath, and so that they may fear from this name and the oath, which was revealed to all the children of men who are beloved.

¹⁵ And this is the power of the oath, because this mighty one is strong and unshakable, and he took hold of this oath and established it in his hand to the holy one, Michael.

¹⁶ And these are strong because of this Oath, and they were established by his Oath. And the heavens were suspended by it, so that the world should be created, and it shall remain forever.

¹⁷ And by it, the earth was established upon the waters, and in faith, the beloved ones shall come to the living waters from the creation of the world and forever.

¹⁸ And by this Oath, the sea was created, and the foundation of time and judgment was established. It remained without moving, and it shall not pass away from the creation of the world until eternity.

¹⁹ And by this Oath, the luminaries follow their paths, the lights move in their courses. They stand firm and do not change their places from the beginning of the world until eternity.

²⁰ And by this Oath, the sun and the moon complete their cycles and do not transgress their command from the beginning of the world until eternity.

²¹ And by this Oath, the stars fulfill their courses, and their names are preserved, and they remain unchanged from the beginning of the world until eternity.

²² And just as the waters have their souls, so do the winds and all spirits, along with their paths, from all the companions of the spirits.

²³ And by it, the storehouses of the voice of thunder and the light of lightning are bound. And by it, the storehouses of hail, frost, mist, rain, and dew are joined together.

²⁴ And all of them are strong, [they believe], and they are united before the Lord of Spirits. They praise with all their strength, with all their power, and with all their thoughts and unity. And they are exalted in his name before the Lord of Spirits forever and ever.

²⁵ And their paths are strong through the Oath, and they are bound by it. Their ways are held together, and their cycles shall not perish.

²⁶ And they rejoiced with great joy, and they blessed and praised, and they were exalted because of what was established for them, his name, [for this one, the Son of Man, the Living One.]

²⁷ And he sat upon the throne of his glory, and his head was given to him. And it was bestowed upon [the Son of Man, the Living One], and sinners shall pass away and perish from the face of the earth, and those who led astray shall be removed forever.

²⁸ They shall be bound in chains, and in their assembly of corruption, they shall be destroyed. And all their deeds shall vanish from before the face of the earth.

²⁹ And from that time, there shall be no destruction, because that one [the Son of Man] was seen, and he sat upon the throne of his glory. And all the wicked shall pass away from before his face, and they shall be destroyed and delivered up to that one [the Son of Man]. And he shall be strong before the Lord of Spirits. This is the parable that Enoch saw.

CHAPTER 70

¹ And it came to pass after this that his name was exalted, the Living One, before him, [the Son of Man], before the Lord of Spirits, from those who dwell upon the earth.

² And he was lifted up in the chariots of spirit, and his name went forth in their midst.

³ And from that day, I was no longer found among them, but I dwelt in the midst of all the spirits, in the midst of the blessed ones. And I was taken up before the throne of the hosts of angels, so that they might show me the dwelling place of the chosen ones and the righteous.

⁴ And there, I saw the fathers, the ancient ones, and the righteous who dwell in that place from eternity.

CHAPTER 71

¹ And it came to pass after this that my spirit was taken up, and it ascended into the heavens. And I saw the offspring of the holy angels, moving upon a blazing fire. Their garments were white, and their faces were bright like snow.

² And I saw two streams of fire, and a pure bright light like a consuming fire that gave illumination. And they fell before my face, before the Lord of Spirits.

³ And Michael, one of the chief angels, took me by my hand, led me, raised me up, and brought me before all the beloved ones of mercy and the beloved ones of righteousness.

⁴ And he showed me all the beloved ones at the extremities of heaven, and all the treasuries of the stars and the luminaries, where they come forth before the face of the holy ones.

⁵ [And the spirit carried Enoch into the heavens], and I saw there the immovable place at the center of the great pillars, and the midst of the faithful ones, and tongues of living fire.

⁶ And I saw in my spirit that which surrounds that house, fire from the four pillars, flowing as a stream of living fire, and it enclosed that house.

⁷ And Seraphiel, Cherubiel, and [Afnin] stood, these are the faithful ones, those who do not sleep. And they guard the throne of glory that belongs to Him.

[8] And I saw innumerable angels, entering and going forth, moving in procession, encircling that house. And Michael, Raphael, Gabriel, and Phanuel stood there, along with the holy angels who fill the heavens, going out and entering into that house.

[9] And they went out from that house, Michael, Raphael, Gabriel, and Phanuel, and with them, the holy angels, those who had not become corrupt.

[10] And their appearance was like a great splendor, but his face was like the fullness of white purity, and his clothing was beyond description.

[11] And they fell on my face, and all my flesh was dissolved, and my spirit was transformed. And I cried out with a great voice, with the spirit of power, and I blessed, praised, and was lifted up.

[12] And blessings came forth from my mouth, and glorifications were established before that exalted one, the Head of Days.

[13] And the Head of Days came with Michael, Gabriel, Raphael, and Phanuel, and they went forth, moving in procession. And the angels who had not become corrupt encircled them.

[14] And that angel came near me, and with his voice, he blessed me and said to me: 'You are a child of humanity, born for righteousness, and righteousness is upon you. It remains with you, and righteousness belongs to the Head of Days; it shall not forsake you.

[15] And he said to me: 'Peace shall be upon you [in his name], for a world that shall not change. For from this moment, peace shall go forth from the creation of the world, and just as it shall be for you, it shall be for the world and for eternity of eternities.

[16] And all shall exist and shall be transformed into your destiny, for righteousness shall not leave you forever. With you shall be their dwelling place, and with you their portion. And your truth shall never be taken away for eternity and for eternity of eternities.

¹⁷ And just as there shall be peace, peace for days with that one, the child of humanity, the one of life, so shall peace be for the righteous. And his portion shall be the reward of the righteous, in the name of the Lord of Spirits, for eternity. The reward of the righteous shall be in the name of the Lord of Spirits, for eternity of eternities.

CHAPTER 72

¹ *And this is the book of the courses of the heavenly luminaries, their dominions, their orders, their cycles, their names, their origins, and their months, which Uriel, the holy angel who was with me, revealed to me. He showed me one by one, as they are governed, and revealed all their laws, for all the years of the world, until a new creation shall be made.*

² *This is the eternal law of the heavenly luminaries, which was shown (to me). From the gates of El (in the west) to its entrance in the east, from the gates of its rising.*

³ *And I saw that the sun goes forth from there, from six gates. These are the gates through which both the sun and the moon pass. They all align: six gates in the east and six in the west, with their governors and the stars. These gates have many windows, arranged in sequence, one after another, and to their left.*

⁴ *And the sun, which is called the great luminary, goes forth first.*

⁵ *In which the chariot burns, shining with fire, filling the heavens as a circuit. The sun moves toward the north but does not enter that gate; instead, the wind carries it until it is lifted toward the east.*

⁶ *From the first gate in the month it goes forth; thus, the waters shine upon the face, illuminating as those six gates lead through the fourth gate.*

⁷ *And twelve open windows are in that fourth gate, from which the sun goes forth in the first month, and flames emerge from them at the appointed times when they are opened.*

⁸ When the sun shines in the heavens, it goes forth through that fourth gate for thirty days. And the day will extend, and the sun will set in the fourth gate, which is in the west of the heavens.

⁹ The length of the day will increase at that time, from day to day, while the night will shorten from night to night, until the thirtieth day.

¹⁰ Two portions of the night are taken from the day, so that the day surpasses the night. And on that day, the day is eight parts, and the night is precisely ten parts, a portion by number.

¹¹ And the sun goes forth from that fourth gate, and it enters into the fourth. Then, it returns to the eastern fifth gate for thirty days, and from there it goes forth and enters.

¹² In the fifth gate, then the day surpasses by two portions, and it increases to eleven parts.

¹³ And the night will shorten, and it will have seven portions. Then, the sun will return to the east and enter the sixth gate, and it will go forth and enter the sixth gate for thirty-one days.

¹⁴ Because of the signs that belong to it, on that day, the day surpasses the night. Its length shall be twice as much as the length of the night, and it shall increase to twelve parts, while the night shortens to six portions.

¹⁵ And the sun will rise up to diminish the length of the day and to add to the length of the night. And the sun will return to the east to enter.

¹⁶ In the sixth gate, and from it, the sun will go forth and enter for thirty days. And as thirty days pass, one portion will be precisely diminished from the day, and it will increase to eleven parts, while the night shall be seven portions.

¹⁷ And the sun will go forth from the west, from that sixth gate, to go eastward, and it will rise in the fifth gate for thirty days.

¹⁸ And it will set again in the west, in the fifth western gate. And on that day, two portions will be diminished from the day, and the day will be ten portions, while the night will increase to eight.

¹⁹ And the sun will go forth from the fifth gate, that same one, and it will enter the fifth gate, which is in the west. Then, it will go forth from the fourth gate, because of its signs.

²⁰ For thirty-one days, and it will set in the west. And on this day, the day and the night are equal in their length, and they will rise to nine portions for the night and nine portions for the day.

²¹ And the sun will go forth from that gate and will set in the west. Then, it will turn and complete the thirtieth day, and it will go forth through the third gate to the east.

²² In the third gate, and on that day, the night will increase in its length over the day, and the day will decrease from day to day until the thirtieth day. And the night will rise to ten portions.

²³ Precisely, and the day will have eight portions. And the sun will go forth from that third gate and will set in the third gate in the west. Then, it will turn to the east and will rise in the second eastern gate for thirty days. And thus, it will set in the second gate in the west.

²⁴ And on that day, they will rise to eleven portions for the night, and to the day seven portions.

²⁵ And on that day, the sun will go forth from the second gate, that same one, and it will set in the west in the second gate. Then, it will return to the east, to the first gate.

²⁶ Thirty-one days, and it will set in the west in the first gate. And on that day, the night will increase in its length, twice as much as the day, and the night will rise to twelve portions.

²⁷ Precisely measured portions. And to the day, six portions. And with this, the sun will complete its cycle and will return once more to this cycle, and it will enter that gate.

²⁸ Thirty-one days, and it will set opposite to it in the west. And on that day, your sign, the night, will diminish, losing one portion, and will lack by one measure. It will rise to eleven portions.

²⁹ And the portions for the day are seven portions, and the sun shall return and enter the second eastern gate. And upon this cycle, it shall return for thirty days, rising and setting.

³⁰ And on that day, the length of the night shall decrease, and the night shall reach ten portions.

³¹ And to the day, eight portions. And on that day, the sun will go forth from the second gate, that one, and it will enter in the west. Then, it will return eastward and rise in the third gate, one.

³² And on that day, the night will diminish, and it will rise to nine portions, and to the day, nine portions. And then, the night and the day shall be equal in their length. And it shall be [the number of days], the reaching of (precisely) three, as they change by the cycle of the sun.

³³ Three hundred and sixty-four days. And the length of the day and the night. And the day and the night will shorten.

³⁴ They will change by the cycle of the sun, and therefore, its motion will increase in the day, from day to day.

³⁵ And it will diminish in the night, from night to night. This is the law of the sun, its cycle, and its return. According to all that it shall return, sixty times it shall return. And the great, eternal luminary will shine.

³⁶ That one, which is called the sun, is for eternity of eternities. And this one that shines is the great luminary.

³⁷ That which is so-called, according to its appearance. Just as the master moves, so it goes forth and comes in. It will not diminish, and it will not rest. Only it will run in its chariot, day and night. And its light will shine sevenfold [from the light] of the moon. But in their greatness, both of them are equal.

CHAPTER 73

[1] *And after this law, I saw a second law concerning the small luminary, which is called the moon's cycle in the circuit of the heavens.*

[2] *And the chariot in which it moves is lifted up from [its course].*

[3] *The wind and the light are given to it in measure. And as each month changes, its emergence and its entrance are like the days of the sun. And when its light is full, it shall be a seventh of the light of the sun.*

[4] *And thus, it will rise. At first, it will go out from the east on the thirtieth day, and it will be seen on that day together with the sun, in the gate from where the sun had gone out. And on the thirtieth day, the new moon is for you.*

[5] *And its first half will contain one-seventh [of all the light that is hers]. And the entire sphere is empty, without light, except for one-seventh from four.*

[6] *Ten portions of instruction. And on the day when it will receive a seventh and a half (of instruction), and it shall be its light—a seventh, and one-seventh and a half.*

[7] *And it will come with the sun. And where the sun rises, the moon will also rise. It stood and received half a portion of the light. And on this night, at dawn, on the first day, the moon will come together with the sun, and they will be counted.*

[8] *On this night, seven and seven portions and a half. And on that day, it will be seen as the seventh portion exactly, and it will rise and incline from the setting of the sun, and it will shine for the remaining days, seven and seven portions.*

CHAPTER 74

[1] *And a second cycle, and another law I saw in it. And in that law, it shall be made its monthly cycle.*

² And Uriel, the holy angel, showed me everything. And he is the one who governs all of them and their divisions. I wrote as he showed me, and I recorded their months and the appearance of their light, until fifteen days pass.

³ And in the seventh divisions, in the sevenths, it will complete its full light in the east, and in the sevenths. In the seventh divisions, the united ones, it will complete all its darkening in the west.

⁴ And in the known months, it will change its cycle. And in the known months, it will run its special course.

⁵ And in those two gates, which are in the middle at the third gate and the fourth gate.

⁶ The moon shall set with the sun together. For seven days, it shall go out, revolve, and return again to the gate from which the sun went out, and there it shall complete all its light. Then it shall turn away from the sun and come for eight days into the sixth gate, from which it went out.

⁷ And when the sun goes out from the fourth gate, the moon shall go out after seven days, until it goes out from the fifth gate. Then it shall return again for seven days in the fourth gate, completing all its light. Then it shall incline and come into the first gate.

⁸ For eight days, then it moves toward [its position] and returns again for seven days in the fourth gate, from where it departed.

⁹ The sun departs. Thus, I saw their cycles, according to the order of their months, measured by a span.

¹⁰ The sun, in its arrival, and in those days, when the five years are completed, they will exceed toward [a measure]. The sun, thirty days, and the days that belong to each of these five years shall be.

¹¹ In their completion, three hundred and sixty-four days. And an excess of six days will be added to the sun and to the stars. And in five years, they will exceed thirty with six days per year. And to the moon, from the number of days of the sun.

12 And the stars and the moon shall govern the years with precision, according to their order. Never shall they precede, nor shall they delay a single day. Only in justice and precision shall they complete their cycles in three.

13 Four hundred and sixty-four days, three years, one thousand and ninety-two days, and five. [Their years and days.] One thousand eight hundred and twenty days, and the number.

14 The days in eight years: two thousand nine hundred and twelve days. To the moon, they shall ascend, and their excess—sixty days. In five years, they will be lacking fifty days. They will be added for upon its number: their excess and sixty days.

15 And the number of days in five years: one thousand seven hundred and seventy days. And the number of the days of the moon in eight years: two thousand eight hundred and thirty-two days.

16 In the shortfall of eight years, it will amount to eighty days. And all the days that will be lacking, in the eight years, they will amount to eighty.

17 And the year shall pass in its order, according to its appointed times and the constellations of the sun, in their going out from the gates from which it shall go out, and in them, it shall enter, thirty days.

CHAPTER 75

1 And the leaders, the chiefs of the thousands, who are over all creation and over all the exalted ones, and with the four that are added, shall not be separated from their place, according to the calculation of the year. And they shall serve the four days, which shall be cut off from the calculation of the year.

2 And in them, the people are mistaken, for those luminaries truly serve the stations of the world: one in the first gate, one in the third gate, one in the fourth gate, and one in the sixth gate. And they shall complete the order of the world's cycle in three hundred and sixty-four divisions.

3 For the signs, the appointed times, the years, and the days were shown to me by the angel Uriel, [whom the Lord of Praises] appointed over all the luminaries in the heavens and on the earth as a parable. On the face of the heavens, to give light upon the earth, and to separate between the day and the night, they are the sun, the moon, the stars, and all the constellations, which complete their cycles in the spheres of the heavens.

4 Thus, Uriel showed me twelve gates opened in the sphere of the chariot of the sun in the heavens, from which the rays of the sun go forth, and from them comes forth heat.

5 Upon the earth, when they are opened at designated times, and also on behalf of the winds and the spirit of the dew.

6 (They) shall open at appointed times, (they are) opened at the edges of the heavens. Twelve gates I saw in the heavens, at the edges of the earth, from which go forth the sun, the moon, and the stars, and the host of the heavens from east to west.

7 And many windows open to their right and to their left. And one window brings forth heat in its appointed time, just as those gates do, from which the stars go forth according to their command. And through them, they shall come according to their number.

8 And I saw spheres in the heavens moving swiftly, throughout the universe, above and below, and the gates. And in them, the stars that are established revolve.

9 And one among them is greater than all the others, and it encircles the entire world.

CHAPTER 76

1 And at the ends of the earth, I saw years, ten gates opened to all.

2 Winds, and a wind shall go forth and settle upon the earth. Three of them are opened opposite the face of the heavens, and three in the west, and three in the north of the heavens.

3 And three (gates) on the left. Three (gates) of the first ones, they are in the west. And three (more). From the north, three.

4 Opposite them on the left, their order. And three from the west. From the four, the winds of blessing and peace shall go forth. And from the remaining eight, the winds of wrath shall go forth. And where they go forth, they shall destroy the whole earth, and the waters upon it, and all who dwell upon it, and all that is within the waters and upon the dry land.

5 And the first wind, which is in those gates, and is called the Eastern Wind, shall go forth from the first eastern gate, which inclines toward the south. And from it go forth dryness and heat, overturning and destruction.

6 And from the second gate, which is in the middle, shall go forth righteousness and rain. And from there shall also go forth rain and dew, and fruitfulness and peace. And from the third gate, which is on the left of the north, shall go forth cold and dryness.

7 And after these winds, the southern winds shall go forth, which inclines toward the east.

8 And from the gate that is adjacent to it, which is within it, shall go forth pleasant fragrances, and dew, and rain, and peace, and life.

9 And from the third gate, which is in the west, shall go forth dew, and rain, and locusts, and desolation.

10 From their openings, the northern winds shall emerge. (And its name is the Sea.) From the seventh gate, which is in the east, inclining toward the south, shall go forth dew, and rain, and locusts, and desolation.

11 And directly from the first gate shall go forth rain, and dew, and life, and peace. And from the third western gate, inclining toward the north, shall go forth (from it) mist, and dew, and rain, and snow, and frost, and locusts.

12 And after them shall go forth the western winds, from the first gate that faces north. And from it shall go forth dew, and rain, and frost, and cold, and snow, and chill.

¹³ And from the gate that is within, shall go forth dew, and rain, and peace, and blessing. And from the final gate, which is in the south, shall go forth dryness, and destruction, and blight, and annihilation.

¹⁴ And thus, the twelve gates that are in the four corners of the heavens are completed, and all their laws, and all the evils and the blessings that proceed from them. I have shown you, Methuselah, my son.

CHAPTER 77

¹ The first wind shall be called the East Wind, for it is the ancient one. The second shall be called the South Wind, for its name is 'The Most High descends there,' the one who blesses forever.

² And the Sea Wind shall be called the West Wind, for its name is 'They set,' and all the lights of the heavens descend.

³ And the fourth wind shall be called the North Wind, and it shall be divided into three parts. The first is for the dwelling place of man, the second is for the seas, and the streams, and the rivers, and the third is for the Garden of Righteousness.

⁴ And I saw seven great mountains, higher than all the mountains that are upon the face of the earth, and snow shall come forth from them. And days shall pass and vanish.

⁵ And I saw seven great rivers, greater than all the rivers upon the earth. And years shall pass and go by. One goes out from the west and pours its waters into the Great Sea.

⁶ And two of them shall go out from the north into the sea, and their waters shall pour into the stream of the Shihor in the east.

⁷ And the four remaining shall go out from the north into the sea. Two of them pour into the stream of the Shihor, and two into the Great Sea. Others say, into the wilderness.

⁸ And I saw seven great islands, in the sea and on the land—two on the land, and two in the Great Sea.

CHAPTER 78

¹ And these are the names of the sun: The first is Oriras, and the second is Tamash.

² And four are the names of the moon: The first is Ashoniya, the second is Avala, the third is Benaashi, and the fourth is Uriya.

³ These are the two great lights. Their cycle follows the circuit of the heavens, and in their separation, both are equal.

⁴ And a seventh of the light of the sphere of the sun is added to the moon, and it is given to her in measure until it is complete.

⁵ And in its setting, it enters the western gates, turns northward, and by way of the eastern gates, it goes out upon the face of the heavens.

⁶ And when the moon begins to appear in the heavens, and at half its seventh part of light. And on the fourteenth [day], it completes all its light.

⁷ And three-fifths of the light shall be given to it. And when it completes all its light on the fifteenth day, according to the signs of the year, there shall be three-fifths in it. And thus, the light of the moon shall come to be from half of the seventh part.

⁸ And as it decreases, it diminishes: on the first day, by fourteen parts of light; on the second, by thirteen parts; on the third, by twelve; on the fourth, by eleven; on the fifth, by ten; on the sixth, by nine; on the seventh, by eight; on the eighth, by seven; on the ninth, by six; on the tenth, by five; on the eleventh, by four; on the twelfth, by three; on the thirteenth, by two; on the fourteenth, by half of the seventh part. And on the fifteenth day, it loses all its remaining light.

⁹ And some months have twenty-nine days for a month, and one has twenty-eight days.

¹⁰ And a second law Uriel showed me: when its light is added to the moon, and where they add to her from the light of the sun.

¹¹ The whole time that the moon revolves in its light, it continues to fill. And on the fourteenth day, it completes its light in the heavens. And when it shines fully, then it has completed all its light in the heavens.

¹² And on the first day, it shall be called 'Molad' (New Moon), for on that day, the light begins [to shine] within it.

¹³ And its light will be full on the day the sun sets in the west, and it will rise at night from the east and shine all night, until the sun rises opposite it, and the moon will be seen before the sun.

¹⁴ And from the place where the light of the moon comes forth, there it will also diminish until all its light is finished. And when the days of the moon have passed, it remains in its orbit, empty and without light.

¹⁵ Three months have thirty days, and three months have twenty-nine days. In them, it diminishes in its first season, in the first gate, in one hundred and seventy days.

¹⁶ And at the end, three months will have thirty days each, and three months will have twenty-nine days each.

¹⁷ And every twenty days, it has the face of a man at night, and its appearance by day is like the essence of the heavens, for there is nothing else in it, only its light.

CHAPTER 79

¹ And now, Methuselah, my son, I have shown you all. And in this, all the laws of the stars of the heavens are completed.

² And he showed me all their laws, for all the days, for all the appointed times, for all dominion, and for all years. And their goings forth according to their ordinance, for every month and every week.

³ The waning of the moon, which diminishes in the sixth gate. For in that sixth gate, all its light will be finished, and it shall be the beginning of the month.

⁴ *And its waning in the first gate, in its time, until one hundred and seventy-seven days have passed. And for the calculation of the weeks, twenty-five [weeks] and two days.*

⁵ *And the deficiency of the five days from the cycle of the sun, and the order of the stars in one time. And at the time that it departs from this place, it shall be seen.*

⁶ *Thus is the appearance and form of all the luminaries, as the prince of the luminaries, the great angel Uriel, showed me.*

CHAPTER 80

¹ *And in those days, Uriel answered me and said to me, Enoch, behold, I have shown you everything, and I have revealed everything to you, so that you may see this sun and this moon, and the leaders of the stars of the heavens, and their courses, their deeds, their appointed times, and their goings forth.*

² *And in the days of the sinners, the years will be shortened, and the seed of their land will be delayed, and their fields. And all existence that is upon the earth will be altered. And they will not come in their time, the rain will not fall, and the heavens will be stopped.*

³ *And in those times, the fruit of the ground will be delayed and will not sprout in its time. And the fruit of the tree will be withheld and will not sprout in its time.*

⁴ *And the moon will change its order, and it will not be seen in its time.*

⁵ *And in those days, the heavens will be seen, and behold, great distress will come at the ends of the chariots that are in the west, and they will shine more than they always shine.*

⁶ *And many will go astray from the heads of the appointed ones of the stars, and they will change their ways and their deeds. And they will not be seen in their appointed time.*

7 *And the order of the stars will cease on behalf of the sinners. And the inhabitants of the earth will go astray in their thoughts concerning them, and they will turn away from all their ways, and they will sin, and they will think them to be gods.*

8 *And many evils will multiply upon them, and judgment will come upon them, so that they will all be destroyed.*

CHAPTER 81

1 *And he said to me, saying, Enoch, observe carefully the book of the tablets of the heavens, and read what is written upon them, and you will know them one by one.*

2 *And I observed all that was upon all the tablets of the heavens, and I read all that was written. And I knew everything, and I read the book, and the writing, and all that was written concerning all the deeds of mankind and all the offspring of flesh that are upon the earth, until the generations of eternity.*

3 *[And afterward, I blessed the Lord, the King, the praised one forever, who created all the creatures of the world. And I praised before the Lord for His patience. And I blessed Him in the name of all the sons of the earth.]*

4 *And I said at that time: Blessed is the man who dies in his righteousness and his goodness, and all the books of wickedness were not written upon him, and no guilt was found in him.*

5 *And those three holy ones brought me and set me upon the earth before the gate of my house. And they said to me: Make everything known to Methuselah, your son, and show it to all your sons. For no flesh shall be justified before the Lord, for He is their maker.*

6 *For one year, you will be left with your sons until you regain strength. Then, a second time, so that you may teach your sons, and write for them and testify to all your sons. And in the second year, they will take you from among them.*

7 Be comforted in your heart, for the good ones will make righteousness known to the good ones. And a righteous one will rejoice with a righteous one, and they will bless one another among them.

8 And a sinner upon a sinner will die, and a transgressor with a transgressor will drown.

9 And the righteous will die because of the deeds of humankind, and they will be gathered away from before the deeds of the wicked.

10 And in the days of the sun, they finished speaking with me, and I will go to the people of my house, blessing the Lord of Eternity.

CHAPTER 82

1 And now, Methuselah, my son, I will recount to you all these things, and I will write them for you. And I will reveal everything to you, and I have given you the books in which all these things are written. Guard them well, Methuselah, the writings of your father, to give them to the generations to come.

2 I have given you wisdom, and to your sons, and to the sons who will be born to you, so that they may give this instruction to their children, for all generations.

3 And those who understand it will not sleep, but will listen with their ears to learn this wisdom. And to those who partake of it, it will be better than good food.

4 They affirm the righteous ones, all those who walk in the way of righteousness and do not sin, as the sinners will sin during the span of all their days. During the time when the sun is powerful in the heavens, in thirty days, it will go out and come in through the gates with the chiefs of the thousands, who are bound by the system of the stars, and with the four others who distinguish the four periods of the year. Their standing will come in four days.

5 And the children of man will go astray concerning them, and will not consider them in the reckoning of the period of the world, for they will err concerning them. And the children of man will not know them exactly.

6 Because in the reckoning of it, they are recorded in truth, eternally, one in the first gate, one in the second, one in the fourth, and one in the sixth. And the year is completed in three hundred and sixty-four days.

7 And trustworthy is the matter, and exact the reckoning that is written, for Uriel revealed to me the luminaries, the months, [the feasts], the years, and the days, and he counted them in my heart as he commanded him [for me, the lord of all creation] and the host of the heavens.

8 And he will govern in the heavens over the day and over the night, to give light upon humanity—the sun, the moon, and the stars, and all the host of the heavens that revolve in their circuits.

9 These are the regulations of the stars that will come in their divisions, in their appointed times, and in their months.

10 And these are their princes who keep their coming in their times, in their orders, in their appointed times, in their months, in their dominions, and in their divisions.

11 At first, four of their leaders will come, who separate the four divisions of the year. After them, twelve overseers divide the months. And the year is divided into 364 days, with the chiefs of the thousands who separate the days, and the leaders of the four additional days—these are the ones who separate the four divisions of the year.

12 And one of the chiefs of the thousands will be placed between the leader and the one who follows, behind the place. But their leaders will separate.

13 And these are the names of the leaders who separate the four divisions of the year, who are arranged: Malkiel, Elimelech, Melayel, and Ner'el.

83

[14] And the names of their leaders are Adnarel, Yehoshua'el, and Ya'alomi'el. These three will go after the overseers, and one will go after the three overseers, who go after the overseers of the places that separate the four divisions of the year.

[15] At the beginning of the year, Malkiel will govern, who is called by his name Teimani, and the sun. And he will shine at first, and all the days of his rule [that he will govern] will be ninety-one days.

[16] And these are the signs that will be seen on the earth in the days of his rule: sweat, heat, and distress will increase in the land. And all the trees will bear fruit, flowers will bloom, the buds will sprout, and the heat will ripen them. And roses and flowers will bloom in the field, but the winter trees will dry up.

[17] And these are the names of the leaders who are under them: Barqel, Zalbasha'el, and one who is added to them, and his name is Elisaf. And the days of his rule are completed.

[18] The second leader who comes after them is Elimelech, and they will call his name 'Shining Sun.' And all the days of his light are ninety-one days.

[19] And these are the signs of these days: scorching heat and drought will be in the land. And the trees will bring forth their fruit, and they will be completed and ripen, but their fruit will also dry up. And the flocks will conceive and give birth, and all the fruit of the earth will be gathered, and all that is in the field. And the wine presses will be full. These will be in the days of his rule.

[20] And these are the names of the subordinate officers who are under the chiefs of the thousands and their guard: Gad'el, Ka'el, and Hiy'el. And the name of the chief of the thousand who is added to them is Aspa'el. And the days of his rule are completed.

CHAPTER 83

[1] And now, Methuselah, my son, behold, I am showing you all the visions that I have seen, and I will recount them before you.

² Two visions I saw before I took a wife, and each one of them was not like the other. The first [I saw] when I learned writing, and the second before I took your mother as a wife. And I saw a terrible vision, and concerning them, [I prayed before the Lord.]

³ I was lying down in the house of Mahalal'el, my grandfather, and I saw in a vision, and behold, the heavens were inclining to fall, and they were crashing into the earth.

⁴ And when they fell upon the earth, I saw the earth, and behold, it was swallowed into a great abyss. And mountains hovered over mountains, and hills were submerged over hills. And tall trees were uprooted from their roots, and they fell and were submerged into the abyss.

⁵ And then a word fell into my mouth, and I began to cry out and said, 'Woe! The earth is perishing!

⁶ And Mahalal'el, my grandfather, woke me, for I was lying down with him, and he said to me, 'Why do you cry out like this, my son? And why do you wail like this?

⁷ And I recounted to him all the vision that I had seen, and he said to me, 'The thing that you have seen is terrible, my son. And the vision of your dream is concerning the secrets of all the sin of the earth, and the earth will be submerged into the abyss, and great destruction will come upon it.

⁸ And now, my son, because trust has been placed in you, therefore arise now and pray to the Lord of Praises, so that a remnant will remain on the earth, and he will not destroy all the earth.

⁹ My son, from the heavens shall come all these upon the earth, and great destruction shall come upon the earth.

¹⁰ And I arose after this, and I prayed and pleaded, and I wrote my prayer for eternal generations. And I shall reveal all to you, Methuselah, my son.

¹¹ And it came to pass, as I went out, that I saw the heavens and the sun as it came forth from the east, and the moon as it descended westward, and the other stars. And I perceived all as before. I blessed [the Lord of Judgment] and gave Him praise, for He brings forth the sun from the windows of the east, and it rises and shines upon the face of the firmament. And it is carried and goes in its path that was shown to it.

CHAPTER 84

¹ And I lifted my hands in righteousness, and I blessed the Holy One and the Great One, and I spoke with the spirit of my mouth and the tongue of flesh, [which Elohim gave to the children of Adam to speak with, and He gave them a spirit, a mouth, and a tongue, so that they may speak with them.]

² Blessed are you, [the Lord], the great and revered King. Lord of all the creatures of the heavens, King of Kings, and God of all the gods. And your kingdom, your dominion, and your greatness shall stand forever and for eternity of eternities. And your dominion in all generations. The heavens are your throne forever, and the earth is your footstool forever and for eternity of eternities.

³ For [you have made everything], and you rule over them, and nothing is difficult before you. And not one of the wisdoms is hidden from you, and nothing is altered before your throne or from before you. And you know, and see, and hear everything. And nothing is hidden from you, for you see everything.

⁴ And now, behold, the angels of the heavens have acted wickedly, and your wrath shall rest upon human flesh until the great day of judgment.

⁵ And now, [Elohim, Lord and great King,] I pray and plead that you may fulfill my request: to leave me a remnant upon the earth, and not destroy all human flesh, and that the earth shall not remain desolate, bringing it to an end forever.

⁶ And now, [Adonai], remove from the face of the earth all flesh that has angered you, and raise up the flesh of righteousness and uprightness to plant seed forever. And do not hide your face from the plea of your servant.

CHAPTER 85

¹ And after this, I saw a second dream, [and visions were shown to me. My son, all of it.]

² [And Enoch answered and said to Methuselah his son,] 'Listen, my son, to the words of this dream, and I will show you the vision of the dream.'

³ Before I took Edna your mother, I saw in a vision, upon my bed, and behold—a bull came forth from the earth, and the dust was white. And after it, a cow [female] came forth, one, and it stood. Then two young bulls came forth—one was black, and the other was red.

⁴ And the black bull rested upon the red one, and pursued him upon the earth. And from then on, I did not see the red bull again.

⁵ And the black bull grew great, and a heifer [female] stood beside him. And I saw, and behold—many bulls came forth from him, in his image and likeness, and they followed after him.

⁶ And that first cow went out from before that first bull to seek the red young bull [that one]. But she did not find him, and she cried out a great cry and searched for him.

⁷ And I saw when that first bull came and comforted her, and she did not cry out anymore from that moment on.

⁸ And after this, she bore another white bull. And after him, she bore many bulls and black cows.

⁹ And I saw in my sleep the white bull, for he also grew and became a great white ox-bull. And many white bulls came forth from him in his likeness.

¹⁰ And they also bore many white bulls in their likeness, and they walked one after the other.

CHAPTER 86

¹ Again I saw with my eyes in my sleep, and I looked above at the heavens, and behold—a star fell from the heavens, and it arose, and mourned, and pastured among those bulls.

² Then I saw the great and watchful bulls, and behold, they all changed their enclosures, their pastures, and their young bulls, and they began to moan one with another.

³ And again I saw in the vision, and I looked upon the heavens, and I saw, and behold—many stars were descending and falling from the heavens near that first star. Among the young bulls and the oxen, and they stood among them and pastured among them.

⁴ And I looked upon them and saw, and behold—they all revealed their nakedness like horses and mounted the females. And they conceived and bore elephants, camels, and donkeys.

⁵ And all the bulls were terrified, and they fled from before them. And they bit them with their teeth and gored them with their horns.

⁶ And they began to eat the bulls. And all the sons of the earth began to tremble and were afraid, and they fled from before them.

CHAPTER 87

¹ Again I saw them, and behold—they all gored each other, and they devoured one another, and the earth cried out.

² And again I lifted my eyes to the heavens, and I saw in a vision, and behold—a being was created. And behold, from the heavens descended many white beings in the likeness of men. One went forth from that place, and three stood still.

³ And those three who descended last took hold of me by my hand, and they lifted me up from the family of the earth and set me upon a high place. And they showed me a high tower upon the mountains, and all the hills were lowered before my eyes.

⁴ And they said to me, 'Sit here, please, until you see all that shall come upon the elephants, the camels, the donkeys, the rams, and all the bulls.

CHAPTER 88

¹ And I saw one of the four who had descended first, as he took hold of the first star that had fallen from the heavens. And he bound its hands and its feet. And he placed it into the valley, and this valley was narrow, deep, dreadful, and dark.

² And one of them drew his sword and gave it to the elephants, the camels, and the donkeys. And they began to strike one another, and the whole earth trembled because of them.

³ And it came to pass, as I saw in the vision, that behold, one of the four who had descended cast [...] from the heavens. And he gathered and took all the wandering stars, whose nakedness was like the nakedness of horses. And he bound them all by their hands and their feet, and he placed them into the abyss of the earth.

CHAPTER 89

¹ And one of the four went to one of the raised ones he led away and he revealed to him a secret. And he trembled a great trembling. And he was born a bull and he became a man. And he made for himself a great box and he sat inside it. And three bulls sat and stood in that box. And he attacked them.

² And I lifted my eyes again to the heavens, and I saw a high roof, and upon it were seven openings. And these openings poured out many waters into one courtyard.

³ And I saw again, and behold, the springs of the earth were opened in that great courtyard. And the waters grew strong and increased greatly upon the earth. And they covered all of that courtyard until the waters forced over all its ground.

⁴ And the waters increased upon it. And the darkness and the vapor. And it was when I saw from above over the waters. And behold, the waters swelled upward above the courtyard that they overflowed from above over the courtyard, and they arose upon the earth.

⁵ And all the bulls that were in that courtyard gathered together, until I saw them drowning, and they were swallowed and drifted within those waters.

⁶ And that vessel floated upon the waters, and all the bulls, and the rams, and the camels, and the donkeys, and all the beasts drowned [in the waters] upon the earth. And I could not see them, for they were unable to escape. And they drifted and drowned within the abyss.

⁷ And again I saw in the vision, and behold, the windows ceased upon that high roof, and the springs of the earth burst open, and other abysses were opened.

⁸ And the waters began to descend into them, until the land was dried. And that vessel rested upon the land. And the darkness moved, and there was light.

⁹ And the white bull that was for Adam went out from that vessel. And three bulls arose, and one of the three bulls was white, like the appearance of that bull. And one was red like blood, and the other was black. And the white bull went away from them.

¹⁰ And they began to bring forth the beasts of the forest and the birds of the sky. And there went out from them a company of kinds—lions, leopards, dogs, wolves, jackals, wild boars, foxes, hyraxes, swine, hawks, vultures, herons, eagles, and ravens. And among them, a white bull was born.

¹¹ And they fought among themselves, and one bit the other. And the white bull that was born among them gave birth to a wild donkey and a white bull. They stood, and the wild donkey increased itself and multiplied greatly.

¹² And that bull, who was born from him, gave birth to a black wild boar and a white lamb. And that wild boar gave birth to many other wild boars, and that lamb gave birth to twelve sheep.

¹³ And when the twelve sheep grew, they gave one to the donkeys. And those donkeys wrongly gave the sheep to the wolves. And that sheep grew up among the wolves.

¹⁴ And the master brought the eleven sheep to dwell. And they remained and grazed among the wolves, and they multiplied and became many flocks.

¹⁵ And the wolves were afraid of them, and they oppressed them and killed their children. And they threw their children into a great river of water. And these sheep cried out because of their children and groaned to their master.

¹⁶ And one sheep escaped from the wolves and fled to the wild donkeys. And I saw the sheep groaning and crying out, pleading to their master with all their strength. Until the master of the sheep descended to the voice of the sheep from his exalted chamber, and he came to them to see them.

¹⁷ And he called to that sheep who had escaped from the wolves and spoke with it concerning the wolves, that he would warn them not to touch his flock.

¹⁸ And the sheep went to the wolves by the word of the master, and another sheep found that sheep and went with him, and the two of them went together to the families of the wolves. And they spoke to them and testified against them, that they should not touch the sheep from now on.

¹⁹ Then I saw the wolves, and behold, they further increased in oppressing the sheep with all their strength. And the sheep cried out.

²⁰ And their master came to the sheep and began to strike the wolves. And the wolves howled greatly, and the sheep became silent. And from that time, they did not cry out anymore.

21 And I saw the sheep as they went out from among the wolves. And the eyes of the wolves were darkened, and they went to chase after the sheep with all their strength.

22 And the Lord of the sheep descended and led them, and all the sheep followed him. And his face shone, and his appearance was terrifying.

23 And the wolves pursued the sheep until they found them at one of the streams of water.

24 And that stream of water was split, and the waters stood before them on this side and on that side. And their Lord led them across and stood between the sheep and the wolves.

25 And those wolves no longer saw the sheep, and they turned white in the midst of that stream of water. And the wolves pursued after them and ran after them into that stream of water.

26 And it came to pass, when they saw the Lord of the sheep, that they turned back to flee from before him. And the waters returned and were as before. And the waters rose greatly and covered those wolves.

27 And I saw when all the wolves that were pursuing the sheep drowned, and they perished.

28 And the sheep came up from the water, and they went out to the wilderness where there was no water. And they opened their eyes and saw, and I saw the Lord of the sheep feeding them, and he gave them water and grass. And that sheep went before them to lead them.

29 And that sheep went up to the top of a high rock, and the Lord of the sheep sent him to them.

30 And I saw after this the Lord of the sheep standing before them, and his appearance was terrifying and exalted. And all the sheep trembled before him.

31 And they all trembled and were afraid before him, and they cried out to that sheep and to the second sheep who was among them, saying: 'We cannot stand before our Lord to look upon his face.

³² And the lamb that led them returned and ascended to the top of the rock. And the eyes of the sheep were darkened, and they strayed from the path which had been shown to them. And that lamb did not know.

³³ And he was enraged at them. The lord of the sheep, a great and exceedingly strong wrath, and it was made known to that lamb. And he came down from the top of the rock and he came to the sheep and he found most of them, for their eyes were darkened, and they strayed from his way.

³⁴ And it happened, when they saw him, they were afraid and trembled before him. And they longed to return to their enclosures.

³⁵ And that lamb took his stand, and more lambs with him, and he came to the sheep that had strayed, and he began to kill them. And all the sheep were terrified before him. And that lamb returned the sheep that had strayed from the path, and they returned to their enclosures.

³⁶ And I saw in this vision, when that lamb became a man, and he built a house for the lord of the sheep. And he brought all the sheep into that house.

³⁷ And I saw as he died that lamb which met the lamb that led the sheep. And I saw until they expired all the large sheep and the small ones stood in their places and they came to a field of pasture and they approached a stream of water.

³⁸ And that lamb, which had become a man and had led them, separated from them, and was removed and wavered. And all the sheep searched for him and cried out for him with a great cry.

³⁹ And I saw when they ceased from their outcry about that lamb, and they passed over the stream of water.

⁴⁰ And I saw when the sheep came to a beautiful place and a pleasant and praiseworthy land. And I saw when the sheep were satisfied, and that house stood among them in the pleasant land.

⁴¹ And sometimes their eyes were opened, and sometimes they were blinded, until another lamb stood up and led them. And he restored all of them, and their eyes were opened.

⁴² And the dogs, and the foxes, and the pigs began to devour the sheep. And they were being devoured until the lord of the sheep raised up one ram from the sheep.

⁴³ And that ram began to gore and pursued with his horns. And he struck against the foxes, and after them, against the pigs. And he destroyed many pigs. And after them, he destroyed all of them.

⁴⁴ And the sheep, whose eyes were opened, saw the ram among the sheep. And they watched until he abandoned his path and began to trample the sheep and wander aimlessly.

⁴⁵ And the lord of the sheep sent this lamb to another lamb, to lift him up as a ram and establish him as a leader of the sheep, in place of the ram who abandoned his path.

⁴⁶ And he went to him and spoke with him alone in silence. And he lifted him up as a ram, and as a ruler, and as a leader of the sheep. And despite all this, the dogs continued to oppress the sheep.

⁴⁷ And the first ram pursued the second ram, and he fled from before him. Then I saw the first ram until he fell before the dogs.

⁴⁸ And the second ram arose and led the sheep. And that ram begot many sheep. And he lay down, and a small lamb arose in his place as a ram, and he became a ruler and leader over the sheep.

⁴⁹ And the sheep grew and multiplied. And all the dogs, the foxes, and the wild boars trembled and fled from before him, for they feared him. And that ram struck all the beasts and killed them. And the beasts could no longer be among the sheep, nor did they plunder from them anymore.

⁵⁰ And that house was lifted up and became exceedingly great. And they built a lofty tower over the house of the Lord of the sheep. And that house was humbled, but the tower was high and exalted. And the Lord of the sheep dwelled within the tower, and before him was set a full table.

⁵¹ And I saw that the sheep strayed greatly, and they walked in many paths, and they abandoned that house. And the Lord of the sheep called some from among them and sent them to the sheep, and they killed the sheep.

⁵² And one of them escaped and was not killed, and she fled and cried out to the sheep. And they sought to kill her, but the lord of the sheep rescued her from their hands. And he lifted her up and returned her to his presence.

⁵³ And he sent many other ewes to the flock. For they will bear witness in them. And they wailed over them.

⁵⁴ And I saw after this, and behold, they abandoned the house of the lord of the sheep and his tower. And their eyes were darkened, and they strayed from his way. And I saw that the lord of the sheep sent many afflictions upon all their flocks, until the sheep cried out because of the afflictions and returned to him.

⁵⁵ And they were abandoned into the hands of the lions, and the leopards, and the wolves, and the jackals, and into the hands of the foxes, and all the beasts. And the beasts of the field began to tear apart the sheep.

⁵⁶ And I saw when he abandoned their house and their tower, and he gave them into the hands of the lions, to tear them apart and to eat their flesh, and into the hands of all the beasts.

⁵⁷ And I began to cry out with all my strength, and I called to the lord of the sheep, and I showed him the sheep, that they were being devoured by all the beasts of the field.

⁵⁸ But he remained silent when he saw this, and he rejoiced that they were being devoured, and swallowed, and taken by force. And he abandoned them to be food into the hands of all the beasts of the field.

⁵⁹ And he drove out the sheep and called seventy shepherds to tend them. And he said to the shepherds and to their attendants, saying: 'Each and every one of you shall now shepherd the sheep, and everything that I command you, you shall do.

60 And I delivered them to you by number, and I have declared to you which of them will perish, and that one you shall destroy. And he gave the sheep into their hands.

61 And he called to the second one and said to him: 'Look and carefully observe everything that the shepherds will do with the sheep, for they will destroy more of them than I commanded.

62 And every destruction and annihilation that will be done by the shepherds, write how many will be destroyed by my command and how many will be destroyed by their own will. And write that which each of the shepherds will cut off.

63 And read before me by number how many they destroyed by their own will, and how many were given to them to destroy, so that it may be a testimony for me against them, and so that I may know all the deeds of the shepherds, and to repay them. And you shall see all their deeds, if they will keep my commandments or not.

64 But they will not know anything about this, and you shall not tell them, and you shall not warn them. Only write everything that the shepherds will destroy, each one in his appointed time, and bring everything before me.

65 And I saw when the shepherds tended in their appointed time, and they began to kill and destroy far more than they were commanded. And they abandoned the sheep into the hands of the lions.

66 And the lions and the leopards ate and swallowed the majority of the sheep, and the wild boars of the forest ate with them. And they burned that tower and destroyed the house.

67 And I was very sorrowful for the tower because it was destroyed, and for the house of the sheep. And after this, I no longer saw the sheep or their return to that house.

68 And the shepherds and their attendants gave the sheep to all the beasts to eat them. And each one took a count, and the second wrote in a book that which was destroyed, each and every one of them.

69 And they were all destroyed, and they killed far more than they were commanded. And I began to weep and wail greatly concerning the sheep.

70 And I saw in the vision that scribe, and behold, he wrote down everything that was destroyed by those shepherds, one by one, each day. And he brought this entire book to the lord of the sheep and placed it before him. And he showed him everything they had done, and everything that was destroyed by each of the shepherds, and everything they were given to destroy.

71 And the book was read before the lord of the sheep, and he took the book in his hand and read in it. And he sealed it and placed it for safekeeping.

72 Then I saw that the shepherds shepherded for twelve hours. And behold, three of those sheep returned, and they came and began to build.

73 And they began to build again as before, and they raised up that tower. And it was called by the name 'The High Tower.' And they began again to set a table before the tower, but all the bread upon it was unclean and was not purified.

74 And over all, the eyes of the sheep and the eyes of their shepherds were blinded, and they did not see. And many were given over exceedingly into the hands of the shepherds to be destroyed. And they trampled upon the sheep with their feet and devoured them.

75 And the lord of the sheep remained silent until all the sheep were scattered over the field, and they mixed among them, and they were not saved from the hands of the beasts.

76 And [the scribe] who wrote the book brought it to the dwelling places of the lord of the sheep, and showed it to him and read it before him. And he pleaded and supplicated before him as he showed him all the deeds of the shepherds, and testified before him against all the shepherds.

77 And he took the book and placed it before him and went out.

CHAPTER 90

¹ And I saw until the time when thirty-seven shepherds had shepherded them, all of them completing their times like the first ones. And others took them in their hands to shepherd them.

² Then I saw in the vision, and behold, all the birds of the sky came—the eagles, the kites, the herons, and the ravens. And the eagles brought them, all of them, and they began to bring destruction upon the flock. And they pecked out their eyes and ate their flesh.

³ And the flock cried out because all the birds ate their flesh. And I wailed and cried out in my sleep against those shepherds who had shepherded the flock.

⁴ And I saw as the flock was devoured by the dogs, and by the eagles, and by the herons, and they left them nothing—no flesh, no skin, nor sinews—only their bones alone they left for them. And even their bones fell to the earth, and the flock diminished.

⁵ And I saw until the time when twenty-three shepherds shepherded them, and in their times, fifty-eight appointed times were completed.

⁶ And small lambs were born from these white ones of the flock, and they opened their eyes, and they saw, and they cried out to the flock.

⁷ And the sheep did not answer them a word, and they did not hear that which was spoken to them. And they were as if deaf, and their eyes were completely blinded.

⁸ And I saw in the vision the ravens swooping upon the lambs. And they took one from those lambs, and they tore apart the sheep and ate them.

⁹ And I saw when horns grew on the lambs, and the ravens cut off their horns. And I saw again when one large horn grew on one of the sheep, and their eyes were opened.

¹⁰ And she looked after them, and behold, their eyes were opened. And she cried out to the sheep, and the young of the sheep saw her. And they all ran to her.

¹¹ And despite all this, the eagles, the lions, the ravens, and the herons tore apart the sheep until that time. And they swooped upon them and ate them. And the sheep became numb, but the young of the sheep wailed and cried out greatly.

¹² [And they fought and struggled, and the ravens took a stand and sought to break his horn. But they could not overcome him.]

¹³ And I saw until the shepherds and the eagles and the kites and the herons came, and they called to the ravens that they should break the horn of that lamb. And they quarreled and fought and stood firm. But he fought against them, and he cried out for help, that it might come to him.

¹⁴ And I saw until there came [the scribe], who wrote the names of the shepherds and brought them before the lord of the sheep. And he helped that lamb and showed him everything, and that his help would come.

¹⁵ And I saw when the lord of the sheep came to them in the fury of his anger. And all who saw him fled, and they all fell before him.

¹⁶ And all the eagles, the lions, the ravens, and the herons gathered together, and they brought their forces and all the beasts of the field. And they all came together and helped to cut off the horn of that lamb.

¹⁷ And I saw when [the scribe] came, the one who wrote the book according to the word of the lord. And he opened the book of the records, which the twelve last shepherds had destroyed. And he placed it before the lord of the sheep, for they had destroyed more than those who were before them.

¹⁸ And I saw until the lord of the sheep came to them. And he took the staff of wrath in his hand, and he struck the earth, and it split open. And all the beasts and the birds fell from upon these sheep, and they sank into the earth, and the earth closed over them.

¹⁹ And I saw when a great sword was given to the sheep. And the sheep went out to the beasts of the field to destroy them. And all the beasts and the birds of the sky yielded before them.

20 And I saw when a throne was set up in the pleasant land, and the lord of the sheep sat upon it. And he took all the sealed books and he opened those books before the lord of the sheep.

21 And the lord called to the seven first white ones and commanded [them] to bring before him [all the stars]—from the first star that walked before those stars, which had testimonies like the mares of the horses. And [the first star] that fell at the beginning. And they brought them all before him.

22 And he called to the man who was writing before him, and he was one of the seven white ones. And he said to him, 'Take these seventy shepherds, to whom I gave the sheep in their hands. And they took them, and they killed more of them than I had commanded them.'

23 And I saw, and behold, all of them were bound, and they stood before him.

24 And the judgment was first upon the stars, and they were judged and declared sinners. And they went to the place of judgment, and they were thrown into the midst of a valley filled with flames of fire and filled with pillars of fire.

25 And the seventy shepherds were judged, and they were declared sinners. And they were thrown into that valley of fire.

26 And I saw at that time, and behold, a valley like this, filled with fire, was opened within the earth. And they brought the blind sheep, and they were judged, and the sinful ones emerged. And they were thrown into that valley of fire, and they were burned. And that valley was to the right of that house.

27 And I saw the sheep as they were burned, and their bones were burned.

28 And I arose to see when they covered that old house. And they lifted all the pillars, all the beams, and all the ornaments of that house, and they concealed them in their place. And they carried them and placed them in one of the places on the right side of the land.

29 And I saw when the lord of the sheep brought a new house, large and taller than the first. And he raised it upon the place of the first, where they had covered it. And all its pillars were new, and its ornaments were new and larger than the first ones that were old and had been removed. And all the sheep entered within it.

30 And I saw all the sheep that remained, and all the beasts that were on the mountains, and all the birds of the sky that had fallen. And they bowed before the sheep and pleaded with them, and they listened to all their words.

31 And after this, they took me, three clothed in white, who lifted me up before this one. And when I held the lamb in my hand, they lifted me up and seated me among these sheep before the judgment took place.

32 And all the sheep were white, and their wool was large and pure.

33 And all the lost and scattered ones, and all the beasts of the field, and all the birds of the heavens gathered in that house. And the Lord of the sheep rejoiced with great joy, for they had all improved their deeds and returned to his house.

34 And I saw until they laid down the sword that was given to the sheep, and they returned it to his house and sealed it before the Lord. And all the sheep entered into that house, but it could not contain them.

35 And the eyes of all of them were opened, and they saw the good. And there was not one among them who did not see.

36 And I saw, and behold, the house grew and expanded exceedingly.

37 And I saw, and behold, a white bull was born, and its horns were great. And all the beasts of the field and all the birds of the heavens were afraid before him and pleaded before him at all times.

38 And I saw until all their families were transformed, and they all became white bulls. And the first among them became a very great beast, and it had great horns, and they were black upon its head. And the Lord of the sheep rejoiced over them and over all the bulls.

39 *And I slept among them, and I awoke, and I saw everything.*

40 *This is the vision that I saw in my sleep. And when I awoke, I blessed the Lord of Righteousness and gave him praise.*

41 *And I wept a great weeping, and my tears did not cease until I could no longer endure it. And throughout all that time, my tears flowed over the vision that I saw, for everything shall come and be fulfilled. And all the deeds of mankind, in full detail, were shown to me.*

42 *And I remembered that night also my first dream, and I wept again when I saw this vision.*

CHAPTER 91

1 *And now, Methuselah, my son, call to me all your brothers and gather to me all the sons of your mother, for the word calls to me, and the spirit has been poured upon me, so that I may show you that which shall happen to you in the last days.*

2 *And Methuselah went and called to him all his brothers, and he gathered all the sons of his family.*

3 *And he spoke to his sons about righteousness and said, ['Hear, my sons, all the words of your father, and listen to the words of my mouth. I testify among you, my beloved, and I will tell you,' Love righteousness and walk in its ways.]*

4 *[And do not draw near to righteousness with a divided heart, nor associate with those of deceitful hearts. Only his heart, my sons, walks in the way of righteousness, and He shall guide you in good paths. And to righteousness you shall cleave.]*

5 *I have known that great devastation shall be upon the earth. However, a great judgment shall come upon it, and all the corruption shall be finished and uprooted from its root. And all its uprising shall be changed.*

6 *And yet again, corruption shall come upon the earth, and all the deeds of violence, and the deeds of oppression and wickedness shall return once more.*

7 And when violence, sin, disgrace, oppression, and all deeds increase, and rebellion, wickedness, and defilement break out, then a great judgment shall come upon them all from the heavens. [And the Holy Lord shall go forth in wrath and fury] to execute judgment upon the earth.

8 In those days, oppression shall be uprooted from its roots, and the roots of violence and deceit from under the heavens.

9 And all the pleasing images and the towers shall perish. They shall be burned in fire, and they shall be erased from the face of the earth. And they shall be cast into She'ol of fire, and they shall be cut off in fury and a great judgment forever.

10 Then [the righteous one shall rise from his sleep, and wisdom shall also rise and be given to them].

11 And after this, the roots of violence (חמס hamas) shall be uprooted, and the sinners shall perish by the sword. And the roots of the blasphemers shall be uprooted wherever they are. And those who scheme violence, and the blasphemers, shall die by the sword.

12 And after this, another week shall come—[the eighth]. A sword shall be given to it to execute righteous judgment upon the workers of iniquity, and the sinners shall perish by the hands of the righteous.

13 And in their final days, they shall acquire houses for themselves in their righteousness, and the House of God shall be built for the great king, in glory, forever.

14 And after this, in the ninth week, righteous judgment shall be revealed to the whole world, and all the works of the wicked shall be removed from upon the face of the whole earth, and they shall be written for eternal destruction. And all mankind shall flow toward the way of righteousness.

15 And after this, in the tenth week, in its seventh part, there shall be an eternal judgment upon the great Watchers who came forth from among the angels, and upon the heavens forever.

16 Then the upper heavens shall pass away and be changed, and new heavens shall appear. And all the host of the heavens shall shine sevenfold forever.

17 And after this, countless weeks shall come, forever, in goodness and righteousness. And from now on, sin shall no longer be remembered for eternity.

18 And now, I testify among you, my sons, and I will show you the ways of righteousness and the ways of wickedness. And I have shown them to you again, so that you may know that which is to come.

19 And now, listen, my sons, and walk in the ways of righteousness, and do not walk in the ways of wickedness. For all who walk in the ways of violence (hamas) shall be cut off forever.

CHAPTER 92

1 [Written by Enoch the scribe, the teaching of wisdom, which is praised in the mouth of all men and which judges the whole earth.] To all the children who dwell upon the earth, and to the last generations who do what is right and pursue peace.

2 Do not let your spirit be troubled about time, for days have been given by the Holy and Great One to all.

3 [And the righteous one shall rise from his sleep, and he shall walk in the ways of righteousness. And all his ways and his journey shall be in goodness and mercy forever.]

4 [And he shall have mercy on the righteous one and shall give him righteousness and dominion forever. And he shall live in goodness and righteousness and walk in eternal light.]

5 And sin shall perish in darkness forever and shall no longer be seen from that day onward forever.

CHAPTER 93

1 [And after this, Enoch began to recount from the books.]

2 [And Enoch said about the sons of righteousness, about the chosen ones of the world, and about the planting of righteousness and uprightness:] Behold, I speak with you. And I, Enoch, will declare to you the words of that which appeared to me as a vision of the heavens, that which I know from the words of the holy angels, and that which I have learned from the tablets of heaven.

3 [And Enoch began to recount from the books and said:] "I am the seventh, born in the first week, at the time when judgment and righteousness were withheld."

4 And after, in the second week, great wickedness shall arise, and deceit shall sprout. During it, they shall come. The first end shall come, and after it passes, violence shall increase. And in it, one man shall be saved, who shall establish law for the sinners.

5 And after this, at the end of the third week, a man shall be chosen to plant justice and righteousness. And after him, the planting of righteousness shall sprout forever.

6 And after this, at the end of the fourth week, the visions of the holy ones and the righteous shall be seen. And his covenant shall be for all generations, and an inheritance shall be given to them.

7 And after this, at the end of the fifth week, a house shall be built for glory and for kingship forever.

8 And after this, in the sixth week, all who live in it shall awaken, but they shall turn their hearts away from wisdom. And in it, a man shall ascend. And at its end, the house of kingship shall be burned in fire, and in it, the entire family of the chosen root shall be shattered.

9 And after this, in the seventh week, a generation of upheavals shall arise, and many shall be its deeds, and all its works shall be upheavals.

10 And at its end, the chosen and the righteous shall be rewarded from the planting of righteousness forever, upon being given the sevenfold law of all creation.

[11] [For who is this, the son of man, who can hear the voice of the Holy One and not tremble? And who will know His thoughts? And who is able to understand all the decrees of the heavens?]

[12] [And who is this who is able to know the works of the heavens, and who can measure his spirit and his soul? And who is able to recount them? Who has ascended and has seen all their extremities, and has understood and is able to do as they do?]

[13] [And who is able to understand the breadth of the earth and its length? And to whom has the measurement of everything been revealed?]

[14] [Is there anyone who can understand the breadth of the heavens and their heights? And upon what they were founded? And how great is the number of the stars? And where do all the luminaries rest?]

CHAPTER 94

[1] And now, behold, I say to you, my sons: Love righteousness and walk in it. For the ways of righteousness are worthy to be chosen, and the ways of violence (hamas) will come to an end swiftly, and they shall be destroyed.

[2] And they shall reveal the ways of violence (hamas) and the ways of death to certain men of that generation, and they shall distance themselves from them and not walk in them.

[3] And now, behold, I say to you, the righteous: Do not walk in the ways of wickedness, violence (hamas), or death. Do not draw near to them, so that you will not perish.

[4] Only seek righteousness and choose for yourselves a good life. Walk in the ways of peace, so that you may live and delight in it.

[5] And you shall keep my words, and they shall not be erased from upon your heart. I know that the sinners will lead the children of Adam astray, to do evil against wisdom, and wisdom shall find no place. Yet all counsel shall not be lacking for them.

6 Woe to them, the builders of violence (hamas) and wickedness, who set deception as their foundation. For suddenly they shall be cut off, and there is no peace for them.

7 Woe to them, the builders of their houses without justice, for they shall be uprooted from the foundation, and by the sword they shall fall. And the treasuries of silver and gold shall be swiftly cut off in judgment.

8 [Woe to you, the rich, for you trusted in your riches. But your wealth and power you shall abandon, for you did not remember the Most High in the days of your prosperity.]

9 And you commit destruction (niklah) and violence (hamas). Therefore, you have consecrated yourselves for the day of bloodshed, the day of darkness, and the day of great judgment.

10 Thus I say to you, and I have made it known to you: for your creator will destroy you. And for your falsehoods, there will be no mercy, and your makers will rejoice at your destruction.

11 And in the days of corruption, your righteous ones will be a disgrace to the sinners and the wicked.

CHAPTER 95

1 Who will tear down? My eyes are water, and I weep over you. Like water, I pour out my tears and sigh from the sorrow of my heart.

2 Who gave you the right to sow hatred and do evil? Justice will find you, sinners.

3 Do not fear, righteous ones, because of the sinners. For still, [YHWH] will give them into your hands to execute justice upon them as you have desired.

4 Woe to you who bind yourselves together as companions. All healing shall be far from you as your sin endures.

5 Woe to them who do evil to their brothers, for by your own deeds, you will be repaid.

107

6 Woe to false witnesses and deceivers, for you shall swiftly perish.

7 Woe to you, sinners, who persecute the righteous, for you will be repaid. And you men of violence (hamas), you will continue to pursue, but darkness will fall upon you.

CHAPTER 96

1 Rise up, righteous ones, for the sinners shall quickly be cut off before you, and you shall rule over them as you have desired.

2 On the day of distress of the sinners, your children will rise and ascend like eagles. You will raise your nests beyond measure. Like rabbits, you shall ascend and enter the holes of the dust and the clefts of the rocks forever before the wicked. And they shall groan and wail before you like goats.

3 And you, do not be distressed in your suffering, for healing is for you. A bright light will shine for you, and you will hear the sound of rest from the heavens.

4 Woe to you, sinners, for in your wealth you make yourselves appear like the righteous, but indeed, your own hearts will convict you. For you are sinners, and this matter will testify against you, the memory of your wickedness.

5 Woe to you who consume the richness of the wheat and drink in luxury, and trample the poor with your power.

6 Woe to you who drink water at all times, for quickly it will be taken from you, and you shall burn and dry up because you have abandoned the source.

7 Woe to you who commit violence and deceit, for your remembrance shall rise up against you for evil.

8 Woe to you, tyrants, who trample the righteous with power, for the day of your downfall will surely come, and the day of your judgment. And to the righteous shall come many good and long days.

CHAPTER 97

¹ Beside the mountain where they swore and cursed their companions, cold, snow, and frost shall never leave it. Dew shall not descend upon it unless as a curse, until the great day of judgment, when the sinners shall be a disgrace and perish.

² At that time, it shall be burned up and brought low. It shall be consumed and melt like wax before fire, and thus it shall burn concerning all its works.

³ And now I say to you, sons of men: Great wrath is against you and against your sons. And this wrath shall not cease from you until the time of the slaughter of your sons.

⁴ And your beloved ones shall perish, and your honored ones shall die from all the earth. Because from now on, their days shall not be more than one hundred and twenty years.

⁵ And do not think to live for more years, for there is no way of escape for them from now on, because of the wrath that has been kindled against you by the King of all ages. Do not think that you shall escape these things.

⁶ And all the words of your lawlessness shall be read before the Great Holy One, before your face. Then all the deeds that were done in lawlessness shall be exposed.

⁷ Woe to you, sinners, who are in the midst of the sea and who are on the dry land. A remembrance of evil is upon you, for you have been reckoned for evil.

⁸ Woe to you who acquire gold and silver not from righteousness. And you will say, 'We have become rich with wealth, and we have acquired and possessed what we desired.'

⁹ And whatever we desire, we will do. For we have stored up silver in our treasuries, and we have many good things in our houses.

CHAPTER 98

¹ And now, I swear to you, the wise and not the foolish, that you shall see much lawlessness upon the earth.

² For men shall put on beauty like women, and their appearance shall be more beautiful than virgins, in kingship, greatness, and authority. And silver and gold shall be for them as food, and in their houses, it shall be poured out like water.

³ They shall have no knowledge and no wisdom. Thus, you shall perish together with all your possessions and all your glory and honor. Into disgrace, desolation, and great slaughter. Your spirits shall be cast into the furnace of fire.

⁴ Sin was not sent upon the earth, but men themselves created it. And those who commit it shall arrive into a great curse.

⁵ Slavery was not given to a woman, but through the works of their hands, it came to be. For she was not destined to be a slave; from above, it was not given, but from oppression, it came into existence. Likewise, neither was lawlessness given from above, but from transgression. Likewise, neither was a barren woman created, but from her own wrongdoing, she was condemned to childlessness and shall die childless.

⁶ I swear to you, sinners, by the holy and the great one, that your evil deeds shall be revealed in the heavens. There shall not be for you a hidden unjust deed.

⁷ Do not assume in your soul, nor in your heart, that they do not know or see, nor that they do not perceive your injustices. Nor are they unrecorded before the Most High.

⁸ From now, recognize that all your injustices are recorded day by day until your judgment.

⁹ Woe to you, fools, for you shall perish because of your foolishness. And you shall not listen to the wise, and good things shall not meet you. [But] evil [...] you.

¹⁰ And now, know that you are prepared for the day of destruction. And you, sinners, do not hope to live. Only go and die, for you shall not know atonement. Be prepared for the great day of judgment, and for a day of distress and great disgrace for your souls.

¹¹ Woe to you, hard-hearted ones, who do evil and eat blood. From where will good things come to you, that you may eat and drink and be satisfied? There is no peace for you.

¹² [... works of] unrighteousness. For do you have good hopes for yourselves? Now, let it be known to you that into [the hands of] the righteous you shall be delivered, and they shall kill you, and they will not spare you.

¹³ Woe to you who rejoice in the suffering of the righteous. Your pit shall not be dug.

¹⁴ Woe to you who seek to nullify the words of the righteous. You shall have no hope of salvation.

¹⁵ Woe to you who write false words and words of deception. You write them, and with your lies, you shall lead many astray.

¹⁶ You yourselves are deceived, and you have no joy. But you shall quickly perish.

CHAPTER 99

¹ Woe to you who commit deception and to those who receive honor and glory through works of falsehood. You are destroyed; there is no salvation for you.

² Woe to you who alter the true words and distort the eternal covenant, and who consider yourselves sinless. You shall be swallowed up in the earth.

³ Then prepare yourselves, O righteous ones, and present your petitions as a memorial. Offer them as a testimony before the angels, so that they may bring the sins of the wicked before the Most High [God] as a memorial.

111

⁴ And then [they shall be shaken] on [the day] of destruction of wickedness.

⁵ In that [time], those who give birth shall cast out and suffer greatly, and they shall abandon [the infant] child. And those who are pregnant [shall miscarry], and those who nurse [shall cast away their children], and they shall not [turn back] to their infants, nor upon those who nurse, nor shall they have pity . . .

⁶ *And behold, I swear to you, sinners, that for the day of bloodshed and destruction, eternal destruction is prepared for sin.*

⁷ Those who carve images of silver and gold, wood, stone, and clay, and worship [phantasms], demons, and evil spirits, to all the deceptions not according to [understanding], and no help shall be found from them.

⁸ And they will be led astray in the foolishness of their hearts, and the visions of dreams will mislead you.

⁹ You and the works of your falsehoods which you have made and worked, and you shall perish in one.

¹⁰ And then, blessed are all those who hear the wise words and learn them, to do the commandments of the Most High, and they will walk in the ways of His righteousness, and they will not go astray with the deceivers, and they will be saved.

¹¹ *Woe to you who spread evil among your brothers, for you will die in Sheol.*

¹² *Woe to you, foundation-layers of sin and deception, who pour out a bitter spirit upon the earth, for because of this, they shall come to an end.*

¹³ Woe to those who build their structures not from their own labor, and who make every building from stones and bricks, for which there is no grace to you.

¹⁴ Woe to those who despise the foundation and the inheritance of their fathers from eternity, for a spirit of deception shall pursue you, and there is no rest for you.

¹⁵ Woe to you who commit lawlessness and aid injustice, murdering your neighbor, until the day of the great judgment.

¹⁶ For at that time, he will wipe out your glory and stir up his wrath against you. He will destroy all of you with the sword, and all the righteous will remember your injustices.

CHAPTER 100

¹ *And in those days, the fathers will be slain with their sons* **in one place** *and they will die together, until their blood flows like a river.*

² And a man will not hold back his hand from his son, nor from his beloved one, to kill him. And the sinner from the honorable one, nor from his brother. From morning until the sun sets, they will be slain in the same place.

³ And a horse will pass through, up to its chest in the blood of the sinners, and the chariot will sink down up to its axles.

⁴ And the angels shall go down, descending into the hidden places on that day—those who helped in wrongdoing. And they will be gathered into one place, and the Most High will arise on the Day of Judgment to execute a great judgment upon all.

⁵ And he will appoint a guard over all the righteous and the holy ones of the holy angels, and they will be preserved like the pupil of an eye until evil and sin vanish. And from that time, the devout shall sleep a sweet sleep, and there will no longer be one who terrifies them.

⁶ Then the wise among men will see, and the sons of the earth will understand these words of this writing, and they will know that their wealth is unable to save them in the fall of injustice.

⁷ Woe to you, the unjust, when you oppress the righteous on the day of great distress and imprison them in fire, for you will be repaid according to your deeds.

⁸ Woe to you, hard-hearted ones, who stay awake to think upon evil. Fear surrounds you, and there is no one to help you.

⁹ **Woe to you, all sinners, for the deeds of your mouth. Woe to you, all sinners, for the words of your mouth and for the deeds of your hands, for you have gone astray from the holy deeds...**

¹⁰ *And now, know that the angels will investigate your deeds in the heavens, from the sun and the moon and the stars. Your sins, which you have committed wickedly against the righteous, shall be examined.*

¹¹ *And it will testify against you,* **the cloud and the mist and the dew and the rain. Every cloud and mist and dew and rain**... *for they were all withheld because of you and did not fall upon you...* **upon your sins.**

¹² **Therefore, give gifts to the rain so that it may not be prevented from coming down to you, and to the dew and the cloud and the mist. Write in gold so that they may come down.**

¹³ **For if snow is cast upon you, and frost, and its cold, and the winds and their ice, and all their plagues, you will not be able to withstand the cold and their plagues.**

CHAPTER 101

¹ **Consider then, sons of men, the works of the Most High and fear to do evil before Him.**

² **If He shuts the windows of heaven and restrains the dew and the rain from descending because of you, what will you do?**

³ **If He sends His wrath upon you and upon your deeds, will you not be pleading with Him? Why do you speak great and harsh words against His greatness?**

⁴ **See the sailors who sail the sea, their ships being shaken under the surge of the waves and the storm.**

⁵ **And being storm-tossed, all are afraid... They throw their possessions into the sea and suspect in their hearts that the sea will swallow them, and in it they will perish.**

⁶ Is not all the sea and all its waters the work of the Most High? And He established their boundaries, and He bound it, and enclosed it with sand?

⁷ And from His rebuke they fear and dry up, and the fish...

⁸ ... the earth and all that is in them? And who gave knowledge to all who move in the sea? The sailors fear the sea *but do not the sinners fear the Most High?*

CHAPTER 102

¹ And when He casts upon you the surge of fire of your burning, where will you flee to be saved? And when He sends forth His voice upon you,

² You will be shaken and afraid by a great sound, as the whole earth is shaken, trembling, and violently disturbed.

³ And the angels fulfill what was commanded to them, and the heaven and the luminaries are shaken and trembling. All the sons of the earth, and you sinners, are cursed forever. There is no joy for you.

⁴ Take courage, souls of the righteous who have died, of the righteous and the pious.

⁵ And do not be grieved that your souls have descended into Hades with sorrow, and were not met with the body of your flesh in your life according to your holiness. For the days in which you lived were days of sinners and the accursed upon the earth.

⁶ When you die, then the sinners will say, 'The pious died according to fate, and what advantage did they gain from their deeds?'

⁷ And they also died just like us. See then how they die with sorrow and darkness, and what advantage did they gain?

⁸ From now on, let them rise and be saved, and they will see forever us eating and drinking.

⁹ Therefore, to seize, to sin, to steal, and to acquire possessions, and [to see] good days.

¹⁰ See then, those who justify [themselves], what became of their destruction, for all righteousness was not found in them until they died and were destroyed.

¹¹ And they became as though they had never been, and their souls descended with suffering into Hades . . .

CHAPTER 103

¹ *And now, behold,* **I swear to you,** *the righteous, by the greatness of His splendor and glory, and by the honor of His kingdom and majesty, I swear to you.*

² I know this mystery. For I have read the tablets of heaven, and I saw the necessary writing. I knew the things [written] in them and engraved [concerning] you.

³ For goodness, joy, and honor have been prepared and recorded for the souls *of the* [righteous] *dead.*

⁴ *They will rejoice,* and the *spirits* of them shall not perish. Nor shall the *remembrance of the generations of the* ages be erased from before the Great One. *Therefore, do not fear* their reproach.

⁵ And you, the dead of the sinners, when you die, they will say about you: 'Blessed are the sinners all the days of their lives, as many as they saw in their lifetime, and gloriously.'

⁶ They died, and judgment did not take place in their lifetime.

⁷ You yourselves know that they will lead your souls into Hades.

⁸ And there they will be in great distress, and in darkness, and in a trap, and in a burning flame. And they shall enter into great judgment, your souls in all the generations of eternity. Woe to you, there is no rejoicing for you.

⁹ For do not say, you righteous ones, being holy in life: 'In the days of affliction, we toiled in hardship, we were exhausted and became few, and we found no helper.'

¹⁰ We were crushed and perished, and we despaired, and no longer expected salvation, day after day.

¹¹ We hoped to become the head, but we became the tail. We labored in work, but we did not gain power over our wages. We were devoured by sinners, and the lawless placed a heavy yoke upon us.

¹² Those who rule over us, our enemies pierce us and enclose us. We sought where [to flee] from them so that we might find relief...

¹³ *We sought to leave them so that we might escape and find rest, but we found no place to sleep or to be saved from them.*

¹⁴ ...We cried out to those who overthrew and oppressed us, but they did not accept our pleas, nor did they want to hear our voice.

¹⁵ And they did not help us, nor did they act against those who oppressed and devoured us, but instead, they strengthened them against us. They killed us and reduced us to few. And they do not speak of our slain, nor do they remember the sins of their sinners.

CHAPTER 104

¹ I swear to you that the angels in heaven remember [you] for good before the glory of the Great One.

² Take courage now, for you have grown old in evils and in tribulations. Like the lights of heaven, you will shine and appear. The windows of heaven will be opened for you.

³ And your cry will be heard, and your judgment, which you cry out, will be revealed over all that was taken from you concerning your tribulation, and from all who participated in oppressing and devouring you.

⁴ *Hope, for your joy will be great, like the joy of the angels of heaven. And do not abandon your hope.*

117

⁵ [Do not fear] the evils on the day of the great judgment, and you shall not be found like the sinners. [But you sinners] shall be plundered, and eternal judgment shall be upon you for all the generations of eternity.

⁶ Do not fear, you righteous ones, when you see the sinners prevailing and prospering. And do not become their associates, but keep far away from all their injustices.

⁷ For do not say, you sinners, '[that] your sins shall not be sought out [from] time.'

⁸ And now I declare to you that light and darkness, day and night, observe all your sins.

⁹ Do not be deceived in your heart, nor lie, nor alter the words of truth, nor deny the [words of the] holy one. And do not give praise to your [images], for they do not lead to righteousness, [but bring all lies and deception]...

¹⁰ They alter the truth and rewrite it, the sinners mislead the many, and they lie, fabricating great falsehoods. And they inscribe the writings upon their own names.

¹¹ And I wish that all my words would be written in truth, in their names, and that they neither remove nor alter these words, but may they write all in truth, which I testify to them.

¹² And again, I know a second mystery: that my books shall be given to the righteous, the holy, and the wise, for the joy of truth.

¹³ And they shall believe in them, and in them they shall rejoice and exult, all the righteous to learn from them all the ways of truth.

CHAPTER 105

¹ *And in those days, the word of [the Lord] said: Call to the children of Adam and bear witness to them concerning their wisdom. Show them that you are their guides, and their reward is great upon the earth.*

² *For I and my sons will be joined with them forever, [and they will walk] in the ways of righteousness all the days of their lives. Rejoice in the valley of righteousness in truth, for peace shall be yours.*

CHAPTER 106

¹ And after a time, Methuselah took a wife for my son, and she bore a son, and he called his name Lamech. Righteousness was diminished until that day. And when he came of age, he took a wife for himself, and she bore him a child.

² And when the child was born, his body was whiter than snow and redder than a rose. All his hair was white, like white wool, curly and glorious. And when he opened his eyes, the house shone like the sun.

³ And he rose from the hands of the midwife, opened his mouth, and blessed [the Lord].

⁴ And Lamech was afraid of him, and he fled, and he came to Methuselah his father and said to him.

⁵ A child has been born to me, different, not like mankind, but like the children of the angels of heaven. And his form is different, not like us. His eyes are like the rays of the sun, and his face is glorious.

⁶ And I suspect that he is not from me, but from an angel. And I fear him, lest something happens in his days on the earth.

⁷ And I beg you, [Father, and] I implore you, go to Enoch, our father, and ask him [...].

⁸ [He came] to me, to the ends of the earth, [where he saw] that I was then, and he said to me: '[My] father, hear my voice and come [to] me.' And I heard his voice and came to him and said, 'Behold, I am here, my child. Why have you come to me, my child?'

⁹ And he answered, saying, 'Because of great distress, I have come here, father.'

[10] And now, a child has been born to Lamech, my son, and his form and his image {are not like mankind, and his complexion} is whiter than snow and redder than a rose. And the hair of his head is whiter than white wool, and his eyes resemble the rays of the sun.

[11] And he rose from the hands of the midwife, and opening his mouth, he blessed the Lord of the Ages.

[12] And my son Lamech was afraid, and he fled to me, and he does not believe that he is his son, but that he is from the angels. [...] the exact knowledge that you have and the truth.

[13] Then I answered, saying, 'The Lord will renew an ordinance upon the earth, and in the same manner, I have seen a child and have made it known to you. For in the generation of Jared, my father, they transgressed the word of the Lord from the covenant of heaven.'

[14] And behold, they sin and transgress the custom, and they unite with women, and with them they sin, and they took wives from them. And they bore, not like spirits, but fleshly ones.

[15] And there shall be great wrath upon the earth, and a flood, and there shall be great destruction for one year.

[16] And this child that has been born shall be left behind, and three of his children shall be saved while those upon the earth perish.

[17] And he will pacify the earth from the corruption that is in it.

[18] And now, say, Lamech, that he is your child, righteous and holy, [and] call his name [Noah]. For he shall be your remnant, upon whom you shall find rest, and [his] sons shall be saved from the corruption of the earth, and from all the sinners, and from all the destructions upon the earth.

[19] He showed me and revealed to me, and on the tablets of heaven I read them.

CHAPTER 107

¹ Then I saw the things written concerning them, that generation after generation will grow more wicked. And I saw this until a generation of righteousness arises, and wickedness will be destroyed, and sin will be removed from the earth, and good things will come upon the earth upon them.

² And now, go quickly, my son, and inform Lamech, your son, that this child who has been born is truly his and not falsely.

³ And when Methuselah heard the words of Enoch his father, for he revealed it to him secretly, he was called Noah, bringing joy to the earth from destruction.

CHAPTER 108

¹ [A second book, which Enoch wrote for Methuselah his son and for all who come after him, that they may keep the law in the latter days.]

² You who have done all these things, wait for those days until all evildoers perish and the power of the wicked is removed.

³ And you, wait until sin passes away and their name is erased from the books of the holy ones. Their offspring will be cut off forever, and their souls will die. They will cry out and wail in the place of their name, and with the sword they will be burned in fire in a desolate land.

⁴ And I saw there something like a cloud, but I did not pass through it. It was deep, and I was also unable to see. And a bright fire was burning inside it, and there were bright mountains surrounding it, moving back and forth.

⁵ And I asked one of the holy angels who was with me and said, 'What is this light? For this is not the heavens, but only a flame of burning fire, and a sound of crying and weeping, and lamentation and great pain.'

6 *And he said to me: This place that you have seen—in this, it is where the souls of the sinners, and the criminals, and the ones who do wickedness shall come. And those who alter all that the [Lord] spoke by the hand of the prophets concerning [the coming days].*

7 *[For they are written and recorded in the heavens above, so that the angels may read them and know what will come upon the sinners, and upon the souls of the humble, and those who afflict their flesh and are reviled by wicked men. And their reward is prepared from Elohim.]*

8 *[And to those who love Elohim, and do not love silver, nor gold, nor all the good things of the world, and they shall give their flesh to be trampled.]*

9 *[And for those who, from the time of their existence, have not craved the luxuries of the earth, and remembered that the spirit of their life, and they guarded it. And the Lord greatly tested them, and their souls were found pure, so that they may bless His name.]*

10 *[And I wrote in these books all of their blessings, and he established their reward, for he found them loving [Elohei] the heavens with their souls forever. And they blessed me at the time when they were trampled by the wicked people, and they heard from them curses and blasphemies and were insulted by them.]*

11 *[And now, behold, I call to the souls of the righteous from the dwelling of light, and I have shined upon all who were born in darkness. And their flesh was not repaid with honor according to their faith.]*

12 *[And I will bring those who love my holy name into a radiant light, and I will seat each one upon a throne of glory.]*

13 *[And they shall shine forever and ever, for God is righteous in his judgment. He will give faith to the faithful in the dwelling of the righteous.]*

14 *[And they shall see those who walk in darkness, for they shall be driven into [a place of] the shadow of death. And the righteous shall shine.]*

15 *[And the sinners shall groan when they see the radiance of the righteous. And they also shall go to [the place] that is written for them for days and times.]*

זה הסוף

Zeh Ha'Sof
(This is the End)

Appendix A
Chapter Summaries & Textual Notes
Chapter 1

Enoch's opening words address both his generation and a distant future one, affirming that his message transcends time. He speaks of the Watchers and the holy ones, celestial beings confirmed in the Dead Sea Scrolls (DSS) but downplayed or altered in later translations.

The earliest Aramaic text simply states that the Holy One, the Great One, will go forth in power, but does not specify from where. Later texts, particularly Ge'ez, insert phrases like "His dwelling" or "the heavens," attempting to define His location. The title "The Great One" (רבה, rabā) was later altered to "Lord of Eternity," introducing theological shifts not found in the original.

As this being manifests in strength, the ends of the earth tremble. In the Aramaic, this is a physical event—a cosmic or terrestrial upheaval. Later versions insert "the Watchers shall tremble," shifting the focus to a supernatural reaction rather than a natural disaster. The Ge'ez expands the scene further, adding imagery of shaking mountains, collapsing hills, and melting wax—all absent from the earliest text.

The phrase "the earth shall be split apart" describes a cataclysmic event, potentially an earthquake or global rupture. Later interpretations frame it as divine judgment, but the original emphasizes sheer destruction rather than moral reckoning.

Enoch then speaks of the q'doshim (קְדוֹשִׁים)—holy ones—who accompany the Divine in executing judgment. These beings, referenced throughout biblical and extra-biblical texts, are celestial rather than human. Some traditions equate them with "saints" or "angels," but the term itself does not specify their nature. Their role is similar to the Mesopotamian Anunnaki or Igigi, celestial beings who act on behalf of a greater power.

A mysterious name, 'ämalak, appears in this chapter. Its meaning is uncertain, though later interpretations associate it with divine rule or a messianic figure. Over time, scribes reshaped this passage to reflect later religious doctrines, shifting its focus toward themes of divine favor and end-times prophecy.

Chapter 2

Enoch calls for reflection, urging his audience to consider their flesh—a phrase that may imply self-awareness, mortality, or the impermanence of human existence. Later interpretations expand on this theme, connecting it to divine judgment or a spiritual reckoning.

The Aramaic presents these verses as an observation of human nature, the earth's works, and celestial signs. However, later translations distort the meaning by shifting the term "signs" (דגלי, diglī) to "seasons," reframing the passage as a calendar reference rather than an omen. Additionally, the original meteorological imagery of "clouds pouring rain" is missing in later versions, revealing a deliberate omission of natural cycles and weather symbolism.

Chapter 3

Enoch directs attention to the trees, observing how they wither yet remain standing for two or three years. This passage originally served as an observation of nature's cycles, possibly as a metaphor for endurance or decay.

Later versions significantly alter this verse, reframing it as a commentary on seasonal cycles rather than long-term resilience. Some translations expand it further by inserting a reference to "fourteen evergreen trees" that endure through winter. This is a later religious reinterpretation not found in the earliest Aramaic text.

Chapter 4

Enoch continues the theme of observing natural signs, directing attention to heat and frost as omens rather than mere weather patterns. The Aramaic uses the term "signs" (דגלי, diglī), establishing the idea that nature conveys divine messages.

Later versions alter this verse, reducing it to a commentary on seasonal weather rather than a reflection on divine order and meaning. The original text also emphasizes shade and shelter as forms of protection from natural forces, but this theme is minimized in later translations.

Chapter 5

Chapter 5 contrasts the righteous and the rebellious, emphasizing divine order, transgression, and consequence. The earliest Aramaic text describes trees that last and remain covered, possibly symbolizing divine glory. Later translations shift this into a religious reinterpretation.

The phrase "consider all works" appears in the original text without a clear subject. Later versions add "His" to suggest ownership, but this is an assumption. However, the phrase "He is forever" (הוא לעלם, hū' l-ʿālam) is confirmed in both Aramaic fragments (4Q201 & 4Q204), proving it was present in the original.

The text then turns to defiance and rebellion. The Aramaic preserves "all of them in defiance" (וכלהן, w-kulhōn) and rebellion (ממרה, mamrāh), but later versions soften or remove this, obscuring the passage's meaning. The Geʿez text, in contrast, describes seas and rivers working together to fulfill their tasks, reinforcing the theme of natural order and obedience. Some later interpretations expand this, linking it to divine law or cosmic harmony, but the original text focuses on the natural world's function.

A stark warning follows: "You will transgress" (ותע[ברון, w-taʿăḇrūn) and on the day of your death (ביום טמתכן, b-yōm ṭĕmāṭkōn). Later translations soften this by removing the direct references to transgression and judgment. The original Aramaic presents a blunt warning about human actions and their lasting consequences.

Further emphasizing this theme, the text states: "Your days will be cursed" (יומיכן תלוט, yōmēḵōn tĕlôṭ) and "the years of your destruction shall be many" (ושני אבדנכן יסגין, w-šănē ʾăḇāḏnēḵōn yisgīn). The final phrase mentioning "mercy" (ורחמ[ין, w-raḥm[...]) is fragmentary, leaving its full meaning uncertain.

A damaged Aramaic fragment preserves "your names shall be ... forever" (שמהתכ[ן עלם, šĕmāṭkōn ʿālam). However, it is unclear whether this implies eternal honor or disgrace. Given the surrounding context of judgment and consequences, it refers to lasting repercussions rather than a blessing.

The Ge'ez version restructures the passage into explicit divine judgment, stating: "Then you shall curse the eternal curse, and all the righteous shall receive peace. But you will be cursed, you sinners, forever, and you shall have no peace." This stark division between the righteous and the wicked does not appear in the surviving Aramaic, revealing that it was a later theological addition.

Later versions expand this contrast between the righteous and the cursed. The righteous are promised light, joy, peace, and faith, while the cursed receive damnation. Since the Aramaic equivalent is missing, it remains uncertain whether this dualistic theme was part of the original text or a later adaptation.

Several later translations soften or modify key elements. The original Ge'ez text states "mercy shall be given" to the righteous, but many versions replace this with "wisdom will be granted." Similarly, the phrase "sin by wickedness, injustice, or arrogance" is specific in Ge'ez but generalized or removed in later versions.

The final section describes the righteous as those who "shall not sin" and "shall not be harmed." Later translations expand this, introducing phrases about breaking divine law, eternal gladness, and increased years of joy. These additions shift the original emphasis on peace and fulfillment toward a more religious doctrine of reward and punishment.

Chapter 6

Chapter 6 describes a pivotal moment in human and celestial history, detailing the multiplication of humanity and the arrival of the Watchers. The Ge'ez term ዐዋፅዕልል (mawa'əl), often mistranslated as "work" or "deed," actually refers to an event. The text describes how offspring were born, beautiful and lovely ones. Later translations smooth over this language, sometimes interpreting it as a divine act, but the original text frames it as a historical occurrence.

The Aramaic uses mal'āk (מַלְאָךְ, "messengers"), which originally lacked the later Christian meaning of "angels." The Ge'ez text translates this as "angels," but the phrase "children of heaven" implies divine origin rather than a fixed classification. A damaged Aramaic fragment (4Q201 6:2) preserves partial dialogue paralleling Genesis 6:2, where the "sons of God" take human wives.

The Geʿez text names Samyāzā (Shemihazah) as "their leader" and refers to the others as "their messengers" (malʾāʾkomä, ⰿⰀⰄⰧⰘⰿ), avoiding a specific term for angels. This aligns with the Aramaic malʾəkt in 6:2, proving that they were envoys, not later religious angels. Samyāzā expresses fear that the others may hesitate, showing doubt before their decision. His declaration, "I alone will pay the price," implies he is willing to take sole responsibility, although the text later shows they all share in the consequences.

The Aramaic text is fragmentary, but it describes an oath and a binding curse. Without a complete source, we cannot confirm if this wording was original, but it aligns with the theme of a sworn pact. The Geʿez states that "all of them together" swore and invoked a curse, but due to missing portions of the Aramaic, it is unclear whether they explicitly bound themselves. The final phrase in Geʿez, "they agreed," may be a later smoothing not found in the original Aramaic.

The Aramaic confirms that the Watchers descended and bound themselves with a curse but does not specify a number, location, or name. The Geʿez version adds that two hundred descended upon "Mount Hermon" and named it after their oath. Since these details are missing in the Aramaic, we cannot confirm if they were original or later additions.

A list of names is preserved in the Aramaic, but it appears without an introduction. Some names are damaged, but those that remain are confirmed. The Geʿez version includes additional names not present in the Aramaic fragments, indicating later expansions. This list represents the earliest known preserved names of the Watchers' leaders and is compiled from multiple Dead Sea Scroll fragments: 4Q201, 4Q202, and 4Q204.

The Aramaic mentions "chiefs and great ones," but it only confirms ten names. The rest of the passage is missing. The Geʿez expands this, stating that the ten were leaders over two hundred "faithful angels," a detail absent from the Aramaic and thus a later theological addition.

Chapter 7

Chapter 7 expands on the events following the descent of the Watchers, focusing on their interactions with humanity, their offspring, and the resulting corruption. The Aramaic confirms that "they took women from all whom they chose" and "taught them sorcery." However, due to fragmentary wording, the number of Watchers involved is uncertain.

The Ge'ez version significantly expands this passage, adding that the Watchers "separated" before taking wives, that the women "became pregnant and bore ḥabēhōn (their offspring, the Tall Ones)," and introducing additional magickal practices such as "spells, root-cutting, and tree magick." These details do not appear in the Aramaic, pointing to later elaboration.

The Aramaic fragments (4Q201, 4Q202) preserve the core meaning that the women became pregnant by the Watchers and gave birth, but portions of the text are missing, preventing full reconstruction. The Ge'ez further expands this passage, adding that they "stood" for 400 years, though it does not mention size or greatness ("giants") in this verse. The later association of these offspring with giants developed from external influences rather than the earliest sources.

The Aramaic confirms that human labor and eating are central themes, but much of the verse is missing, leaving its full meaning uncertain. The Ge'ez adds phrases such as "until they exhausted" and "the children of men," which do not appear in the Aramaic. These additions may have been intended to emphasize hardship and suffering. No Greek or Latin manuscript exists for this passage.

The Aramaic (4Q201) clearly states that the Watchers conspired to kill men, but part of the verse is missing. There is no mention of giants devouring mankind in the Aramaic. The Ge'ez expands the text, adding that "the great ones" were "enraged" and "devoured men," but these details do not appear in the earliest source. No Greek or Latin manuscript exists for this passage.

The Aramaic (4Q201, 4Q202) confirms that this conspiracy extended beyond humans, involving winged ones (birds), creatures of the earth (beasts), creeping things, and those of the sea (fish). The phrase "to consume their flesh" is present, but the missing portions prevent identifying who was consuming whom. The Ge'ez expands this passage, adding corruption, destruction, and suffering, which are not present in the Aramaic. No Greek or Latin manuscript exists for this verse.

The Aramaic (4Q202) is fragmentary but suggests that something occurred affecting the earth. However, the exact nature of this event is unclear. The Ge'ez explicitly states that "the earth cried out against the lawless ones," but the Aramaic does not confirm this directly. The Greek and Ge'ez represent a later interpretations.

Chapter 8

Chapter 8 focuses on the forbidden knowledge taught by the Watchers, emphasizing advancements in metallurgy, warfare, adornment, and divination. The Aramaic (4Q202) confirms that Azazel taught the use of iron for weaponry, metallurgy, and adornment, including gold, silver, and antimony for cosmetics. This passage confirms that the Watchers had physical bodies, as they directly influenced human craftsmanship and beauty practices.

The Ge'ez aligns with the Aramaic but adds minor embellishments, such as "mighty" swords. The Greek (Gizeh, Syncellus) expands Azazel's role further, calling him a "ruler" and emphasizing "angelic teachings," neither of which are present in the earliest text.

The Aramaic explicitly names antimony (kḥl', כוחלא), the root of "kohl," an ancient metallic compound used in Egyptian and Mesopotamian eye makeup. Ground into stibnite (Sb_2S_3), it was a staple cosmetic material, confirming that the Watchers' influence extended beyond warfare into chemistry and beauty. This knowledge shaped traditions for millennia.

The Aramaic (4Q202) preserves only the phrase "they were reckless," without explicitly mentioning ungodliness or fornication. The Greek (Gizeh, Syncellus) expands the text, introducing "great ungodliness" and "fornication," neither of which appear in the earliest manuscript. Similarly, the Ge'ez adds "wickedness" and "deception," further emphasizing moral corruption. The root of "reckless" (פחז, pḥz) can imply unchecked behavior, but it does not specify the exact nature of their actions.

The Aramaic (4Q201, 4Q202) confirms that Shemihazah (later Semjaza) and others taught spells, divination, and star knowledge to their women, though some text is missing. The Greek (Gizeh, Syncellus) expands this list, adding potions, plant lore, categories of teachings; none of which are found in the Aramaic. The Ge'ez follows the Greek, introducing extra Watcher names, visions, plant knowledge, and lunar omens, all of which are absent from the earliest texts.

The name Semihazah (שמיחזה) means "He who sees the Name" or "He of the Name and Vision," connecting him to forbidden knowledge. Later Greek and Ge'ez versions modify Watcher names, further obscuring their original meanings. This follows a pattern of altering celestial names over time, making it more difficult to trace their true origins.

The Aramaic (4Q201, 4Q202) is fragmentary but contains a reference to "deeds from the earth rising before..." with the subject unclear due to missing text. The Greek versions (Gizeh, Syncellus) drastically expand this passage, adding a cry of the perishing, human suffering, and an appeal to divine justice. The Ge'ez follows this expansion, inserting explicit references to sin and divine judgment.

A variant in 4Q202 includes "voice" (קל א), which may explain why the Greek and Ge'ez introduce a "cry," but the rest of their additions are later theological developments.

Chapter 9

Chapter 9 describes the reaction of four celestial beings to the corruption on Earth, their plea for intervention, and the expanding consequences of the Watchers' actions.

The Greek (Gizeh) and Ge'ez both confirm that four archangels witnessed the bloodshed on Earth, though they differ in details. The Greek names Michael, Uriel, Raphael, and Gabriel, while the Ge'ez replaces Raphael with Suriel, indicating a textual alteration. The Greek version focuses solely on bloodshed, whereas the Ge'ez expands the narrative, adding "all transgression," a known pattern of theological embellishment by Ge'ez scribes.

No Aramaic or Latin survives for this passage. The Greek states, 'They spoke together, a loud voice rising to the gates of heaven,' while the Ge'ez adds 'with their understanding,' emphasizing supplication.

Some translations insert "reaching the gates of the earth and up to the ends of heaven," but this phrase is absent from both Greek and Geʻez, perhaps a later theological addition or mistranslation.

Both the Greek (Gizeh) and Geʻez describe a demand for justice, but they frame it differently. The Greek states, "They make a strong appeal," implying a legal demand rather than a humble request. The phrase πρὸς τὸν ὕψιστον (pros ton Hypsiston) is traditionally translated as "to the Most High," but it simply means "the highest," which may have originally referred to a supreme authority, a galactic force, or a high place, rather than a specific deity. Later scribes reinterpreted it as a divine title.

Some translations insert "lifting up the souls of men," but this phrase is absent in both Greek and Geʻez, and suspected as a later assumption rather than an accurate rendering. The Greek ἀνθρώπων (anthrōpōn), meaning "men," was a collective term for humanity, including both men and women, though later translators debated its inclusivity unnecessarily.

The Greek Κυρίῳ (Kyriō) is traditionally translated as "Lord" but can also mean "Master" or "Overlord," implying rulership by dominion rather than devotion. The phrase "King of the Ages" (βασιλεὺς τῶν αἰώνων) has often been misrendered as "King of Eternity," though aiōn (αἰών) originally meant "age" or "era," indicates rule over vast but finite time periods, possibly linked to celestial cycles. The Geʻez further expands the hierarchy, adding "their Lords of the mighty ones" and "their Gods of the gods," phrases absent from the Greek and clearly later theological insertions.

The Greek and Geʻez confirm that this passage describes creation, power, and wisdom. The final statement, "nothing is hidden or concealed from You," follows the Greek φανερὰ καὶ ἀκάλυπτα ("manifest and uncovered"), conveying the idea of total awareness. This aligns with ancient understandings of omniscience but does not necessarily imply the later theological concept of absolute foreknowledge.

Both the Greek and Geʻez confirm that Azazel spread forbidden knowledge. The phrase "mysteries of the age" (μυστήρια τοῦ αἰῶνος) is often mistranslated as "secrets of eternity," but aiōn (age) refers to a specific time, not infinite duration. This points to Azazel's teachings being tied to celestial cycles or advanced sciences.

The text states that these mysteries were practiced in the heavens before being taught to men. Azazel's teachings included metallurgy and cosmetics, which are the very foundation of alchemy, and require physical, hands-on practices. If these arts existed in the heavens, it confirms that the Watchers were not purely spiritual beings.

The Greek and Ge'ez confirm that Semjaza was a leader alongside Azazel, but his exact role is unclear. The Greek explicitly states that he was given "the authority to lead" (τὴν ἐξουσίαν ἄρχειν), not necessarily to rule, as later translations suggest. The Ge'ez emphasizes his position but does not explicitly state rulership. The phrasing implies organization and is evidence that the descent of the Watchers was not a chaotic rebellion, but a deliberate decision.

The Greek and Ge'ez confirm that the Watchers went to the daughters of men and became defiled with them. The Ge'ez word ḥəbərä means "companions," reflecting both union and defilement. The Ge'ez also identifies certain individuals specifically as sinners, rather than simply recipients of knowledge, implying a deliberate exposure or separation among humanity. The exact meaning of this identification process remains unclear.

The Greek and Ge'ez confirm that beings were born from human women. The Greek calls them Titans (τιτᾶνας, titânas), linking them directly to Greek mythology. The Ge'ez uses Tall Ones (rä'äyta, ረአይት), a neutral term unrelated to mythology. Since the Aramaic is missing, it is unclear whether these beings were originally described as giants or if this interpretation developed later. The original text does not blame these offspring for pre-flood chaos; later traditions recast them as villains, rewriting the history of when the Titans ruled the earth.

The Greek and Ge'ez confirm that the souls of the dead cried out, their voices reaching heaven's gates. The Greek states that they made appeals to heaven, their voices constant and trapped without resolution. Both texts state that the voices rose before the face of lawlessness, emphasizing that the dead bore witness to chaos and could not be silenced.

This passage, found in both Greek and Ge'ez, confirms that everything, past, present, and future, is already known to the one being addressed. The Greek reads, "You see these things and allow them," showing dismay at inaction, while the Ge'ez emphasizes "what has been done and what exists," accounting for both past and present. The Greek asks, "Why have we not been told what to do?" while the Ge'ez shifts to, "How long will judgment last?" This suggests that earlier versions focused on uncertainty about action, whereas later traditions became more concerned with the duration of punishment.

Chapter 10

Chapter 10 describes the judgment of the Watchers, the destruction of their offspring, and the renewal of the earth. This passage outlines the punishment of Azazel, the fate of the Nephilim, and the coming restoration of humanity and nature.

The Greek and Ge'ez preserve a major anomaly in the angel's name. The Greek calls him Israēl (Ἰστραὴλ), linking him explicitly to Jacob, while the Ge'ez gives the otherwise unattested Arsyalalyur (ለአርስያላዩር), meaning "God's Light upon the Earth." This directly corresponds to Uriel ("God is My Light"). The name Israēl originally belonged to a celestial being predating Jacob, but later traditions erased or misunderstood this celestial origin, reducing it to a purely human context.

The Greek preserves the command, "Hide yourself," warning someone of an impending flood. However, the Ge'ez removes this phrase, suppressing the original warning. The Greek explicitly announces the coming flood, while the Ge'ez avoids direct mention, stating only that waters will never return. This deliberate change separates 1 Enoch from its Mesopotamian origins, confirming that it preserves an older flood narrative than Genesis.

The Greek preserves a survival message, stating that someone is taught how to escape and that his offspring will endure. The Ge'ez reverses this into judgment, erasing survival and declaring destruction, a clear redaction. This confirms that 1 Enoch originally contained a divine warning about the flood, aligning directly with Mesopotamian tradition before being later suppressed.

The Greek preserves the command, "open the wilderness in Dudael," while the Ge'ez removes it, softening Azazel's punishment. The term 'əgzī (አግዚእ) is ambiguous, meaning "lord" or "ruler," not necessarily "God." Later traditions assumed the speaker was the Most High, but the original text remains vague.

The phrase "until the time" appears only in Ge'ez but is absent in the Greek, indicating it was added to imply a temporary punishment. The Greek, being older, indicates that Azazel's exile was permanent. His punishment is physical confinement, not moral judgment. He is buried beneath jagged stones, completely isolated. The phrase "cover him with darkness" defines entombment, not exile.

The Greek phrase "for the age" (εἰς τὸν αἰῶνα) has been misrepresented as "forever." Aiōn means "age" a long but finite period. If eternity was intended, we would expect aiōnios, which does not appear. Later traditions forced an eternal meaning onto this verse to align with evolving doctrines of eternal punishment. However, the earliest text specifies only a long but undefined imprisonment, not necessarily forever.

The Greek states "on the great day of judgment" (τῆς κρίσεως), while the Ge'ez removes this, pointing to later softening of Azazel's fate. The Ge'ez phrase "when the appointed time has come" (ኩነኔ, kunənē) confirms a future event but does not specify eternal damnation. It simply states that at the appointed time, Azazel will be cast into fire.

The term mala'əkt (መላእክት) means "messengers" rather than "angels." The phrase "heal the earth" indicates that the Watchers caused physical or environmental damage beyond moral corruption. The Greek explicitly names these beings Watchers (ἐγρήγοροι, egrēgoroi), meaning "beings who do not sleep," emphasizing their physical nature. The Ge'ez replaces Watchers with "mighty ones" (ትጉሃን, təguḥan), deliberately obscuring their identity.

The Greek and Ge'ez both place all sin solely on Azazel, sharply contrasting later traditions which spread blame among the Watchers or humanity. The Greek uses "devastated" (ἠρημώθη, ērēmōthē) instead of "defiled," emphasizing global ruin. Azazel bears responsibility for all sin, making him the entity upon whom guilt rests, possibly the origin of the scapegoat ritual in *Lev.* 16:10.

The Greek explicitly calls these beings "offspring of the Watchers" (ἐγρήγοροι, egrēgoroi), while the Ge'ez replaces this with "offspring of the mighty ones" (ትጉሃን, təguḥan) to obscure their origin. The phrase "cast them out among themselves" indicates these beings turned on each other. Only Noah is preserved, aligning with *Genesis* 6:9 in both righteousness and pure lineage.

The offspring of the Watchers beg for mercy but are denied. The Greek states, "they hope to live eternal life," confirming they expected immortality, believing their hybrid nature ensured it. Their extended lifespan exceeded the later 120-year human limit. Mercy was also denied to their fathers, sealing both their fate and the Watchers' as irreversible.

This passage commands Michael to deliver judgment to Semihazah and the Watchers for their unions with human women. Their defilement was total, corrupting themselves, their offspring, and the earth itself. The Greek states the offspring of the Watchers will be "slaughtered," while the Ge'ez softens this to "killed."

The Greek states, "he shall be burned up and destroyed," referring to Semjaza, leader of the Watchers. The Greek "burned up" (κατακαυθῇ) signifies complete destruction, while the Ge'ez "cast down" weakens his fate. The phrase "until the completion of the generation of generations" (τελειώσεως γενεᾶς / ተወáይ ተወáይ) implies a long but finite sentence or indefinite imprisonment. Earlier verses set it at seventy generations, but this phrase may extend it, even until the end of time.

The Watchers are cast into "the abyss of fire" (χάος τοῦ πυρός), a consuming realm, while the Ge'ez calls it the "house of correction" (bēta moqǝh), defining it as a prison, not annihilation. Their fate is endless suffering, not destruction.

This passage describes a complete renewal of the earth, eradicating all injustice and evil while firmly establishing righteousness. The phrase "let the seed of righteousness be revealed" indicates righteousness is not just restored but propagated, leaving the door open to referring to genetic lineage rather than symbolism.

The final section describes a transformed world where humanity flourishes. The Greek states, "One measure shall yield a thousandfold," reflecting divine multiplication, establishing a restored paradise. The Ge'ez adds "filth" (ርኩስ, rūkəs) to emphasize impurity being wiped away. The earth is permanently cleansed, marking the final restoration of peace and righteousness.

Chapter 11

Chapter 11 describes a future age of divine blessings, prosperity, and lasting harmony.

The first verse depicts a time when blessings will pour from the heavens into human labor and deeds. This divine abundance will alleviate toil, bring prosperity, and restore harmony between heaven and earth. The emphasis is on a transformation where human effort is rewarded, and the struggle for survival is eased.

The second verse describes an age of enduring peace, truth, and righteousness. The phrase "in all the days of the world" indicates the perpetual nature of this harmony, while "in all generations of the world" ensures its continuity across time. Peace and truth coexist, not merely as the absence of conflict but as a foundation of divine integrity and order.
This passage represents a complete renewal of the world, where righteousness prevails and divine balance is restored.

Chapter 12

Chapter 12 introduces Enoch's unique role, his connection to celestial beings, and the fate of the fallen ones.

The first verse establishes Enoch's unique status as being "hidden" before the unfolding of events. This phrase suggests either a physical or spiritual removal, implying a transformation or ascension. The statement "and from that, he was" may allude to a state of being that transcended the human realm, demonstrating Enoch's exceptional nature. No other human received divine knowledge or instruction as he did, making him distinct among mankind.

The second verse illustrates Enoch's work with both the "holy ones" and the "mighty ones." The "holy ones" refer to divine beings, while the "mighty ones" could refer to the Watchers, Nephilim, or other powerful celestial figures. The phrase "in the days of those" points to a specific era, though the exact identity of these groups remains ambiguous.

The third verse describes Enoch receiving a divine blessing from "the Most High and the King of the Ages," emphasizing his special status. The "mighty ones" (the Watchers or other celestial beings) cause him distress, setting up a critical dialogue where Enoch, the scribe, is called to receive further instructions. His title "scribe of righteousness" makes his role as a recorder of divine revelations crystal clear.

The fourth verse commands Enoch to deliver a message of judgment to the mighty ones of the heavens who defiled themselves with women, mimicking human behavior. Their actions led to great deception and turmoil on Earth. This passage drives home the severity of their transgressions and sets the stage for their coming punishment.

The fifth verse confirms that peace and forgiveness will not be granted to the fallen ones. The phrase "upon the earth" alludes to their judgment as a perpetual condition for as long as they remain here. The lack of forgiveness makes the severity of their crimes undeniable. It is unclear whether this applies solely to the fallen ones or extends to their offspring, but the focus on their defilement and rebellion strongly suggests it applies to both.

The final verse describes the eternal suffering of the fallen ones. They will witness the death of their loved ones and the destruction of their offspring. They will mourn and beg forever, yet no mercy or peace will be granted to them. This passage emphasizes the unending nature of their punishment, sealing their fate.

Chapter 13

Chapter 13 depicts Enoch's confrontation with Azazel, the Watchers' desperate plea for mercy, and their ultimate rejection.

The first verse captures Enoch's direct confrontation with Azazel, declaring that peace will not be granted to him. The phrase "a great punishment has gone out upon you" suggests that Azazel's judgment is not only inevitable but has already begun. The words "it shall bind you" imply that his restraint and fate are imminent, foreshadowing the consequences of his actions.

The second verse makes it clear that Azazel will not receive any form of mercy or intercession. His teachings—violence, oppression, and sin—are declared unforgivable. The phrase "you have shown to the children of men" emphasizes that his knowledge was actively imparted, spreading corruption throughout humanity.

The third verse describes the intense fear of the fallen ones upon hearing

Enoch's message. The phrase "fear and trembling seized them" illustrates their terror, portraying that they knew their punishment was certain and near. Their reaction indicates the weight of their impending judgment, leaving no room for denial or escape.

The fourth verse shows the fallen ones pleading with Enoch to record their request for mercy and forgiveness. They hope he will intercede on their behalf before the Most High. Their desperation shows recognition of their sins and a belief that they may still have a chance, despite their seemingly sealed fate. The Ge'ez emphasizes Enoch's role as their only hope for mercy.

The fifth verse (Greek) states that the Watchers are completely silenced, unable to speak or even lift their eyes toward heaven due to overwhelming shame. Their condemnation is absolute, and their guilt renders them powerless. The Ge'ez adds a slight expansion on their speech but does not alter the core meaning. This moment marks the full realization of their downfall, those who once descended with authority can no longer even look upon the divine realm.

The sixth verse connects the Watchers' fate to ancient mythic traditions. In Atra-Hasis, the Igigi gods rebel against Enlil but are replaced by humanity rather than being cast down. In the Anzû Myth, a rogue divine being defies Enlil by stealing his authority but is ultimately defeated, restoring order. The Watchers' fate in 1 *Enoch* mirrors these traditions, divine beings breaking cosmic law and suffering exile, silence, or destruction as a result.

The seventh verse confirms that the Watchers filed a formal plea for mercy, which Enoch recorded as a written petition. The Greek word ὑπόμνημα (hypomnēma) suggests an official memorandum or legal record. Their request is not just for physical deliverance but for their very spirits, showing a deeper fear of permanent condemnation. The Greek "prolongation" (makrotēs) to prolong, they sought a delay in judgment, while the Ge'ez changes this to "rest" (nuhatə), indicating a softened theological reinterpretation.

The eighth verse establishes a significant location, at the waters of Dan, west of Mount Hermon. Mount Hermon is already central to The Book of Enoch, as it is where the Watchers descended and made their pact (cf. 6:6). Enoch's act of reading their petition aloud he makes a formal, sacred proclamation, an attempt to intercede. The Greek confirms this was a legal document (hypomnēma), presenting the nature of their plea.

The ninth verse marks a turning point. Instead of Enoch merely acting as a scribe, he is now given direct authority to confront the Watchers. The phrase "visions of wrath" indicates that their plea for forgiveness has been rejected, and divine judgment is imminent. The Greek structure makes it clear that Enoch is experiencing something involuntary and overwhelming; the visions fall upon him, rather than him seeking them out. This further illustrates that Enoch is merely a messenger, not an intercessor with actual influence. The phrase "sons of heaven" directly confirms that the Watchers are celestial beings, not humans.

The tenth verse captures the Watchers at their lowest point. They are gathered, sitting in mourning, covering their faces, universal signs of grief, despair, and possibly shame. The mention of Lebanon and Senisel (Sēnēsēr) places this event in a real geographical region, tying in the physical reality of their punishment.

The name Senisel (Sēnēsēr) corresponds to Senir (שְׂנִיר / Šənîr), an ancient name for Mount Hermon. This identification is supported by:
- *Deut. 3:9*: "The Sidonians call Hermon Sirion, and the Amorites call it Senir."
- *1 Chr. 5:23*: "The half-tribe of Manasseh lived in Bashan, as far as Baal-Hermon, Senir, and Mount Hermon."

These references confirm that Senir was historically associated with Hermon, further anchoring this passage in real-world geography.

The eleventh verse mentions the name Ebelsata (Ubelsyael in Ge'ez), an unclear term that may be a lost geographical or mythological reference. Given its proximity to Dan and Hermon, it could be a corrupted form of Banias (Paneas), a major cult center near Mount Hermon. This indicates the Watchers' gathering place was not an obscure wilderness but a real location tied to their descent.

Enoch's movement from Dan to Ebelsata within walking range proves their proximity, further linking the Watchers, their rebellion, and the real-world geography of Hermon. Their mourning and covered faces indicate full awareness of their fate. This was not just symbolic, but a memory of a real place associated with divine descent and judgment.

The final verse marks Enoch's transition from messenger to prophet of judgment. He declares his visions before the Watchers and openly rebukes them, delivering the "words of righteousness." The Greek calls them "Watchers of heaven," while the Ge'ez refers to them as "mighty ones of heaven," preserving their celestial nature.

This moment cements Enoch's role as a divine intermediary, not as an advocate for the Watchers, but as the one who seals their fate.

Chapter 14

Chapter 14 presents a formal proclamation, emphasizing that this section of 1 Enoch is a written record of both righteousness and judgment. The Watchers are described as "those from eternity," reinforcing their ancient, celestial origins. The rebuke issued against them is not of human origin but is commanded by "the Holy and Great One," proving its divine authority. The phrase "in this vision" confirms that this is not merely a verbal decree. Enoch is experiencing a revelation that he is compelled to record. The close alignment between the Greek and Ge'ez manuscripts suggests that this introduction has been preserved with minimal corruption.

Enoch affirms that his vision is not his own; it was revealed to him and is now spoken in human language. The phrase "a tongue of flesh" suggests that divine knowledge is normally beyond human comprehension but is being translated into a form men can understand. The "spirit of my mouth" emphasizes that this is not merely speech but divinely inspired revelation. This passage does not explicitly reference Babel but describes its predecessor, the original, unified language that existed before humanity's tongues were divided. The Tower of Babel event in Genesis marks the loss of this divine tongue, while 1 Enoch preserves a remnant of the era when divine speech was still accessible. This passage may retain echoes of the antediluvian language of the gods, spoken before linguistic fragmentation.

Throughout history, esoteric traditions have sought to reclaim this lost celestial language. John Dee (1527–1609), mathematician and advisor to Queen Elizabeth I, and Edward Kelley (1555–1597), a scryer and alchemist, claimed to have received a divine angelic language through spiritual communication. They called this system "Enochian," believing it to be the original tongue spoken by angels and the pre-Flood world. Dee believed that divine speech could still be accessed through angelic revelation, mirroring 1 *Enoch's* account of receiving and transmitting sacred knowledge. Whether their work represents a full reconstruction or a speculative attempt, it demonstrates that the pursuit of the primordial language of heaven has continued throughout history.

The text then shifts to reinforce divine authority over the Watchers. The "One who created" (the Great One) is the source of judgment, ensuring that the Watchers' actions do not go unchecked. The Greek focuses purely on their rebuke, while the Ge'ez introduces "words of understanding" and intelligence given to men. This addition may reflect a later scribal emphasis on wisdom, but the core meaning remains intact. The Watchers, called "the sons of heaven," are held accountable for their transgressions.

Enoch confirms that he recorded the Watchers' petition but reveals that it has been rejected. The phrase "in my vision, this was revealed" establishes that their fate is not subject to negotiation. It has already been decided. The Greek presents this statement simply, while the Ge'ez adds a stronger sense of finality, tying their rejection to a broader cosmic judgment. This moment marks the realization that their plea for mercy has failed, sealing their doom. The Watchers are permanently exiled from heaven and bound within the earth for eternity. The "bonds of the earth" signify total separation from their celestial origins, with their punishment lasting forever. They will witness the destruction of their children, the Nephilim, who will fall by the sword. Their rebellion brings no gain, only loss, as their bloodline is wiped out before their eyes.

This section emphasizes that their petition is not only rejected but that they will be rendered silent. They were unable to speak or even hear the decree against them. Their judgment is final.

The text then transitions into Enoch's celestial ascent. The natural elements, clouds, mists, stars, lightning, and winds, actively engage with him, lifting him into heaven. The Ge'ez adds that he was frightened, emphasizing the intensity of this supernatural experience. This marks a turning point; Enoch is no longer just an observer but is being transported into the divine realm.

Enoch describes his entry into a surreal structure where fire, ice, and stone merge into a luminous, otherworldly environment. The walls, ceiling, and floor are crystalline, composed of hailstones and ice, yet he passes through tongues of fire to reach them, stepping beyond human comprehension. If he had never encountered metal or artificial light, he would describe them using familiar terms. A smooth, reflective surface might appear as "ice," while contained illumination or energy fields might be "tongues of fire." Rather than a symbolic palace, this description indicates a metallic environment with glowing lights and unknown energy fields. This is an encounter beyond the limits of human experience.

A ceiling shifting like stars and lightning reinforces that he is in a celestial or otherworldly domain. The presence of fiery cherubim indicates that this space is sacred, heavily guarded, and restricted. The phrase "their heaven was water" is particularly intriguing. If taken literally, it may describe a reflective, liquid-like barrier above the structure, akin to the "waters above the firmament" in *Genesis*. If metaphorical, it may indicate a luminous, shifting sky or an atmospheric effect beyond human understanding.

The entire building is engulfed in fire, as a perimeter, and directly over its entry points. This is more than symbolic. The fire may function as a security measure, an energy field, or even an impassable barrier. If Enoch lacked a frame of reference for controlled energy fields, he would describe them as walls of flames encircling the building, with doors that "burned." If the fire did not consume the walls or doors themselves but instead acted as a moving, ever-present force, it alludes to a technology beyond anything known in the ancient world.

The Greek and Ge'ez align closely in their descriptions, though the Ge'ez uses "ice" (በረድ) instead of "snow" (χιών), likely due to regional adaptation. The phrase "no nourishment of life" suggests total desolation. There is no food, warmth, or sustaining energy. The paradox of fire and ice coexisting hints at a space beyond natural law, a liminal or artificial environment. Enoch's fear and trembling emphasize that he is encountering something utterly alien.

Inside, the absence of living beings is striking. If the fiery cherubim from earlier verses were animate, Enoch should have seen them, but he does not. Positioned 'between the moving stars and lightning,' they may be mechanical or technological rather than biological.

Enoch entered a non-organic domain beyond human comprehension.

Overwhelmed by the sheer intensity of the vision, Enoch physically collapses, though he remains conscious. As he is drawn deeper into this realm, he enters a larger structure built entirely of tongues of fire. The escalating imagery instills the idea that he is moving beyond mortal experience.

Both the Greek and Ge'ez emphasize that what Enoch saw was beyond human expression. The phrase "so that I was unable to describe it" confirms that his experience defied words. The ground itself is fire, making it uninhabitable for biological beings. The upper part contains lightning and celestial movements, a sky filled with artificial energy or orbital mechanics. The roof blazes with fire, indicating the image of an intense, possibly plasma-like structure.

Enoch's description proves he entered a high-tech control center, possibly with a dome-like celestial display. The fiery floor could be illuminated from below, while the upper section pulsed with electrical currents and star maps. His inability to articulate what he saw aligns with the idea that he was witnessing something far beyond his time.

The rivers of fire beneath the throne resemble a power source, energy discharge, or a controlled plasma system. The phrase "I was not able to see" indicates an intensity too great to observe directly. This was not ordinary fire but a radiant, overwhelming energy field. The positioning of the throne above these flows makes known it was not merely symbolic but functional, an advanced control interface powered by the energy below.

The enthroned presence is described as too bright to behold, radiating an overwhelming intensity. Whether this was a being infused with energy or one wearing advanced protective shielding, Enoch perceives it as impossible to look upon. Even the celestial beings could not withstand its radiance, proving that it was far more than an ordinary divine manifestation. The fire surrounding it functioned as an active barrier, preventing any from approaching.

Finally, Enoch is directly addressed. He has not moved since collapsing earlier, yet now, he is lifted by one of the "holy ones" and brought to the entrance of the command center. This moment marks a critical shift. He is no longer an observer but a summoned participant, standing before the supreme intelligence governing this entire operation.

Chapter 15

Chapter 15 marks the moment of direct communication between the supreme intelligence and Enoch. The being addresses him as "true man, man of truth, scribe," confirming his role as the chosen recorder of divine knowledge. The command "Do not be afraid" proves the overwhelming nature of this encounter, while "Come here and listen" signals that Enoch is about to receive a message of great significance.

The message begins with a direct rebuke of the Watchers. Originally tasked with guiding humanity, they reversed their role, interfering instead of overseeing, and now expecting divine intervention for themselves. The statement "You should have asked about mankind, not men about you" is a clear condemnation. They were never meant to seek mercy but to provide guidance, not indulgence, and certainly not rebellion. The Watchers abandoned their celestial station, descended to earth, and corrupted the natural order, permanently altering creation.

The offspring of the Watchers are explicitly called "Tall Ones" (rä'äytä), confirming that they were not only large but visibly distinct. Past translations have caused confusion. While the Septuagint (LXX) mistranslated Nephilim as "giants" (γίγαντες), the original meaning refers to beings who "fell" or "descended," not merely their physical stature. This verse cements the Watchers' crime, not just interbreeding with humanity but fundamentally changing what was meant to be. Their actions resulted in the birth of a hybrid race whose presence would shake the world.

The Watchers, originally immortal and incorruptible, altered their very nature by taking human wives. By intermixing with mortal flesh, they became entangled in the cycle of life and death. The phrase "defiled in the blood of women" makes known that their union was not only forbidden but also irreversible. The reference to "begot in the blood of flesh" confirms that their reproduction was physical, producing a hybrid race that could no longer claim celestial purity. The supreme intelligence makes it clear that their actions mirrored those of mortals, meaning they could no longer claim their former status. Once beyond birth and death, they had now tied themselves to the same fate.

A stark contrast is drawn between the roles of humanity and the Watchers. Humans were given females for reproduction to sustain labor and civilization. The phrase "so that no work may cease upon the earth" proves that reproduction was a necessary function of human existence, ensuring continuity. The Watchers, however, were never meant to participate in this process. Their interference disrupted the natural order, corrupting a system that was structured with a specific purpose.

The original text does not describe the Watchers as "eternal spirits" in the later theological sense. The words used for "spirit" (pneuma in Greek, mänfäs in Ge'ez) originally meant breath, wind, or life-force, rather than an incorporeal entity. This confirms that the Watchers were corporeal beings with an extended lifespan, not truly eternal. The phrase "for all generations of the ages" clarifies that they were meant to exist for a long but finite period. Later scribes distorted this into "eternal spirits" to align with theological doctrines that depicted angels as purely non-physical beings, an idea that does not align with the original Book of Enoch. This verse further establishes that the Watchers were corporeal, biological entities who fundamentally altered their existence through their choices, binding themselves to mortality.

The Watchers were never meant to reproduce. The phrase "spirits of the heavens" follows both the Greek (πνεύματα τοῦ οὐρανοῦ) and Ge'ez (መንፈሳውያን ውስተ ሰማይ), indicating celestial beings associated with the heavens. Later theology reinterpreted "spirits" as purely immaterial, but the original meaning likely denoted beings of divine essence or breath, not necessarily non-corporeal entities. "Their dwelling is in the heavens" suggests a separate domain or state of existence, distinct from the human world. The key takeaway is that the Watchers' actions violated the structure in which they were created, fundamentally altering their nature.

The fate of the Nephilim is then described. As the hybrid offspring of the Watchers and human women, they possessed both spiritual and physical essence, but after their deaths, their spirits persisted. The phrase "shall be called mighty spirits upon the earth" indicates that they continued to exist in a non-corporeal form after their bodies perished. The Ge'ez subtly alters this meaning by implying that these spirits became wicked, prior to their later identification as malevolent entities. 'Their dwelling shall be within the earth' affirms a continued presence on the terrestrial plane.

The spirits of the Nephilim remained on Earth after their bodies died. Both the Greek and Ge'ez confirm that evil spirits emerged from them, indicating a transformation upon death. The phrase "born from above" makes known their mixed nature, part celestial, part human, while their connection to the "holy Watchers" proves that their origin was tied to the rebellion of the fallen ones. The final statement "they shall be called evil spirits" marks the transition of the Nephilim from living beings to disembodied entities, forever bound to the earthly realm.

A final distinction is made between the divine beings and the spirits of the Nephilim. The heavenly spirits retain their domain in the heavens, while the earth-born spirits remain bound to the earth. The phrase "those who were born on the earth" explicitly refers to the Nephilim, confirming that their hybrid nature permanently ties them to the terrestrial realm. Unlike their celestial progenitors, they have no place in the heavens.

The spirits of the Nephilim are described as chaotic, oppressive forces. They do not consume food, yet they hunger and thirst, existing in an insatiable, restless state. The Greek and Ge'ez agree that they continue to exist on the earth, bringing destruction and disorder. Their inability to find fulfillment or rest indicates they are cursed to wander, neither truly alive nor fully gone.

The chapter concludes with a final confirmation that the spirits of the Nephilim remain hostile toward humanity. They do not ascend or move on but instead continue to afflict and oppose the living. Their origin from human mothers permanently ties them to the earthly realm. Unlike their divine progenitors, they are bound to the world of the living, forever influencing mankind in unseen ways.

Chapter 16

Chapter 16 confirms that the spirits of the Nephilim remain active on earth after their physical destruction. They continue to bring chaos and disorder, yet they are not judged immediately. Instead, they persist in this restless state until the appointed time of the great judgment, which marks the completion of an age. The phrase "without judgment" implies that they exist in an interim period. They are neither fully condemned nor fully free. Their influence is tied directly to the larger astronomical timeline, emphasizing that their existence is not random but part of a greater unfolding plan.

The text then reaffirms that the Watchers, before their fall, resided in heaven. The Greek explicitly uses ἐγρηγόροις (egrēgorois, "Watchers"), while the Ge'ez softens the term to "mighty ones" (la-təguhan), indicating a possible theological redaction. The phrase "sent you" indicates that Enoch was functioning as an intermediary, perhaps pleading on behalf of the Watchers. This aligns with earlier passages where the fallen Watchers sought divine intervention regarding their fate.

A direct rebuke follows, emphasizing that while the Watchers had access to divine knowledge, there were mysteries they were never meant to understand. Yet, they uncovered a mystery from God and revealed it to humanity, specifically to women. The phrase "mystery that was not revealed to you" confirms that divine knowledge was not equally accessible, proving that the Watchers overstepped their boundaries. Their true transgression was not just taking human wives, but teaching forbidden knowledge.

The phrase "through this mystery, the women multiplied" is ambiguous. It could refer to the birth of hybrid Nephilim, a population boom from technological advancements, or the spread of esoteric wisdom tied to femininity and the divine womb. Regardless, the passage makes it clear that the knowledge imparted by the Watchers led to human corruption and increased wickedness. The teachings they provided were not neutral, and they had catastrophic consequences.

The phrase "stubbornness of heart" makes it obvious that the Watchers acted out of arrogance, not ignorance. They knew the risks but proceeded anyway. Enoch does not portray them as tragic figures but as rebellious beings who knowingly disrupted the divine order. Their punishment was not just for breaking laws, but for unleashing knowledge that humanity was never meant to wield.

The chapter concludes with a final, unambiguous declaration: "There is no peace." The Greek and Ge'ez align perfectly, leaving no room for alternative interpretations. The response is absolute, there will be no negotiation, no redemption, no second chances. The Watchers pleaded for mercy, but their fate was sealed. Their transgressions had irreversibly altered the world, and now they would face the consequences. This definitive rejection marks a complete and final separation between them and the divine order.

Chapter 17

Chapter 17 begins with Enoch being taken to an unknown location where he encounters luminous beings that shift between blazing fire and human form at will. The Greek phrase "become like fire" indicates a transformation rather than merely being composed of fire. These entities exhibit a dual nature, existing as both radiant, fiery beings and as human-like figures. This closely parallels ancient descriptions of the Djinn, who were said to be created from smokeless, scorching fire (Qur'an 55:15) and could manifest in human form. The ability to transition between energy-based and corporeal forms reveals a level of control over matter and perception beyond normal human experience.

The similarities between these fiery beings and the Djinn cannot be ignored. Both the Watchers and Djinn were said to interact with humanity, sometimes as teachers of forbidden knowledge, and both were believed to exist in a parallel plane, unseen unless they willed otherwise. Some Djinn were said to have once been divine but fell from grace, mirroring the Watchers' rebellion. This raises the possibility that the Watchers, or at least some of them, survived in later traditions as Djinn. If the Watchers were bound beneath the earth for generations (cf. 10:12), those who remained free may have been remembered under a different name. This passage preserves one of the oldest records of the Djinn phenomenon, describing the same type of entities under a much older framework.

Enoch is then taken into a place of thick darkness before arriving at a mountain reaching into heaven. This fits with the ancient axis mundi concept, where sacred mountains bridge the divine and earthly realms. Many traditions describe such peaks as meeting points between gods and humans. The phrase "thick darkness" often signifies supernatural realms or divine judgment. Enoch is entering a forbidden domain, linking it to the Watchers' punishment or the boundaries of divine space.

Enoch witnesses a celestial storage realm where stars, thunder, and lightning are kept and controlled. The "bow of fire" and arrows clearly symbolize lightning, tying it to the idea that storms were seen as divine weapons, not random events. The phrase "deep places of the air" makes known he has entered a supernatural atmospheric domain, similar to myths where gods wield thunderbolts stored in heavenly armories. This passage reveals that lightning, like divine power, was summoned and unleashed at will, a concept reflected in Mesopotamian, Vedic, and Greek traditions.

He is then taken to a place where the sun's descent is controlled, described as the "setting of fire." This aligns with ancient beliefs that the sun traveled through gates, portals, or an underworld before rising again. The Ge'ez addition of "waters of life" are a connection to celestial renewal. This passage makes known the idea that sunset was not a random event but governed by a cosmic mechanism.

Enoch next witnesses a river of fire flowing like water into a great western sea, describing a form of volcanic or molten activity. The imagery is consistent with ancient beliefs and describes lava flows meeting the ocean, forming new land when seen from above. This could be an early account of island formation, solar plasma, or even electromagnetic currents.

He then sees great rivers, a single "great river," and a mysterious "great darkness" before returning to where all living beings exist. This indicates he traveled through a boundary or unknown realm before re-entering familiar territory. The "great darkness" is a void, celestial abyss, or threshold between worlds.

Enoch then observes storm winds of darkness and winter alongside the abyss releasing all waters. This indicates a controlled cosmic water system, aligning with ancient beliefs in divine reservoirs regulating storms and floods. The abyss is a void and a source of celestial and subterranean waters.

Finally, Enoch witnesses the entry and exit points of Earth's waters, linking surface rivers to the abyss. This points to an ancient understanding of the hydrological cycle, where water flows between the surface, underground reservoirs, and the abyss. The "mouth of the abyss" represents a deep chasm, a subterranean ocean, or a gate on a universal level regulating water on Earth.

Chapter 18

Chapter 18 describes Enoch's journey through the celestial storehouses of wind, reinforcing the idea that natural forces are controlled and stored, not random. The text connects these winds to the ordering of creation, implying they play a structural role in stabilizing the world. The "cornerstone of the earth" hints at a metaphysical foundation, possibly referencing the earth's axis, a literal geological feature, or an esoteric concept of galactic balance.

Enoch sees four winds supporting both the earth and the heavens, portraying them as stabilizing forces rather than mere air currents. The Ge'ez adds "pillars of the foundation," which proves atmospheric balance or Earth's axial forces. This passage presents planetary stability in pre-scientific terms, hinting at an early cosmological framework where unseen forces uphold the heavens and the earth.

Enoch then observes a firmament upheld between earth and heaven. The Ge'ez expands upon this by adding "pillars of heaven," which could represent atmospheric layers, celestial mechanics, or literally, pillars that support the sky.

Enoch describes galactic winds that direct the sun and stars, implying that celestial bodies move in accordance with an unseen order rather than at random. This aligns with ancient cosmological models where divine winds, celestial spheres, or unseen forces controlled planetary motion. These descriptions reflect an early attempt to explain the movement of the heavens through a purposeful system.

He then witnesses earthly winds carrying clouds, providing the link between celestial mechanics and weather patterns. The reference to the "ends of the earth" may indicate horizons, boundary points, or even atmospheric limits. The mention of "the foundation of heaven" indicates a structural element holding up the sky, while the Ge'ez addition "boundaries of the angels" implies a supernatural separation between divine and earthly realms.

Enoch is taken to a place of continuous fire, surrounded by seven mountains composed of valuable minerals. The specific directional placement lends itself to an intentional design, linked to spatial alignment. This brings to mind a volcanic region, a supernatural domain, or even an astronomical observatory.

The seven mountains exhibit distinct mineral compositions, with references to pearl, carved stone, and red minerals. The presence of carved stone indicates human (or non-human) intervention, proving the possibility that this site was artificially modified. If this location represents a mining or extraction site, it evidences a deeper connection to ancient operations tied to the Watchers or other celestial beings.

Enoch then sees a towering building of unknown stone, topped with sapphire. The Greek states that the fire is "beyond the mountains," while the Ge'ez locates it "within all the mountains," pointing to a scribal shift or theological redirection. The phrase "fire that does not cease" describes a perpetual blaze, which could signify a volcanic site, an energy source, or a supernatural phenomenon. If this fire was connected to the Igigi mining operations, it could represent an advanced smelting site or power source. The fact that it is positioned beyond the mountains indicates it was hidden or forbidden.

The Greek states that the heavens "come to an end" at this location, while the Ge'ez states that "waters are gathered." This could indicate a cosmological boundary or an attempt to harmonize the passage with later traditions. The phrase "end of the great earth" is either a literal boundary or a cosmic threshold where the known world transitions into something unknown.

Greek and Ge'ez diverge on the depiction of fire descending into a chasm. The Greek states that "columns of fire" descend into an immeasurable chasm, while the Ge'ez says the fire "does not descend." This could reflect a scribal error or a theological shift. The description of the chasm as immeasurable gives the idea of a bottomless abyss, a place beyond human comprehension.

Beyond this chasm, both the Greek and Ge'ez describe an absolute void, no sky, no land, no water, no life. The Greek states that there is "no water beneath it," while the Ge'ez states "no water above it," a simple minor scribal shift. This could represent a boundary where the natural order breaks down, a wasteland, or an area outside of creation itself.

Enoch then witnesses seven burning stars like mountains. The Ge'ez adds that these stars "do not move" and "did not answer." This indicates they are fixed in place, possibly imprisoned in an astronomical penitentiary.

The Greek describes this as "the end of heaven and earth," while the Ge'ez calls it "the completion," but both confirm that this place serves as a prison for "stars" and "heavenly forces." This indicates that the passage refers not just to celestial bodies but to celestial beings, rebellious angels or fallen entities.

The Greek states that these stars "roll in fire," while the Ge'ez says they are "bound in fire." Their transgression is linked to their initial rising, implying a failure to follow order. The Greek further adds that "a place outside heaven is empty," implying that they were cast out and removed from creation.

The final section describes the duration of their punishment. The Greek states that their suffering lasts for "thousands of years," while the Ge'ez calls it "a secret number of years." Both confirm that these beings are bound until their sins are fulfilled, indicating a fixed sentence rather than an eternal condemnation.

Chapter 19

Chapter 19 introduces the term daimoniis in Greek, referring to spirits or guiding powers that exert malevolent influence. The corresponding Ge'ez term l'āgānnät conveys a similar meaning, encompassing both spirits and entities that lead humans astray. While these beings are not yet equated with the later Christian concept of demons, this passage marks an early stage in the evolution of that idea. These spirits mislead humanity, directing people toward evil forces until the great judgment, where they will be judged and condemned to destruction. The Ge'ez mäl'āk'ät refers to messengers, beings that deliver messages, but not in the later theological sense of "angels."

The Greek text introduces the term σειρῆνας (seirēnas), referring to sirens, the mythological beings known for their deceptive and alluring nature, leading humans to ruin. This makes known that the wives of the transgressing angels undergo a transformation into deceptive entities, luring people toward corruption. The Ge'ez equivalent, አስሒቶን (asīhīton), carries the same implication of transformation into misleading beings. This passage drives home the idea that the Watchers' influence extends beyond their direct rebellion, as even their human wives are caught in the

153

consequences of their transgression.

The chapter concludes with Enoch alone witnessing "the ends of all things," a vision no other human has seen. This statement proves his unique role as a divinely chosen scribe, granted insight beyond mortal comprehension. His access to these revelations sets him apart from humanity, affirming his status as the sole witness to these hidden cosmic truths.

Chapter 20

Chapter 20 introduces a celestial hierarchy of divine beings, described in the Greek as "Angels of the Powers." The Ge'ez expands on this, describing them as holy messengers who stand guard, making clear their roles as watchers and protectors of celestial order. This passage outlines the distinct functions of several named archangels, each presiding over different aspects of divine governance and enforcement.

Uriel is identified as a holy messenger with authority over both the world and Tartarus, establishing him as a celestial overseer. The Greek preserves the connection between Uriel and the underworld, while the Ge'ez omits Tartarus, a later redaction.

Tartarus, in Greek cosmology, is the deepest abyss beneath Hades, where the Titans were imprisoned. However, in 1 Enoch, it is not the realm of the Nephilim (Titans) but rather the prison of the Watchers, the divine rebels who descended to Earth. This brings in the Greek concept of Tartarus inherited from an older Enochian tradition. If Uriel is "over Tartarus," he is the one ensuring that the Watchers remain bound within their designated prison.

Raphael is given dominion over the spirits of humanity, a role in guiding, protecting, and overseeing human souls. The phrase "spirits of men" (πνευμάτων τῶν ἀνθρώπων) referring to the living, the dead, or disembodied souls, illustrating his authority over spiritual matters. That both the Greek and Ge'ez align perfectly indicates this passage was preserved without later redaction.

Raphael's name means "God has healed" (רְפָאֵל), and in the Book of Tobit, he is portrayed as a divine healer and exorcist, sent to cure blindness and cast out the demon Asmodeus. His authority over spirits in 1 Enoch may imply a broader role, one who intervenes in the affairs of souls, healing bodies and spiritual afflictions, as well. Unlike Uriel, whose dominion is confined to Tartarus, Raphael's role spans both the earthly and spiritual realms.

Raguel is described as "the avenger," a celestial enforcer who exacts retribution upon both the world and the luminaries (φωστῆρες, ብርሃናት). These luminaries could represent celestial bodies, divine beings, or galactic forces, proving his role involves judging rebellious celestial entities; fallen angels or corrupted stars. Unlike Uriel, who oversees Tartarus, and Raphael, who heals spirits, Raguel enforces divine justice, ensuring cosmic balance.

The question arises: who or what is Raguel avenging? If luminaries were seen as divine intelligences, then his role may extend beyond Earth, upholding divine law over both the heavens and the celestial order itself. His function as an avenger implies that judgment is not just for human transgressions but also for cosmic violations.

Michael's role is twofold. He is responsible for "the good things of the people," which could mean divine favor, blessings, or protection, but he also holds authority over chaos (χάος). The Ge'ez omits "chaos," alluding to the idea that later scribes may have removed it to avoid associating Michael with disorder.

What does it mean for Michael to be "over chaos"? This implies that he is not merely a protector but also a force of order, maintaining the balance between divine will and primordial disorder. Unlike Raphael, who heals, or Uriel, who oversees Tartarus, Michael governs both stability and upheaval, shoring up his role as a warrior and guardian of divine law.

Sariel's role is unique. He presides over spirits who sin against the spirit, implying he deals with a specific category of transgressors. The phrase indicates he is responsible for fallen spirits, corrupted souls, or those who commit spiritual offenses. The Ge'ez adds "of those who live," hinting that his oversight extends to both disembodied spirits and living beings who engage with them. Unlike Raphael, who heals, Uriel, who oversees Tartarus, or Michael, who maintains order, Sariel's function is directly tied to the judgment of spiritual wrongdoing.

Gabriel is given authority over Paradise, dragons, and the Cherubim, positioning him as a protector and gatekeeper of divine realms.

The mention of dragons (δράκοντες) is striking, as later Ge'ez manuscripts deliberately remove it, pointing to an effort to erase celestial beings that no longer fit later theological frameworks. The inclusion of Cherubim, often portrayed as guardians of divine access, enforces Gabriel's role in governing entry to sacred domains.

Additionally, the Greek text from Gizeh 2 includes Remeiel, an archangel who presides over resurrection. His complete absence in the Ge'ez text implies a deliberate suppression of his role, reducing the full list of seven archangels. This follows a broader pattern of textual redaction in later traditions, minimizing the original Enochian angelology and obscuring earlier teachings about celestial hierarchy and the afterlife.

Chapter 21

Chapter 21 takes Enoch to an unformed void, a place where nothing was made, a realm beyond creation, a primordial chaos or a boundary to an even deeper abyss. This passage presents a galactic wasteland, separate from both heaven and earth, calling forth the idea that divine creation has limits beyond which only desolation exists.

Enoch arrives at a terrifying emptiness where neither heaven nor earth exists. The Greek word ἀκατασκεύαστος and the Ge'ez phrase empty wasteland indicate a place outside divine order, the abyss, a pre-creation void, or a prison for the forsaken. This parallels Tartarus in Greek thought or the primordial chaos before *Genesis*, pointing to a region that exists outside the realms of existence.

He then sees seven stars of heaven, bound and cast into the void, burning like great mountains of fire. Both the Greek and Ge'ez agree on their imprisonment, though the Ge'ez indicates they are suspended above the abyss. The imagery implies these are not merely celestial bodies but celestial beings. Fallen Watchers, punished and confined in a realm beyond creation, where neither heaven nor earth exists.

The Greek states that Uriel was the leader of the messengers present, but the Ge'ez subtly minimizes his authority by altering "he was their leader" to "he led me," making him appear as merely Enoch's guide rather than a commander. Additionally, while the Greek simply asks what Enoch inquires about, the Ge'ez expands his inquiry into "seeking, inquiring, striving," in a more intense personal quest for knowledge.

These types of adjustments reflect a later scribal effort to reframe divine hierarchy and emphasize human agency.

The Greek confirms that the Watchers are "of the stars of heaven," describing their celestial nature, while the Ge'ez adds "Most High Lord" as an embellishment. The most significant change concerns the length of their imprisonment. The Greek states "ten thousand years," while Ge'ez alters it to "until the end of the world," shifting the sentence from a finite period to an eternal punishment. This reflects later theological influence, transforming the Watchers' fate from long-term confinement to permanent damnation.

The Greek and Ge'ez mostly align in describing a pit of fire that is never extinguished, its perpetual nature never-ending. Both confirm a deep, endless chasm with pillars of descending fire, describing something celestial, volcanic, or industrial. The scale of this abyss is beyond Enoch's comprehension, marking it as a cosmic-level punishment zone, possibly the Watchers' final prison.

Enoch's reaction is one of overwhelming horror. The Greek and Ge'ez closely align in describing the abyss as "dreadful in appearance," emphasizing its vastness and otherworldly nature. The fear it instills in Enoch makes known it is a place of ultimate judgment.

While the Greek only refers to "one of the holy messengers," the Ge'ez explicitly names Uriel, further cementing his role as Enoch's guide. This minor difference does not affect the overall meaning but reflects a slight redaction to clarify Uriel's identity in later versions.

The chapter concludes by confirming that this abyss is the eternal prison of the fallen messengers. The Greek uses the term prison (δεσμωτήριον), while the Ge'ez expands it to house of imprisonment, a minor elaboration. The phrase "until eternity, forever" remains unchanged, emphasizing the inescapable nature of their punishment. This abyssal prison is where the Watchers remain bound until the final judgment, sealed away from the heavens and the earth.

Chapter 22

Chapter 22 describes Enoch's westward journey, where he encounters a massive, immovable mountain of solid rock. This directional shift is significant. Many ancient texts associate the west with the underworld or the afterlife. Enoch's movement in this direction indicates that he is entering a realm related to the dead or divine judgment. The solid rock imagery implies permanence, linked to cosmic foundations or divine structures.

The Greek version includes a spring of water, but the Ge'ez omits it, a later redaction. Enoch observes four hollow places, which appear deliberately shaped, indicating that they serve a specific purpose. The contrast between light and darkness are distinct fates for the dead, casting this scene as a depiction of judgment. The nature of these hollow places resembles descriptions of the afterlife or judgment realms in later traditions, making this passage crucial for understanding Enoch's cosmology.

Raphael confirms that these hollow places serve as gathering sites for the spirits of the dead. The Greek states they were "judged," while the Ge'ez alters this to "made," subtly shifting the meaning. The Greek emphasizes that these places were "made for gathering," while the Ge'ez softens this to "dwelling," altering the implication of their purpose. The reference to an "appointed and determined time" confirms that a final judgment is expected, aligning with earlier references to souls awaiting their fate. The Ge'ez uniquely adds "their life span," as in a fixed duration before judgment, a concept absent in the Greek.

The Greek text emphasizes that the dead are pleading, while the Ge'ez shifts to calling them "spirits" and describes them as "crying out," slightly altering the nuance. Their voices reaching heaven implies that they seek justice, connecting to later passages where souls cry out for vengeance.

Enoch asks about the identity of one particular pleading spirit, a detail missing in the Ge'ez. The Greek emphasizes urgency, relaying that this is no ordinary soul but one actively seeking divine intervention. The fact that its voice reaches heaven brings in the theme of divine justice responding to the cries of the afflicted.

This passage extends the narrative found in *Genesis* 4:10, confirming that

Abel's cry for justice continues beyond death. Both the Greek and Ge'ez affirm that Abel demands the complete destruction of Cain's lineage, revealing an early concept of blood vengeance persisting in the afterlife.

The Greek specifies "enclosures" for the dead, while the Ge'ez generalizes this to "these things," softening the meaning. Enoch's question confirms that souls are divided into separate locations, proving the idea of a afterlife with designated realms for different categories of spirits.

The text clarifies that there are three divisions for the dead, separating the righteous from others. The mention of a "bright spring of water" conveying an idea of purity, renewal, or divine favor in the nature of the afterlife.

The passage introduces a postmortem judgment for sinners, establishing that divine justice extends beyond mortal life. This affirms the idea that some individuals may escape justice during their lifetimes, but ultimate accountability is unavoidable.

Both the Greek and Ge'ez depict a place of torment for sinners, where suffering continues until the final judgment. The references to "scourges and afflictions" convey the idea of an ongoing punishment, with eternal binding as retribution for their deeds.

The Greek and Ge'ez confirm a separate place for spirits seeking justice, proves the theme of cries for vengeance, as seen with Abel. The mention of "days of sinners" is a period of great wickedness, paralleling the pre-Flood corruption described elsewhere in 1 *Enoch*.

The passage describes a realm specifically designated for the unholy, distinct from the righteous. The sinners remain with the lawless, indicating a hierarchy of punishment. Some spirits suffer less than others, pointing to degrees of torment based on their transgressions. The most striking statement is that these spirits will "never rise again," marking a permanent separation from the divine order.

The chapter concludes by reaffirming divine justice and eternal rule. The titles "Lord of Glory" and "Lord of Righteousness" proclaim both majesty and moral authority, emphasizing that true justice is unchanging.

The shift from "Lord of Glory" (accusative) to "Kyriō" (vocative) mirrors 1 *Enoch* 9:4, a direct address to a distinct figure. This vocative form is not used for "Lord of Eternity" (cf. 1:3) or "Lord of the Heavens" (cf. 13:4), establishing that this is a unique divine title. While later traditions frequently applied Kyrios to Christ, 1 *Enoch* itself does not specify who is being addressed, maintaining an earlier, non-Christian theological framework.

Chapter 23

Chapter 23 continues Enoch's westward journey, bringing him to what is described as the "ends of the earth." Both the Greek and Ge'ez use terms (πέρατα, perata in Greek and አጽናፈ, 'aṣṣǝnafä in Ge'ez) that allude to a geographical extremity, but leaves open the reference to a mythological or cosmological boundary. The phrasing in both texts remains nearly identical, with only minor linguistic shifts and no significant theological alterations.

Enoch encounters an ever-moving fire that never rests or deviates from its path. Both the Greek (ἡμέρας καὶ νυκτὸς, "day and night") and the Ge'ez (መዓልት ወሌሊት, "day and night") gives rise to the concept of perpetual motion. This fire is depicted as following a fixed course, which describes a cosmic force, volcanic activity, or even plasma discharges in the sky. The description makes it obvious something astronomical or a natural energy phenomenon that was perceived as eternal and self-sustaining.

Enoch is perplexed by this fire, which never stops. Both the Greek (Gizeh) and the Ge'ez emphasize its lack of rest but do not explicitly define what it is. The fact that Enoch is explicitly questioning it indicates that this is not an ordinary fire, it exhibits behaviors that seem unnatural or extraordinary. This fire could symbolize a cosmic force, an astral phenomenon, or an unceasing natural event such as a volcanic fissure or an eternal flame.

The chapter then describes the Sun as a celestial force that guides the movement of the stars and planets. The phrase "driving" does not indicate repelling, but rather leading and compelling their motion. This passage reflects an early understanding of celestial mechanics, where the movement of the Sun influences all other luminaries. While not fully developed as a scientific model, this passage preserves an early recognition of the Sun's dominant role in maintaining cosmic order.

Chapter 24

Chapter 24 describes Enoch's encounter with a landscape of fiery mountains and a sacred, eternal tree. The Greek states that the mountains of fire burned at night, while the Ge'ez expands this to include burning during the daytime and Enoch actively traveling. The shorter Greek text is likely original, the scene describes volcanic activity or an unknown cosmic phenomenon.

The Greek and Ge'ez largely agree in depicting seven mountains composed of precious stones. Three are positioned toward the east, three toward the south, and one stands at the center. The mountains do not touch each other, and deep valleys separate them. The phrase "glorious and magnificent" implies the presence of precious metals or gemstones, bringing to light that these were ancient mining sites or sacred locations. This description aligns with other accounts of divine or hidden places associated with rare materials, these locations were considered of cosmic significance.

The Greek and Ge'ez closely align in describing the seventh mountain as the tallest and central, shaped like a throne. The presence of trees surrounding it could indicate a sacred grove, indicating its divine or supernatural importance. The throne-like imagery makes known that this is as a place of celestial rule, potentially linked to Enoch's later visions of the divine throne.

Both the Greek and Ge'ez describe a unique, eternal tree with an unmatched fragrance, stating that its scent surpasses all perfumes. Its fruit clusters like dates, linking it to sacred or divine nourishment. The phrase "never withering" brings to mind immortality or divine essence, recalling the reference to a pre-Flood Tree of Life. This tree is clearly distinct from normal vegetation, with its role as a supernatural or divine entity.

The Greek and Ge'ez both emphasize the tree's beauty and powerful fragrance, with the Ge'ez adding that its fruit is splendid. This enforces the tree's sacred nature, linking it to the cosmic Tree of Life, a symbol found in many ancient traditions. Its presence near the throne-like mountain indicates that it is intimately connected to divine realms, even as a source of celestial sustenance or wisdom.

Michael then appears, taking charge of the scene. The Greek keeps his role straightforward, while the Ge'ez elevates his status by calling him "holy and great." This passage is one of the clearest confirmations that Michael held authority among the divine messengers, at least in this section. The original Aramaic would have used "mal'āk" (messenger), not the later Christianized "angel." Calling into question if originally Michael was just a high-ranking envoy of the divine council rather than the warrior-angel later traditions depict, evolution or promotion

Chapter 25

Chapter 25 continues Enoch's dialogue with Michael, focusing on the mysterious sacred tree and its divine significance. Michael questions why Enoch is so intrigued by its fragrance and nature. The Greek emphasizes Enoch's pursuit of "learning the truth," while the Ge'ez simplifies it to "understanding." This distinction indicates that the tree holds deeper meaning beyond its physical presence and Michael's response implies that its nature is not immediately apparent, requiring divine revelation to comprehend.

Enoch confirms that while he seeks knowledge about all things, his greatest curiosity is this tree. The Greek intensifies his eagerness with "very much so," while the Ge'ez rephrases it as a strong desire to understand. This exchange further emphasizes the tree's exceptional importance, even among all the celestial wonders Enoch has witnessed, this tree stands out as something uniquely profound.

Michael reveals that the seventh mountain is the divine seat of God, with its peak resembling a throne. The title "King of the Age(s)" (τοῦ αἰῶνος, tou aiōnos) indicates rulership over time periods or cycles rather than an eternal, unchanging state. The Ge'ez states "King of the World" (ንጉሠዓለም), which reflects a later theological shift. The divine descent to this mountain is specifically for good, implying favor or blessing rather than judgment. This passage directly ties the throne-like mountain to the dwelling place of the divine, proving its cosmic significance.

The sacred tree remains untouchable until the Great Judgment, when all things are avenged and completed. After this, the tree is given to the righteous and holy, declaring it has a restorative or sacred purpose. This is one of the clearest indications that the tree represents divine nourishment, renewal, or eternal life.

The fruit of this tree grants life to the chosen. It is later moved to a holy place near God's house, with both the Greek and Ge'ez associating this location with the north. The repetition of "King of the Age(s)" intensifies the concept of divine rulership across different time cycles, further emphasizing the connection between the tree, divine favor, and the unfolding of cosmic destiny.

The chosen will rejoice and enter the holy place. The tree's fragrance will be within them, possibly symbolizing a form of divine restoration or transformation. They will live longer than past generations, free from pain and suffering, confirming that the tree provides not just sustenance, but a return to an ideal state. This aligns with traditions of a Tree of Life, enforcing the idea that it is linked to the renewal of the righteous after judgment.

Enoch blesses, calling "the King of the Age(s)," a divine title consistent with earlier titles. The passage emphasizes divine preparation that both created and designated these blessings for the righteous, ensuring their inheritance in the post-judgment world.

Chapter 26

Chapter 26 describes Enoch's arrival at the "middle of the earth," where he encounters a sacred place that is cut off or separated. The Greek describes it as "separated," while the Ge'ez adds imagery of a tree that no longer grows, signaling abandonment or loss. This detail hints at a once-holy site now in decline, with the idea that this location was significant in the past but has since become desolate.

Enoch then sees a holy mountain with water flowing from the east and moving southward. The Greek confirms this direction, while the Ge'ez mistakenly states "north," scribal error or an alternate tradition. The presence of flowing water from the sacred mountain indicates divine or global significance, as many ancient traditions associate sacred geography with supernatural water sources.

Next, Enoch observes a second mountain, which is higher than the first and located toward the east. A deep and narrow valley lies between them, with water flowing beneath the mountain. The description hints that this geographical arrangement is not random, it reflects a sacred, or galactic landscape, tied to divine water sources.

163

Moving further, Enoch sees a third mountain westward, which is lower than the others and positioned near two deep, dry valleys. One valley lies between the mountains, while another is at the peaks of the three mountains. This deliberate arrangement of mountains and valleys indicates a sacred geography or galactic terraforming design, linking it to divine judgment, celestial order, or remnants of a lost holy site.

The valleys are described as deep and composed of strong rock, completely barren with no trees growing upon them. The text strongly emphasizes the harshness and uninhabitable nature of this landscape, giving the idea that this is a place of desolation and significance. The barrenness may symbolize a divine curse, abandonment, or a threshold between realms.

Enoch expresses astonishment at the valley, emphasizing its extraordinary nature. The Ge'ez adds "the rock" as an object of wonder, possibly drawing attention to the valley's barren and unyielding terrain. This repetition of amazement proves that this location held a deeper meaning or purpose, marking it as a place of importance.

Chapter 27

Chapter 27 presents Enoch's vision of a stark contrast between a blessed, fertile land full of trees and a cursed valley within it. This passage proves the concept of sacred geography, where certain areas are set apart for divine favor or judgment. The existence of both a blessed land and a cursed valley within the same region indicates that divine presence and punishment can coexist within the same space, shaping the fate of different beings according to their deeds.

The Greek text does not name an angel, while the Ge'ez later added Raphael, and some versions replaced him with Uriel. This reflects a scribal tradition of inserting specific angels over time to align with evolving theological frameworks. The Greek preserves the original form, making it the more reliable witness for understanding how the text originally presented this scene.

A pivotal moment occurs when even the wicked will bless the "Lord of Glory" during the final judgment. This event unfolds before the righteous, signifying that all beings, even those who were once opposed to divine order, will ultimately acknowledge divine authority. The Greek phrase "for all time" conveys a long-lasting state, while the Ge'ez expands it to "eternity," suggesting a later theological embellishment. The Ge'ez also introduces "vision of judgment," implying that this moment will be an unveiled, revelatory experience, similar to the "Great Day of Judgment" described elsewhere in 1 Enoch.

The phrase "in the days of their judgment" does not refer to a single moment of sentencing, it describes an ongoing state of divine justice being carried out. This indicates that judgment is not an instantaneous event, but a process unfolding over time. The blessing the wicked receive comes through mercy, which here represents divine favor rather than just a legal judgment. The final phrase emphasizes that this mercy is not arbitrarily given, it is something already assigned to them, part of the divine order.

Enoch then magnificently praises the Great One, using language that conveys an exalted and powerful form of worship. The wording emphasizes that this is not merely speaking about glory, but actively proclaiming and declaring it. The final phrase demonstrates that this praise is not excessive or unnecessary it is exactly what is due, laying out the righteousness of divine authority.

Chapter 28

Chapter 28 describes Enoch's arrival at a desolate and abandoned land. The Greek refers to this place as "Mandobara," while the Ge'ez alters the name to "Medbera" and adds "toward the east." Despite this geographical shift in the Ge'ez, both texts agree that this land was left uninhabited, emphasizing its isolation and abandonment.

A mysterious water source is described. The Greek text calls it "rainless water," while the Ge'ez describes it as "flowing from above." This implies a supernatural or hidden origin, possibly a spring, mist, or an underground river. Although the land is uninhabited, trees still grow naturally, proving that the region is not barren, only forsaken.

The Greek compares this water source to a rich aqueduct, while the Ge'ez calls it a "path of moisture." Both texts describe the water flowing endlessly in a westward direction, indicating that this may have been a natural spring, an underground river, or even an ancient irrigation system. The continuous flow of water implies that life still thrives beneath the surface, despite the desolation above.

165

Chapter 29

Chapter 29 introduces a new location as Enoch continues his journey. The Greek names the place "Babdera," while the Ge'ez calls it "Medbera." This discrepancy is caused by scribal error, or intentional modification over time. Despite the naming difference, both texts agree that Enoch traveled east toward a mountain.

Enoch encounters "trees of judgment" that release a fragrant resin, which is clearly a reference to frankincense and myrrh. These resins were historically used in sacred rituals, purification rites, and burial practices, proving the spiritual and divine significance of this place. The Greek describes the trees as "like nut trees," preserving the original meaning. However, the Ge'ez oddly states that "they were not similar," introducing an inconsistency resulting from a misunderstanding or an attempt to alter the description.

The presence of frankincense and myrrh in the east, near a sacred mountain, aligns with ancient traditions of sacred groves and divine sanctuaries where celestial beings or priests performed rituals. The phrase "trees of judgment" implies that this site was associated with divine justice, purification, or offerings, serving as a threshold between the earthly and heavenly realms.

Chapter 30

Chapter 30 describes a water-filled valley, with the Greek calling it "a valley of water" and the Ge'ez making it plural and "unknown," making it a remote or hidden gorge.

The text then describes the fragrant vegetation in this valley. The Greek specifically mentions "fragrant bark," while the Ge'ez uses a broader term, "fragrant trees." Both versions compare this to the mastic tree, a plant known for its prized aromatic resin, widely used in ancient trade and medicine.

Along the edges of the valley, both the Greek and Ge'ez confirm the presence of cinnamon. This detail indicates that the valley is a lush and fertile region, pulling in links to ancient cinnamon trade routes. Given the historical significance of cinnamon as a highly valued commodity, this passage alludes to knowledge of distant lands known for their rich botanical resources.

Chapter 31

Chapter 31 describes mountains with groves of trees producing a flowing nectar. The Greek mentions a substance called "Sarran," which is unknown, while galbanum is a real resin used in incense and medicine. The Ge'ez accidentally repeats "flowing," likely a scribal slip.

Both versions place this mountain at "the ends of the earth" and describe trees with almond-like fruit. The Ge'ez adds that the trees were "high and beautiful."

Crushing the fruit releases a fragrance stronger than all others. The Ge'ez emphasizes this, stating, "its scent surpasses all," accentuating its uniqueness and intensity.

Chapter 32

Chapter 32 describes seven mountains covered in valuable aromatic plants. The Greek specifically lists cinnamon, while the Ge'ez only mentions "fragrant trees."

The Greek names "Zotiel," while the Ge'ez calls it "the angel Zotiel," leaving ambiguity as to whether it refers to a being or a place. Enoch crossing the Red Sea hinting at sacred geography.

The Greek states that "holy ones" eat from the tree of wisdom, but the Ge'ez simply says "they." The Ge'ez repeats "beautiful and great," emphasizing the trees' majesty.

The Greek describes the tree's leaves as resembling a carob tree, a detail the Ge'ez omits. The fruit is "grape clusters" in Greek but "small, beautiful" in Ge'ez. Both confirm its fragrance spread far, and the Ge'ez repeats "beautiful" twice, emphasizing the tree's striking appearance.

Chapter 33

Chapter 33, preserved only in Ge'ez, describes unique beasts and birds at the earth's boundary, distinct in form, size, and voice. Their differences implies beings beyond the known natural world, possibly lost or otherworldly.

Enoch then sees the boundary of the earth, where the sky ends and stretches over a vast expanse. The imagery describes reaching the edge of the known world, witnessing a transition between earth and sky. The phrasing forms an ancient perception of a firm boundary or dome-like structure over the earth.

Under Uriel's guidance, Enoch observes the stars, learning their movements, names, and cycles. The phrase "divided according to their paths," an ordered galactic structure, aligning with early astronomical knowledge. The emphasis on recording names and cycles implies a precise celestial catalog rather than mere visions. Uriel's presence confirms that Enoch is receiving accurate wisdom.

Enoch describes celestial knowledge recorded on a "tablet," proving the theme of divine revelation through written records. The repeated mention of names, commands, and deeds implies an ordered system, linking to astronomical laws, and divine decrees governing celestial bodies. The concept of a sacred or mystical tablet aligns with ancient traditions where wisdom is inscribed on stone or heavenly records.

Chapter 34

Chapter 34 describes Enoch traveling westward to the earth's edge, where he witnesses a vast assembly encompassing its boundaries. The term "assembly" implies a gathering of significant figures, entities, celestial beings, watchers; a representation of divine order. The repeated emphasis on boundaries implies that Enoch is mapping the astronomical or terrestrial limits within ancient cosmology.

Enoch then observes heavenly gates from which winds emerge, arranged in three-by-three formations, reflecting an ordered cosmic system. This aligns with early meteorological and cosmological models where specific winds controlled weather patterns. The mention of cold, hail, frost, heat, mist, and rain indicates that Enoch is witnessing the mechanisms governing climate and seasonal changes.

The passage also describes a powerful force from the heavens, emerging from a hidden source and establishing itself on earth. The imagery of breath, blowing, and power describes cosmic winds, divine energy, an ordered celestial system. The reference to a singular cavern hints at a controlled release, assuring Enoch's role as an observer of intentional cosmic or planetary phenomena.

Chapter 35

Chapter 35 describes Enoch's continued journey toward the region of 'Arab, reaching the edge of the earth. There he witnesses three heavenly winds stretching forth, just as he had seen in the east. This parallel reveals an intentional balance within the natural order, pointing to an ancient awareness of directional forces, celestial symmetry, or elemental design woven into the framework of the world.

Chapter 36

Chapter 36 continues Enoch's cosmic exploration as he ventures to the earth's extremities. Traveling south, he observes three heavenly winds, described as gentle, emerging alongside mist, rain, and wind. This is an ordered system governing both celestial and atmospheric forces, proving the link between natural elements and divine mechanics.

Enoch then moves north, where he witnesses three gentle winds similar to those in other directions. Above them, more powerful winds are present, describing a layered structure in celestial forces. This structured depiction aligns with ancient cosmological models, portraying a highly organized divine system rather than chaotic natural phenomena.

He then describes powerful winds moving through the stars, disturbing the west with force, driving home the idea of a cosmic system with organization where celestial forces influence both the heavens and the earth.

This closing doxology, a later interpolation. While the Ge'ez text is grammatically sound, the tone abruptly shifts from cosmic observation to theological praise. The mention of "souls of men" and the exaltation of the "Lord of glory" proves a scribal insertion intended to reframe Enoch's cosmology into a worship-centric worldview.

Chapter 37

Chapter 37 marks the beginning of a new vision, explicitly described as one of wisdom. It opens with Enoch's genealogy, tracing his descent from Adam. However, since this section survives only in Ge'ez, this introduction was later added to bolster Enoch's authority or distinguish this vision from previous ones. The formal structure and sudden emphasis on lineage point to interpolation.

Enoch then issues a proclamation of wisdom, calling for earthly listeners to hear both past and future revelations. The phrase "before the Lord of Spirits" invokes divine authority, while the contrast between former and latter things indicate a continuum of knowledge, linking past wisdom with future prophecy. This introduction further proves the idea that this section was shaped by later editorial hands.

The text contrasts the wisdom of the past with the ignorance of future generations. It infers that earlier people possessed great knowledge ("passed away in power"), while later ones will struggle to attain true wisdom. This reflects the recurring theme of lost sacred knowledge, common in esoteric traditions where wisdom is progressively hidden or diminished over time.

Enoch states that divine wisdom is not freely given but must be sought. He was not granted wisdom outright but received a portion of eternal life, an intrinsic link between immortality and knowledge. This hints at forbidden knowledge leading to longevity, a theme found in both 1 Enoch and Mesopotamian traditions. The phrase "as it was decreed" points to predestination, only what was permitted by the Lord of Spirits could be revealed.

This chapter also introduces The Book of Parables, a distinct section within 1 Enoch. The phrase "I lifted them up" indicates that these parables were physical, divinely inspired, and received. Unlike earlier revelations, which often addressed the watchers or angelic beings, these teachings are explicitly directed at humanity. The implication of what follows will contain mystical knowledge, esoteric insights, or prophetic warnings meant for mortal dwellers of the earth.

Chapter 38

Chapter 38 opens The First Parable with a stark contrast: the righteous shall rise while the sinners are forsaken for their transgressions. The phrase "shall be seen upon the dry land" indicates that this separation is not just spiritual but will be visibly manifested on earth. This sets the stage for divine judgment, where the fate of both groups is publicly revealed. The distinction is absolute. The righteous are gathered, while the sinners are abandoned.

The bracketed verse introduces theological language, such as "the Righteous One" and final annihilation, that contrasts with the tone of the surrounding text. These elements implicate later editorial additions. The core focus remains the visible separation of the righteous and the wicked.

The separation between the righteous and the wicked is noted. The righteous are "covered," signifying divine protection or transformation, while the sinners are rejected and removed from their presence. This establishes that righteousness and wickedness cannot coexist in the coming judgment.

The fall of the mighty and exalted rulers of the earth is then described, emphasizing their permanent removal. They will no longer see the holy ones, who instead receive divine light before the Lord of Spirits. This signifies a reversal of power, where those who once dominated the earth are erased, while the righteous are elevated and illuminated.

A divine transfer of power follows. Rulers of the world fall, and dominion is given to the righteous. The once-mighty face humiliation and destruction, while the holy ones assume control. This brings home the theme of justice, where oppressors are overthrown and the righteous take their place.

The chapter concludes with the absolute and irreversible judgment of the wicked. Unlike earlier passages where divine mercy was possible, here it is explicitly denied. The condemned do not simply die—they are cast out of existence entirely. This final and unchangeable separation between the righteous and the wicked reveals the full severity of divine justice, where those who defied the Lord of Spirits are erased forever.

Chapter 39

Chapter 39 confirms the return of divine offspring to the earthly realm. The "children of the elect and the holy ones" are descendants of divine-human unions, showing that celestial and mortal lineages will continue to mingle post-Flood.

Enoch is lifted up during a time of divine revelation and judgment. The "books of zeal and wrath" record divine justice, while the "books of confusion and weeping" contain the fate of the condemned. The Lord of

Spirits declares that mercy is no longer available, signaling an irreversible judgment. This indicates Enoch's vision of a cosmic reckoning where the righteous are elevated, and the wicked face absolute condemnation.

Enoch ascends into the heavens, carried by clouds and lifted by the wind. He is placed within the firmament, a celestial boundary described in ancient cosmology. The wording implies he was positioned in a fixed place within the heavenly realm, proving his role as one granted unique access to divine knowledge and realms beyond human reach.

He is then shown the dwelling place of the righteous and the resting places of the holy ones, a designated realm distinct from the earthly domain. The text does not explicitly describe it as "heaven" in the later theological sense but rather as a prepared habitation for those deemed worthy. The righteous dwell among angels, interceding for humanity as righteousness flows before them and mercy descends to earth.

The elect are beyond counting, standing before Him eternally, proving their permanent place in the divine order. They dwell beneath the wings of the Lord of Spirits, a sign of divine protection. They radiate like fire, their very presence exuding holiness. Their lives are defined by unceasing praise, and righteousness remains unshaken forever.

Enoch experiences a deep longing to remain in the celestial dwelling, recognizing that his place here was predestined before the Lord of Spirits. This affirms his unique role and purpose within the divine order. He witnesses a collective act of praise, where all bless and glorify the One who has been exalted from the beginning and will remain so forever. This illustrates the eternal nature of divine worship and the continuous reverence shown by all present.

The passage affirms divine sovereignty over creation. Before the world existed, there was no division, only unity before Him. The world came into being by His command and shall continue across all generations.

We see a celestial chorus of beings "who do not sleep," standing before the Lord of Spirits. However, the liturgical phrase "Holy, Holy, Holy" is from later biblical formulations such as *Isaiah* 6:3 tell-tale signs it was inserted into the text. The claim that "the earth will be filled with spirits" also deviates from the visionary logic of the chapter. For these reasons, this section has been bracketed as an interpolation.

As Enoch witnesses this eternal assembly, he observes their chant of "Blessed are You, and blessed is His Name," reinforcing divine sovereignty and cosmic order. This continues the celestial liturgy theme, aligning with other ancient visions of divine enthronement.

Finally, Enoch undergoes a physical transformation in response to the overwhelming intensity of the divine presence. The phrase "my face was transformed" mirrors other ancient accounts of radiance or altered appearance due to proximity to divine beings. His trembling reaction makes the immense power of the celestial realm unmistakable, which even he, a chosen scribe, could barely withstand.

Chapter 40

Chapter 40 opens with Enoch beholding an innumerable celestial multitude standing before the Lord of Spirits. This imagery mirrors descriptions in *Daniel* 7:10 and *Revelation* 5:11, driving home the concept of an eternal heavenly host beyond human calculation. The phrase "without number or calculation" indicates a limitless divine order that transcends human comprehension.

Enoch then witnesses four distinct celestial beings stationed at the four sides of the Divine Presence. This vision parallels Ezekiel and John's descriptions of heavenly creatures, and establishing the divine chain of command. Enoch had never heard their names before, indicating they belong to a hidden hierarchy. His angelic guide reveals their strengths, emphasizing their role in divine governance.

The four celestial beings continuously praise the Divine, aligning with *Isaiah* 6:3, *Daniel* 7:10, and *Revelation* 4:8, and cementing their role as eternal praisers within the heavenly order.

The passage then describes the First Word, a divine emanation that blesses the Lord of Spirits for eternity. This concept aligns with Da'ath, the hidden Sephirah in Jewish mysticism, where Wisdom (Chokmah) and Understanding (Binah) unite into Knowledge. This reveals that the First Word is not just speech but a fundamental expression of divine reality, the first vibration that sets creation into motion.

A divine blessing follows upon the righteous and chosen, making known a hierarchy based on humility before the Lord of Spirits. The phrase "those who bow down" (säqʷulan) emphasizes reverence rather than mere worship. The Ge'ez text contains theological rewording, but its core meaning remains consistent with earlier passages.

The next passage contains clear evidence of Christian tampering. The phrase "in His name" (ba-səmu) is a direct theological insertion absent from earlier manuscripts. No Aramaic or Greek witness supports this wording, making the Ge'ez text highly suspect. The idea of prayers for the dead and invoking a divine name reflects post-Enochic religious developments introduced by Christian Ge'ez scribes. The phrase "in His name" is removed from the restored text, and the rest of the verse remains bracketed as dubious.

Another heavily corrupted verse follows, containing the plural "Satans" (säytānāt) either a mistranslation or later theological addition. The intercession theme is also Christianized and lacks verification in earlier Enochic traditions. The entire verse is bracketed as an interpolation.

Enoch then describes the messengers of peace who do not sleep, a phrase consistent with earlier Watcher traditions. The mention of "those with four faces" strongly resembles the four-faced cherubim in *Ezekiel* and refers back to 40:3, where they were first described. The phrase "they recorded them" points to divine scribes, again proving the idea of celestial record-keeping.

The chapter concludes by naming four archangels and assigning them distinct roles. Michael, Raphael, and Gabriel align with earlier traditions, while Phanuel is identified as the angel over repentance and the hope of eternal life. In later traditions, Uriel replaces Phanuel as the fourth archangel, marking a shift in angelological developments. The four archangels stand before the Lord Most High, speaking with four voices, proving the divine and ordered nature of the celestial hierarchy.

Chapter 41

Chapter 41 reveals a heavenly order and the measurement of human actions. The phrase "divided" (tətəkəfəl) implies a system of celestial governance, while "measures" (mədalu) indicates a standard by which deeds are weighed, reminiscent of judgment concepts in ancient Mesopotamian and Egyptian traditions. This points to a divine law and order system predates later religious interpretations.

The text establishes a clear division. Righteous and holy ones have

174

designated dwelling places, while sinners are driven away. The phrase "no escape from torment" contrasts with the peace of the righteous, emphasizing divine authority over both reward and punishment. The term "expelled" (yəsədədəw) describes enforced separation, implying exile rather than destruction.

Enoch then observes a celestial system governing weather. The "gathering of lightning and winds" indicating controlled forces rather than random storms. The "emergence and scattering" of clouds and mist from a specific place indicates a central origin point for these meteorological forces, implying divine or supernatural control. The mention of "storehouses" (mäzagəbtä) validates this, describing a deliberate containment and regulated release of winds, hail, mist, and clouds, either an advanced natural phenomenon or technological control over atmospheric conditions.

The text then shifts to celestial mechanics, explicitly stating that the Sun and Moon operate within a controlled system. Their "storehouses" (mäzagəbtä) function as points of emergence and return. The statement "they do not deviate, they do not rest, they do not cease" emphasizes an unbreakable cosmic order. The Sun is the first to move in its cycle, following a designated path, enforcing the concept of an established celestial law rather than randomness.

The passage continues with a reinforcement of this fixed, unchanging celestial order. The Sun and Moon follow their courses without deviation or rest, maintaining an enforced system of movement. The phrase "one is exalted and is observed before the Lord of Spirits" highlights a hierarchy within celestial operations. Their function is continuous and unwavering, governed by a set law that does not permit variation.

The Sun and Moon are described as not just celestial bodies but as forces of blessing, judgment, and cosmic balance. The Sun represents both light and judgment, while the Moon's course influences righteousness and darkness. The division of light and darkness is deliberate, part of an intentional system set in place by the Lord of Spirits. The phrase "divided His spirit for mankind" indicates that divine influence is woven into existence, with a strengthened portion reserved for the righteous.

The chapter concludes with a hierarchical contrast. Celestial messengers (angels) are unable to speak, yet earthly rulers and their exalted ones are granted vision. The text presents a scene of judgment or revelation, with a central figure standing firm. The reason why the messenger cannot speak is ambiguous. Whether due to divine restraint, awe, or another factor is unclear. The phrase "before him" describing a singular figure before whom rulers and exalted ones are gathered, indicating the theme of an ultimate, unwavering authority.

Chapter 42

Chapter 42 presents wisdom as an entity seeking a home, implying the ancient theme that wisdom is not easily attained or retained in the earthly realm. The text describes wisdom attempting to settle but finding no suitable place, leading to its return to the heavens. This proves that wisdom is divine in nature, inaccessible to those unworthy or unwilling to embrace it. Similar traditions exist where wisdom is granted by the divine yet remains elusive to humanity.

The passage continues this imagery, portraying wisdom (Sophia) as seeking to dwell among humanity but being rejected, forcing its return to the celestial realm. The phrase "enthroned in the midst of the angels" confirms that wisdom's rightful place is among the divine, where it is honored rather than ignored. This aligns with Qabalistic and Gnostic traditions, where wisdom (Chokhmah/Sophia) is an exalted cosmic force but remains elusive to those who fail to recognize its value. The text implies that wisdom was offered to humanity, but they were either unwilling or incapable of housing it. In contrast, the angels embrace and honor wisdom, illustrating the divide between earthly ignorance and celestial understanding.

Transgression's return is a recurring pattern in 1 *Enoch* and other ancient texts. Here, it goes out to gather but is instead scattered and finds no refuge. The wilderness symbolizes moral exile, a world overtaken by corruption rather than wisdom. The phrase "concealed upon the earth in silence" confirms that it was not destroyed but remains hidden, waiting for those who will one day uncover it.

Previous translations, particularly R.H. Charles (1855–1931) and his successors, introduced a major mistranslation by rendering "wisdom" as "unrighteousness," completely inverting the original meaning. This distortion shifts the focus from wisdom's rejection to unrelated wickedness, a mistake repeated in later versions.

When restored to its true meaning, this passage is not about wickedness but about wisdom's fate: rejected, returning to its place, and waiting in silence upon the earth.

Chapter 43

Chapter 43 presents a vision where Enoch observes celestial bodies, lightning, stars, and heavenly forces. A key detail is that these stars are named and respond to their names, implying an intelligence and order behind their existence.

The passage describes a divine system governing celestial phenomena, where righteousness itself is measured through light, space, and time. This aligns cosmic order with moral law, intimating the idea that divine justice is woven into the fabric of creation.

Enoch follows his established pattern of questioning celestial beings, a core feature of his journey. After witnessing the phenomena in 43:1-2, he immediately turns to his angelic guide for an explanation.

The chapter concludes with a declaration that celestial knowledge is for the righteous those who guard and uphold the divine way. The "Lord of Spirits" is its source, and wisdom is preserved through action, not just belief. 1 Enoch consistently ties righteousness to observing divine order and maintaining balance, driving home the point that true wisdom is not passive but actively maintained through alignment with cosmic law.

Chapter 44

Chapter 44 presents a brief but significant vision in which Enoch observes the nature of lightning. He distinguishes it from the stars and notes its unique behavior, how it continues or ceases, and how new flashes are born. This passage reveals that lightning is treated as a distinct force, separate from both celestial bodies and other natural weather phenomena, making known the unique position it holds within the design of creation.

Chapter 45

Chapter 45 introduces a new parable, focusing on those who reject the divine name. The mention of the "dwelling place of the holy ones" contrasts the fate of the righteous with the consequences for those who deny the divine order. Throughout 1 *Enoch*, righteousness is portrayed as alignment with cosmic law, while rejection of the sacred leads to separation and judgment.

The passage describes a planetary upheaval linked to the judgment of sinners. The heavens tremble, and the earth is removed, symbolizing the destruction of the old order. The focus remains on those who reject the name of the Lord of Spirits, pointing to 1 *Enoch's* recurring theme that denying divine authority leads to downfall. The phrase "a portion of the sinners" suggests that judgment is not universal, some are set apart for destruction, while others may be spared.

A figure called the Chosen One is introduced suddenly, seated in judgment and revealing hidden thoughts. This language parallels messianic doctrine rather than Enoch's earlier cosmology. The phrase "they will see the Chosen One who was revealed" strongly reflects post-Enochic eschatology and later theological developments.

The divine presence dwells among the righteous, centered around the Chosen One. The phrase "it shall be exalted to the heavens" may refer either to the glorification of the Chosen One or the establishment of divine rule. The emphasis on blessing and eternal light brings forth the vision of a new divine order, where righteousness prevails.

The passage further establishes the separation of the righteous and the wicked. The exaltation and strengthening of divine order is reserved for the righteous and the chosen ones, while the sinners and evildoers are excluded from their presence. This reflects earlier themes in 1 *Enoch*, where the unrighteous are not only judged but also barred from the presence of divine light.

The chapter concludes by solidifying this separation. The righteous are blessed in the presence of the divine, while the wicked face imminent judgment and removal from the earth. The phrase "their end is from the face of the earth" is a clear statement of their annihilation, aligning with earlier passages about divine justice cleansing the world of corruption.

Chapter 46

Chapter 46 opens with Enoch confronted by a vision of two luminous beings. The first is ancient, his presence radiant and pure, with hair resembling white wool. The second figure, standing beside the first, carries the visage of a man yet shines with an angelic grace. At this moment, neither name nor divine role is assigned, leaving their identities shrouded in tantalizing mystery.

Enoch, intrigued by the unknown, immediately turns to one of the holy angels accompanying him, demanding clarity: Who is this mysterious figure, and from where did he come? Enoch's question reveals his uncertainty and intrigue about the identity of the figure standing beside the one now explicitly named the Ancient One of Days.

The angel answers clearly, identifying the second figure as a son of humanity who has become righteous. He embodies righteousness itself, possessing all treasures of wisdom. Yet despite possessing such immense wisdom and authority, his position remains explicitly temporary, deliberately appointed and hidden by the Lord of Spirits for a set time. He is raised from humanity, appointed to fulfill a specific, finite role, not as an eternal divine ruler, but as a vessel of divine purpose and justice.

What follows is no coronation but a reckoning. This mortal-born figure is set forth as an agent of justice, toppling the kings and rulers who have abused their positions. He forcefully removes kings from their thrones, dismantles their oppressive control, and confronts sinners and transgressors alike. Their downfall is explicitly tied not to religious devotion or worship, but solely to their unjust deeds: oppression, injustice, and abuse of power. Their disgrace is complete and irreversible; their legacies crumble, kingdoms taken from them, and authority handed to another.

Yet, a clear interpolation emerges in the text. The phrase, "[for they did not exalt the name of the Lord of Spirits]," is bracketed because it starkly interrupts the ethical logic of the vision, redirecting moral accountability toward religious devotion. This insertion blatantly follows the recognizable pattern of Second Temple scribal tampering, seeking to shift ethical judgment into religious condemnation. Such tampering attempts to reshape Enoch's vision into a form more aligned with later theological agendas, but here it is clearly exposed and bracketed.

The mighty ones fall in disgrace, never to rise again, their downfall tied to their failure to exalt the name of the Lord of Spirits. Their rule is marked as corrupt, and their end is final.

The chapter concludes with a contrast between the righteous and the wicked. The faithful will shine like the stars and follow the ways of the Most High, while the wicked face judgment and destruction. Their rebellion is exposed, and their downfall is tied to false allegiances and the denial of the Lord of Spirits. The text makes it clear. Both actions and allegiances determine one's fate.

Emphasizing the separation between the righteous and the wicked, the final passage describes how some will be cast out of their dwellings and gatherings, while the chosen ones remain. The reference to being "in his name" declares allegiance to the Lord of Spirits, confirming the theme of divine selection. This distinction reflects an early concept of spiritual division, rather than the later theological emphasis on absolute moral judgment.

Chapter 47

Chapter 47 marks a pivotal moment where the prayers of the righteous and the blood of the just rise up before the Lord of Spirits. The imagery suggests that their cries for justice have reached a critical point, but no immediate judgment is declared. The focus remains on divine recognition rather than response, implying that the suffering of the righteous is acknowledged but not yet avenged. This aligns with earlier esoteric concepts of cosmic balance, without the overt moralizing seen in later redacted sections.

The passage then describes heavenly beings uniting in prayer and praise in response to the suffering of the righteous. The acknowledgment of their prayers and shed blood indicates that divine justice is inevitable, though not immediate. The phrase "vengeance will not be delayed forever" reinforces 1 Enoch's theme of shifting power. While this aligns with earlier justice themes, its structured phrasing and collective prayer indicate possible later redaction or harmonization with apocalyptic traditions.

The Head of Days is then seen seated on his throne, a figure previously introduced in 46:1. While later traditions attempt to equate him with the "Ancient of Days" from Daniel 7:9, the text itself does not support this identification. The Head of Days represents an eternal celestial authority unique to Enochic tradition. The Books of the Living are opened before him, recording deeds, but no immediate judgment is declared. The presence of heavenly powers standing before him confirms his authority, yet his exact nature remains distinct from later theological interpretations.

The chapter concludes with the culmination of the righteous' prayers being heard and their suffering acknowledged. The holy ones rejoice as righteousness prevails, but the text remains vague on how justice unfolds. Rather than detailing judgment, the emphasis is on divine recognition as the decisive turning point. Though it echoes apocalyptic themes, the focus here is resolution rather than retribution.

Chapter 48

Righteousness is opened and never ceases. Many drink from it, especially the wise and the thirsty. Wisdom is fulfilled, and those connected to it dwell with the righteous, the holy, and the chosen. The phrasing is deliberately esoteric, emphasizing mystery over clarity.

This verse presents two separate naming events, one feminine, one masculine, before two distinct divine entities. "Purity" is named before the Lord of Spirits, and "his name" is named before the Head of Days. The Ge'ez grammar confirms they are not the same being, but two divine witnesses.

The passage presents a name proclaimed before the creation of the sun, the signs, and the stars of heaven, placing it in a context of pre-existence. No subject is introduced, yet the name is declared before the Lord of Spirits. The phrasing is abrupt and structurally distinct from surrounding verses, raising the possibility of later theological influence. However, due to the lack of older manuscripts, the passage is preserved as-is while its unusual tone is noted.

This next part of the chapter describes the same unnamed figure or force as a support for the righteous and holy ones, those who have chosen it. They will not fall, and this same presence is called the light of the nations and the hope of the troubled. The identity remains deliberately vague, but the phrasing echoes later theological language, pointing to redaction intended to align with external doctrines.

Appendix A: Ch 48

The passage introduces a reverence scene in which the oppressed bow, bless, and sing, yet no subject is named. The phrase "before him" appears without context, and the praise is directed not to a being but "for the name of the Lord of Spirits," echoing theological constructs found nowhere else in authentic Enochian material. The entire structure mirrors post-temple salvific formulas, revealing this verse has been redacted to support external doctrines. Without Aramaic or Greek for comparison, the intrusion cannot be fully proven, but its tone betrays its origin.

This verse uses eternal language to describe someone or something chosen and given "before him," from before the creation of the world and lasting forever. No subject is named. The phrasing directly mirrors later predestination doctrines, meaning the verse was constructed to support a theological framework foreign to authentic Enochian thought. Without earlier manuscript support, the identity remains ambiguous, but the structure betrays its agenda.

The passage goes on to say wisdom was established for the holy and righteous, because their portion was preserved through prayer and endurance in a world of transgression. It states they prayed "in his name" before the Lord of Spirits, and that "in the name of this one, they shall be delivered." The phrase reflects legalistic theological language foreign to early Enoch, shifting the focus to name-based salvation. With no subject identified and no earlier manuscript support, this verse shows clear signs of theological redaction designed to insert later doctrinal concepts.

The passage then shifts to the humbling of earthly rulers and oppressors, who face judgment for their misdeeds. Their power does not shield them from consequences, and their cries will go unanswered. The focus remains on divine justice, reinforcing 1 Enoch's recurring theme: the balance of power will shift, and those who rule through oppression will not escape the reckoning.

The final destruction of the oppressors is then described. They are seen and despised by the chosen ones, their fate compared to hair burning in fire and foam dissolving in water, imagery that signifies complete erasure. The statement that "no bond shall be honored by them" confirms a permanent reversal of power. Unlike later theological developments that emphasize punishment in an afterlife, 1 Enoch focuses on total obliteration. Those who ruled through oppression leave no trace behind.

This chapter survives only in Ge'ez and shows clear signs of theological redaction. From verse 2 onward, it introduces name-based salvation, ambiguous figures, and "his Messiah," a title absent from early Enoch. The language mirrors post-temple doctrine, shifting from vision to structured worship. Though preserved in translation, the chapter's tone and construction betray an agenda foreign to authentic Enochian cosmology. This is not prophecy. This is theology retrofitted into the scroll.

Chapter 49

Chapter 49 opens with a vivid image of wisdom as a life-giving force poured out like water. This elemental metaphor holds onto 1 *Enoch's* core message: wisdom is accessible, sustaining, and enduring. The line "glory shall not cease before him forever" bringing to mind the eternal presence of divine light, not the glorification of a figure.

The second verse begins in harmony with this tone, stating that the Lord of Spirits is mighty among both the righteous and the transgressors. The latter are described as shadows and vapors. None shall remain standing. But the moment this image closes, the verse pivots sharply: an unnamed figure is glorified before the Lord of Spirits, his strength declared eternal. This sudden shift in tone and structure reveals a theological insertion.

The next two verses continue this redacted style, presenting wisdom as dwelling "in him," and portraying a gentle, accepted figure who speaks without force. These passages mirror later theological patterns foreign to Enoch's original vision, centralizing salvation in a person rather than in wisdom, justice, or divine law.

Only the opening verse and the first half of verse two preserve authentic Enochian cosmology. The rest reflects a post-temple redactor's hand, reshaping divine wisdom into messianic worship.

The contrast between this chapter and what follows is striking. The next chapter immediately returns to Enoch's distinct voice, esoteric, bold, and unapologetically just. This shift supports the likelihood that the original scroll from which the Ge'ez was copied had been damaged at this point. In trying to repair the loss, the scribe may have drawn from surrounding context, their own beliefs, or both. The result is a section that feels patched rather than revealed, shaped more by theological imagination than prophetic transmission.

Chapter 50

Chapter 50 describes a future event where the holy and elect are covered and illuminated by light. While later traditions may interpret this as divine intervention, the text itself does not specify its nature. The mention of honor, praise, and majesty points to recognition rather than deliverance. The "day of trouble" frames this event as occurring during a time of upheaval, staying true to 1 Enoch's theme of transformation rather than simple retribution.

The passage then describes a gathering where the wicked perish and the righteous rise. The text does not indicate a direct act of divine judgment, but rather a natural separation based on actions. The phrase "they shall flee because of their deeds" brings to mind consequence rather than punishment. The rising of the righteous symbolizing ascension, enlightenment, or the restoration of balance. While later traditions may have imposed theological interpretations, the text itself remains focused on action and consequence rather than external judgment.

The wicked cannot stand before the divine, not due to punishment but by nature. Mercy here is depicted as understanding rather than salvation, aligning with Enoch's emphasis on wisdom over judgment.

The text then contrasts the endurance of the righteous with the downfall of the sinners. The righteous remain firm, while the sinners collapse entirely under the presence of divine glory. This recurring theme in 1 Enoch confirms the inevitability of judgment. The phrase "shall not stand" proves more than a simple fall. It implies total collapse, a removal from existence itself.

The chapter concludes with the statement "they shall no longer be taught," indicating a divine restriction on knowledge. This could indicate a final decree silencing further revelation, the end of an age, or a transition in divine order where wisdom is no longer granted to those who have rejected it.

Chapter 51

Chapter 51 describes the earth, Sheol, and the abyss giving back what they have held. This is not resurrection or redemption, but rather a release of what was contained. The focus is on restoration. Everything that was entrusted to these realms must return in its appointed time.

The passage then shifts to the joy of the righteous and holy ones as the appointed day arrives. Their deliverance marks the fulfillment of what was awaited, driving home 1 *Enoch's* consistent theme of divine order and timing rather than immediate or arbitrary judgment.

Wisdom is then described as dwelling in those days, with a sign marking its presence. The treasures of wisdom will be spoken, granted by the Lord of Spirits. This does not imply a theological interpretation or eschatological prophecy but simply the revelation of wisdom at the proper time. Unlike later traditions that associate wisdom with a singular figure, this passage presents wisdom as an accessible force granted to the righteous.

A great cosmic event follows, marked by upheaval and transformation. The desert burning like a furnace indicates intense purification, while the abyss being torn open like churned milk implies a deep disruption in the geological order. The reaction of the angels is twofold, trembling in awe or fear, yet shining with joy, indicating that this event is both terrifying and significant.

The chapter concludes with the righteous inheriting the earth permanently, contradicting later traditions that emphasize a separate heavenly realm. The repetition of "dwell" emphasizes stability and finality, making it clear that this is not a temporary state but an eternal restoration. The earth itself rejoicing pointing to a cosmic renewal undoing the corruption introduced by the Watchers. The phrase "they shall shine" echoes *Daniel* 12:3, where the righteous are described as glowing like stars, hinting at a transformation or return to a divine-like state. The closing statement, "they shall find rest," signals the end of struggle and suffering, marking the completion of their journey and the establishment of an incorruptible order.

Chapter 52

Chapter 52 marks a transition as Enoch is carried by a whirlwind into the desert. The "exalted place" refers to where he witnessed mighty appearances before being taken. The imagery of being carried by the wind aligns with other prophetic journeys where the seer is transported to receive further revelation.

Enoch then witnesses heavenly treasures, eternal things that "do not perish," which have descended to earth. The mountains of iron, copper, silver, gold, molten metal, and clay represent distinct elements of creation, reflecting the structured order within the earth. These materials, often associated with wealth and power, are shown as part of a divine plan but not permanent sources of authority.

Enoch directly asks his angelic guide to explain the vision he has just seen. The phrase "hidden thing" making known that what he witnessed is not immediately understandable and requires divine interpretation. The emphasis on "mighty" indicates its great significance.

The angel explains that everything Enoch has seen relates to the authority of the Anointed One. The "hidden thing" implies a pre-established divine order, and the phrase "it shall be strong upon the earth" emphasizes permanence. However, the term "Anointed One" (መሲሕ - mäsīhu) may reflect later Messianic expectations rather than the original text. Without an Aramaic source for comparison, this remains uncertain.

Enoch is then taken by an angel (the same one from the previous verse) to meet the angel of peace, who will reveal the next vision. The focus shifts from witnessing to understanding, Enoch is now being given deeper insight into what has been "planted by the Lord of Spirits". This phrase implies an intentional act of divine establishment, reinforcing divine order and strength.

The vision then turns to the destruction of the metallic mountains, signifying that their power will not last before the chosen ones. The imagery of wax melting before fire and water failing to flow emphasizes complete dissolution. The phrase "they shall be as nothing beneath the earth" implies that whatever these mountains represent, whether earthly kingdoms, material wealth, or hidden organization, they will ultimately be rendered powerless. This enforces the idea that only the divine order remains unshaken.

The next passage continues the theme of impermanence, emphasizing that gold, silver, and wealth will no longer hold value. The "exalted place" remains, but material possessions will not bring honor or security. This signifies a shift from earthly power to divine authority, showing that wealth and possessions have no place in what has been revealed to Enoch.

The dismantling of earthly power continues. Iron will no longer serve as a weapon, nor bronze as a source of strength. The mention of armor and war points to a future where military force becomes obsolete. The inability to cut or shape these materials signifies the end of their utility, making clear the idea that power structures built upon them will no longer exist.

The chapter concludes with the final removal of material power. Everything described in previous passages, including metals, wealth, and war, will be wiped away. The destruction of these things prepares the way for the chosen ones to be revealed before the Lord of Spirits. The phrase "shall appear" declares a moment of divine recognition or transformation, where those who are chosen will stand in the presence of divine authority.

Chapter 53

Chapter 53 begins with Enoch witnessing a deep, open chasm prepared for judgment. Those gathered for judgment, along with fire, torment, and "the sea," are cast into this abyss. The phrase "and the sea" is unusual in this context, possibly signifying chaos, destruction, or a cosmic flood event. The final line, "which is never filled," brings in the idea of an insatiable place of punishment, revealing its role as an eternal destination for the condemned.

The passage then describes the final fate of the condemned, emphasizing inescapable torment and judgment. The phrase "all that does not cease from suffering shall consume the sinners" putting forth that their own punishment leads to their destruction, provoking a sense of relentless, never-ending judgment. The trembling before the Lord of Spirits signifies divine authority enforcing their fate. The final statement, "they shall not escape forever and ever," is absolute, confirming that there is no redemption or release from this judgment.

A following verse is bracketed due to textual corruption. In 1 Enoch, the Angels of Punishment serve divine judgment, NOT an adversary figure. The reference to a singular "Satan" (säyṭan) contradicts 1 Enoch 40:7, where "Satans" (säytänät) appear in the plural as adversarial figures, but not as rulers of punishment. The idea of angels preparing instruments for a singular "Satan" is entirely foreign to early Enochic tradition, aligning instead with much later theological interpretations. This is a clear case of scribal tampering.

The passage then shifts back to expected Enochian themes, with the Angel of Peace witnessing the instruments of punishment. Unlike the corrupted reference to Satan, this passage remains consistent with 1 *Enoch's* framework. The Angels of Punishment are preparing divine judgment, not serving an adversary. The Angel of Peace (ሰላም, sälam) serves as a witness, staying with the theme of divine justice.

Judgment is then declared upon the kings and mighty ones who ruled the earth. The instruments of punishment have been prepared to terrify them, emphasizing divine retribution against corrupt rulers.

The passage then promises preservation and honor for the righteous and the chosen ones after judgment. Some translations render this as "shall be saved," but this is a later theological corruption that does not fit the original Enochian framework. The correct meaning is "shall be preserved," reflecting divine guardianship rather than later religious salvation concepts. Additionally, the reference to "the name of the Lord of Spirits" contradicts the earlier corrupt passage about "the name of the anointed one," exposing a scribal inconsistency. This further confirms the messianic insertion in the previous chapter as an interpolation.

The chapter concludes with mountains and water as imagery for judgment and transformation. The mountains, once mighty, are now as insignificant as the earth, while the abyss, often a symbol of chaos, is likened to disturbed waters. The final statement about the separation of the righteous from sinners follows a common 1 *Enoch* theme, the divine sorting of the faithful from the corrupt.

Chapter 54

Chapter 54 opens with Enoch witnessing another part of the earth, a deep valley where fire shakes and moves. This is more than a simple blaze; the fire is active, unsettling the land. Whether this is a volcanic chasm, a site of divine punishment, or something else remains unclear, the scene absolutely reveals instability and power rather than mere destruction.

The kings and mighty ones are led to the fiery valley and cast in without resistance. The text does not specify who enacts this judgment, but their fate is sealed in the flames.

Enoch then sees the very instruments of punishment he had been shown earlier, iron chains forged by the Angels of Punishment, designed to restrain the kings and mighty ones. Unlike the corrupted version of 53:3, which falsely inserted "for Satan," this passage clarifies that these bindings were always intended for the rulers who oppressed the earth. The chains are described as unbreakable, emphasizing the permanence of their judgment. This moment directly continues the earlier vision, where the Angel of Peace confirmed that these tools had been prepared to terrify those who misused their power.

The Angel of Peace then lifts the unbreakable chains, signifying that their judgment is inevitable. The act of lifting the chains may symbolize the final stage before their punishment is carried out, marking the moment when their fate is sealed. Unlike the corrupted reading in 53:3, there is no mention of Satan; the focus remains solely on the oppressive rulers and their impending downfall.

The fallen rulers are cast down as a spectacle for Azazel, revealing their punishment is meant to be seen. This does not imply the punishment is for Azazel or his followers. Unlike corrupt translations that insert an "abyss of complete condemnation" or a false reference to covering jaws with stones, the original text emphasizes their inescapable fate beneath the heavens. The phrase "the weight of their oppression" confirms their punishment is tied to their actions.

The four archangels, Michael, Gabriel, Raphael, and Phanuel, seize the rebellious ones and throw them into the trembling fire. This unstable, consuming force is now revealed to be the final destination for those who defied divine order. The Lord of Spirits repays them for their rebellion, not just for their own actions but for leading astray those who lived on the earth. This makes known the idea that corruption was not limited to the heavenly beings alone but had direct consequences for humanity as well.

The wrath of the Lord of Spirits is unleashed, causing a cosmic upheaval. The imagery describes a destabilization of the natural order. Both the waters above the heavens and the springs beneath the earth are affected. The reference to "storehouses of water" above the heavens recalls ancient conceptions of the firmament holding back waters, while the mention of springs beneath the earth aligns with older beliefs about subterranean waters feeding rivers and seas. Unlike the Great Flood, which symbolized purification, this event is tied directly to divine judgment.

The cosmic order unravels completely. Both the waters above and the waters below are destroyed. This goes beyond the imagery of a flood, marking a final event rather than a cyclical one.

The destruction extends beyond the elements of creation, emphasizing that all inhabitants of the earth, both those on land and those dwelling beneath the edges of heaven, will perish. The repeated phrasing "those who lived" proves the totality of the judgment. The mention of the "ends of heaven" is ambiguous, possibly referring to remote or hidden places, indicating that no refuge exists from this judgment.

The chapter concludes with the confirmation that the earth was destroyed due to rebellion, both human and divine. Their actions brought ruin, and as a result, they will suffer judgment. The repetition emphasizes that their punishment is a direct consequence of their corruption, confirming 1 Enoch's theme of divine justice restoring order.

Chapter 55

Chapter 55 contains clear indicators of later theological tampering, particularly in the sudden introduction of repentance and mercy after absolute judgment. This contradicts previous passages, where judgment was presented as final with no escape or second chances. The Ge'ez text reflects only the core phrase present in the manuscript, stripping away the clear later additions meant to force 1 Enoch into biblical alignment.

A later insertion attempts to mirror Genesis 9, introducing a divine oath, a heavenly sign, and an eternal covenant, all directly lifted from the Noahic Covenant. 1 Enoch consistently emphasizes inescapable judgment, making this abrupt shift a clear scribal addition meant to soften the original text. The structure, wording, and themes of this passage do not align with the rest of Enoch, further proving its later origin.

Immediately after this fabricated repentance narrative, the original text resumes with absolute judgment. The decree is final. There is no escape, no negotiation. The punishment is handed over to the angels for execution, casting forth the spectacle of divine wrath. The repetition of "punishment" and "wrath" further emphasizes the severity of the sentence, making it clear that 55:1-2 were later theological insertions. The true stance of 1 Enoch is restored here. The sentence has already been passed, and no one is spared.

The passage then describes a moment of reckoning where the kings and mighty ones, rulers influenced by the fallen Watchers, are gathered in a barren wasteland to witness an event that leaves them astonished. The reference to "the chosen one" sitting on the throne of glory describes a being of power and judgment, but given the previous evidence of theological tampering, the identity of this figure remains uncertain.

What is clear, however, is that Azazel and his assembly are acknowledged in this moment, proving his continued presence in the unfolding divine judgment. This is not an act of repentance, but rather a forced recognition of power. A final confrontation where even the condemned must acknowledge the authority before them.

Chapter 56

Chapter 56 provides a direct and uncompromising vision of judgment. The angels of punishment are seen in motion, actively going forth, carrying whips and instruments of torment. This signifies both suffering and affliction, making known that divine retribution is ongoing. There is no repentance, no salvation, only execution of punishment. The fact that the angels are actively holding these instruments of wrath shows that this is not a warning. It is already happening.

A major alteration occurs in later translations, completely rewriting the second verse. The Ge'ez text states that the "angels of peace," previously uninvolved, were stirred up, leading to celestial disturbance and internal conflict. However, popular translations erased this, inserting a fabricated dialogue where Enoch questions an angel and forcing the scene into a judgment narrative that does not exist in the actual text. This deliberate rewrite removed the complexity of celestial upheaval, replacing it with a rigid theological framework. The restored translation reveals that even among the divine, neutrality is breaking, and even the angels of peace can no longer remain uninvolved.

The text overturns expectations as both the "chosen" and "beloved" are cast into the valley of confusion, signifying chaos, not organized punishment. The Ge'ez offers no redemption. Only descent into disorder.

Their fate is sealed. The chosen and beloved cry out from the abyss, their existence erased. They are no longer counted, implying not only punishment but total removal from divine order. This contradicts later theological claims of restoration. The text presents a finality that later interpretations sought to obscure.

A chaotic war and deception follows, where both human rulers and divine forces converge for battle. The phrase "a spirit of confusion" pointing to a divine or supernatural force actively disrupting their plans, causing betrayal among allies. The imagery of wild animals and starving dogs highlights their desperation, implying a descent into uncontrollable violence. Unlike later interpretations that frame this as an orderly divine judgment, the original text presents an unpredictable and frenzied war, one that spirals into madness rather than controlled execution.

Another major alteration occurs here. Later translations forced the text into a biblical framework of conquest and exile. The phrase "tread underfoot the land of his elect" does not exist in the original Ge'ez but appears in later versions. The actual text describes war, destruction, and a land being shaken, not divine punishment of the chosen. This alteration undeniably made to align 1 *Enoch* with later exile theology, distorting its original meaning.

The text then describes an apocalyptic level of destruction and internal strife. The righteous ones are exiled, but rather than a unified enemy rising against them, their own descendants turn on each other in slaughter. The lack of mercy across all generations, elders, children, parents, indicates a total societal collapse rather than an external conquest. Unlike later interpretations that frame this as divine punishment for disobedience, the original text presents internal division and annihilation rather than divine wrath. This is not about judgment. It's about a complete breakdown of order, where no one is spared and suffering is inescapable.

The chapter concludes with absolute destruction as Sheol opens to consume them, sealing their fate. The phrase "as a testimony to the sinners" displaying their downfall serves as a warning, though whether for the living or the condemned remains unclear. The mention of "before the chosen ones" is ambiguous. Later insertions attempt to force repentance or salvation, but the text offers only annihilation and a grim finality.

Chapter 57

Chapter 57 introduces a new vision, filled with movement and storm-like imagery. The mention of chariots lifted by the wind describing celestial or extraterrestrial transportation, divine or otherworldly. The phrase "men were speaking" is ambiguous. Were they commanding the chariots, or simply present as the storm carried them forth? The east-to-west motion implies a vast, almost galactic scale event, culminating in a "turmoil of the day," which describes a cataclysmic upheaval. Later theological interpretations attempt to frame this as angelic warfare or an eschatological battle, but the original text presents only a mysterious and powerful spectacle.

The vision escalates with a deafening roar from the chariots, followed by a great commotion initiated by the holy ones from heaven. The pillars of the earth shake, describing a cosmic-level disturbance, not a localized event. The phrase "from the ends of the earth to the ends of heaven" describes the massive scale of the event, global or even celestial in nature. Unlike later retellings that frame such occurrences as purely divine judgment, the original text ties this disturbance to celestial forces and the movement of the holy ones.

The vision closes with a dramatic act of submission. Whether voluntary or forced remains unclear. The phrase "they all fell" indicating reverence or collapse under overwhelming power. The mention of "another parable" makes known this event is part of a greater cycle of judgment and submission, rather than a singular moment of worship.

Chapter 58

Chapter 58 marks a transition into a new section, the third parable, focusing on the righteous and chosen. The deliberate numbering of these parables indicates a narrative rather than random visions. Unlike the previous chapters centered on cosmic upheaval and judgment, this shift turns toward those who are preserved rather than condemned.

The righteous and chosen are now declared blessed, set apart from those who faced destruction. They are granted splendor, a term that alludes to divine favor, radiance, or transformation. The contrast with earlier passages confirms the recurring theme: judgment for the wicked, elevation for the righteous. This sets the stage for what follows, focusing on the rewards of the righteous.

The righteous exist in a state of divine illumination, both physically ("the light of the sun") and spiritually ("the light of eternal life"). Their days will not end, marking a stark contrast to earlier passages of final destruction. Instead of facing judgment, they enter a timeless existence, where life continues without limit.

This passage brings in the eternal state of the righteous, who seek the light and find rest in righteousness. The promise of peace in the presence of the Lord of Spirits contrasts sharply with earlier destruction, emphasizing the final separation between the judged and the redeemed.

The holy ones ascend into the heavens, marking their transition from the earthly realm. The "treasures of righteousness" and "portion of that which is steadfast" indicate something unshaken and enduring, rather than a belief system or religious faith. The comparison to the sun indicates permanence, while the disappearance of darkness signals the final removal of all that opposes righteousness.

The permanence of light is declared, both literal and symbolic. Unlike earlier cycles of destruction and renewal, here the text states that "the completion of days shall not come," implying an unending state of existence. The reference to "darkness being overturned" confirms a past corruption now undone. The phrase "the light of righteousness shall remain forever" cements this as a final, unchangeable reality, where darkness no longer holds power.

Chapter 59

Chapter 59 presents a vision of cosmic forces, lightning, luminous phenomena, and their movement, functioning as both a blessing and a warning. The "treasures of lightning" indicate something beyond natural storms, indicating celestial or energetic forces under divine control. Their dual nature, "for blessing and for a warning," implies they signal important events, linked to judgment or revelation. Their movement and flashing are deliberate, confirming the idea that these celestial signs are part of a controlled design, not chaotic occurrences.

Enoch's vision continues with the "treasures of thunder," portraying thunder as a controlled force, not just a natural phenomenon. Its resonance in the heights of heaven infers an intelligent or divine mechanism behind it. The passage confirms thunder's dual nature. It can be a sign of divine favor ("peace and blessing") or an omen of destruction ("a curse"). The earth's dwellings shake, indicating physical impacts from storms, celestial movements, or even technological forces wielded by divine entities. This indicates that the heavens communicate with the earth in powerful and unmistakable ways.

A sudden shift follows. The appearance of a pillar, surrounded by lights and flashing energy. The word for "pillar" (lita) is unusual, referring to a beam of light, a structured object, or even a celestial gateway. The connection between "lights" and "treasures" indicates a controlled, stored, or harnessed energy source, a form of technology or divine phenomenon. The flashes serve as both a blessing and a symbol of prosperity, confirming their intentional function rather than being random displays of power. The phrase "they flashed for blessing and prosperity" indicating that this is neither a destructive force nor a chaotic event, but a structured and intentional, beneficial occurrence.

Chapter 60

Chapter 60 begins with a precise date, anchoring Enoch's vision within his 500th year. A great cosmic upheaval follows. The heavens shake violently, and celestial order is thrown into chaos. The Most High's power forces the angels to retreat, an act of divine intervention disrupting even the highest realms. The disturbance of the "outposts of heaven" describes a disruption to celestial fortresses, boundaries, or hierarchies. This is not a passive event but an immense act of power causing the heavens themselves to tremble.

A shift occurs as divine authority is revealed. The "chief of the vision" appears, an ambiguous title that may refer to the Most High, a high-ranking celestial being, or Enoch himself in a transformed state. The "throne of his glory" signifies divine judgment or supreme rulership, with angels and the righteous gathered in reverence. This enthronement scene stands in stark contrast to the prior chaos, marking a pivotal moment in cosmic events.

Enoch's overwhelming reaction reflects absolute awe and terror. He loses strength, collapses, and is lifted up by Michael, who intervenes by restoring Enoch both physically and spiritually. The phrase "I was flung... heaven.." conveys disorientation, not ascent, highlighting the sheer intensity of divine encounters. Other translations have smoothed over or interpolated explanations into the Ge'ez for the gap between "flung" and "heaven," but our version does not assume what might be missing.

Michael declares that the time of mercy has ended, and divine wrath is now set upon the earth. His question, "Why has this vision been revealed?" implies that these events were meant to remain hidden until the appointed time. Judgment is now inevitable, and the separation between the righteous and the wicked is absolute. The Lord of Spirits executes justice, rewarding those who uphold righteousness while condemning those who reject it. The phrase "day of covenant for the chosen and reckoning for sinners" makes it unmistakably clear that this moment is both a reward and a final sentence, ensuring divine order prevails.

The vision then shifts to the introduction of Leviathan, the great primordial sea creature described as a female serpent, assigned to the depths of the sea above the fountains of the waters. Behemoth is hidden in Duidain, a concealed land in the east near the Garden, reinforcing his connection to a primordial order. The "seventh from Adam" is almost certainly Enoch, marking a divine timeline. The separation of Leviathan and Behemoth mirrors cosmic balance, one ruling the sea, the other the land.

Their separation occurs on a single day, a deliberate act rather than a natural evolution. The term "monsters" (አስሕተ, ʾəlkətu) indicates they are more than mere animals, aligning with ancient mythological beings rather than ordinary creatures. The unusual mention of male and female raises the possibility that they were originally counterparts in a cosmic balance of power rather than adversaries. Their forced separation, rather than destruction, indicates that both still exist but in hidden or inaccessible realms.

The angel's explanation implies that this division carries a hidden meaning. Leviathan and Behemoth are part of a greater divine order. The title "son of man" is used not in a later Messianic sense but to emphasize Enoch's humanity in contrast to the knowledge he is receiving. The phrase "you will understand" indicates that Enoch is being granted access to secrets beyond human reach. The "great signs" refer to cosmic or divine mysteries governing creation, confirming the idea that these beings are not just creatures but integral parts of the universe's structure.

The vision expands into the structure of creation, distinguishing between what moves and what is fixed. This describes an early understanding of celestial mechanics and divine laws governing the universe. The reference to the depths, the ends, and the foundations of the heavens implies a layered cosmos with distinct boundaries. This could relate to astronomical bodies, divine laws, or esoteric principles shaping reality.

The scene then erupts into a cosmic upheaval. Winds, spirits, and celestial forces are divided, destroyed, or bound. The "power of the spirit" governs both natural and supernatural elements of divine order. The alignment of light, the moon, and righteousness describe that celestial bodies follow moral and spiritual laws. The division of stars by their names signifies an ordered universe, referencing astronomical cycles or spiritual hierarchies.

A sudden, destructive event follows. Lightning imagery signals divine intervention and judgment. The phrase "their vision was as a creation" indicating that this moment is a fundamental reshaping of existence. The words "they shall be heard" imply that this event will be recognized, recorded, or echoed throughout time. The grand scale of this vision makes its cosmic significance obvious, where destruction, reordering, and divine power are manifest visibly and audibly.

A galaxy emerges from this chaos. Even forces like thunder, lightning, and wind are contained within assigned chambers, reflecting an ancient belief in divinely governed natural events. The phrase "they shall not be separated" confirms these forces remain bound to their roles, ensuring balance in creation. Lightning, thunder, wind, and storms operate in cyclical patterns, never straying from their predetermined paths. The statement "shall be seized, changed, and driven" describes natural transformation, hinting at seasonal cycles or atmospheric shifts.

The wind of the sea is described as a distinct force, moving predictably yet influencing the highest places of the earth. The nature of these winds aligns with divine control over celestial and atmospheric elements. Winds are governed by angels, emphasizing spiritual oversight of natural phenomena. The east wind is simply named, but the north wind is described as "good," indicating a positive role, in cooling, balance, or seasonal change. Each wind is distinct in purpose, enforcing the structured atmospheric environment.

The west wind, uniquely named "Dedek," is associated with moisture and mist, potentially regulating rainfall and seasonal shifts. The anomalous "Gimē" wind does not reside in the same storehouse as the others, rather it operates outside the normal order. The west wind's storehouse is described as "light," with an angel assigned to oversee its functions, linking it to transitions between abundance and drought.

The vision continues with the system governing dew, rain, and clouds. The presence of storehouses for rain reflects an ancient belief in precipitation as a regulated resource. The wind of dew is tied to agriculture, ensuring balance between harvest and drought. The "Gimē" wind reappears, connected to clouds, pointing to a role in storms or moisture distribution. The reciprocal relationship between these forces implies divine control over the earth's needs.

The angels are described as opening storehouses to release rain in a regulated cycle. This confirms an ancient understanding of weather as divinely managed. The joining of rain with existing waters maintains the cycle of life, emphasizing renewal. The phrase "exalted ones from the heavens" referring to celestial beings overseeing the water cycle, divine beings regulate seasonal balance.

The vision culminates with Enoch witnessing the Garden of the Righteous, a celestial or restored Eden, suggesting that the forces of nature and divine order are ultimately connected to a higher reality. Behemoth and Leviathan are revealed to have offspring and lineage, implying that their presence extends beyond their own existence. Their final destruction is tied to divine judgment, and their "stirring up" suggests a future moment when they will become active before their demise.

The chapter concludes with the final transition. Divine judgment has ended, and a new order begins. The era of suffering and chaos gives way to a world governed by mercy and justice. This marks a cosmic reset, restoring balance to creation and ensuring the righteous dwell in peace.

Chapter 61

Chapter 61 describes a major celestial event, where a throne is given to an unnamed figure, and the angels respond by standing, spreading their wings, and flying in service. The lack of a specific name is significant, as later texts have attempted to impose a Messianic or divine figure into this role. The scene confirms that angels possess wings and can fly, and they are sent on a mission of measurement, indicating divine judgment, preparation, or cosmic order. One angel is specifically appointed for this task, confirming the hierarchy among celestial beings.

A great gathering follows, where the faithful and righteous are exalted in the name of the Lord of Spirits. Their elevation suggests a transition to a higher existence. The repetition of "the holy ones with the holy ones" raises questions about whether an artificial distinction was introduced into the text. The phrase "those who were gathered will be given faith" is unusual, as 1 Enoch traditionally emphasizes righteousness based on actions rather than belief. The introduction of "faith" suggests a later alteration to align with theological ideas that were not present in earlier sections. The concept of being "strengthened in the word of righteousness" reads as a doctrinal reinforcement, shifting the text's focus from divine justice to a more organized religious system.

A moment of final judgment unfolds, where those who were gathered are divided. Some are exalted, while others are punished and cast down. The phrase "beloved ones" indicates that even those once favored are not exempt if they have been corrupted. The imagery of being taken by the wilderness, the sea, or beasts may symbolize different paths of defilement or destruction. The "day of the holy ones" marks the decisive moment where righteousness is separated from corruption. There are no exceptions and no last-minute redemptions. Divine justice is absolute.

A divine command is issued to the exalted ones of the heavens, unleashing a powerful celestial event. The reference to "one voice" and "one light like fire" describes a unified force responding to the call. This moment signals the final phase of the divine plan, a cosmic battle, a descent of divine beings, a final judgment upon creation. The scale of power described is immense, driving home the magnitude of what is unfolding.

Signs of theological insertion are evident in the sudden introduction of "the Word" as an object of praise and the phrase "spirit of life." These additions shift the focus from divine justice to a more grace-based theological framework. The influence of later religious doctrines, particularly the New Testament, is evident here. The original text focuses on the exaltation of divine command, without these later embellishments.

The celestial beings receive recognition for their service to the righteous.

The spirits take their place in the divine throne room, acknowledging their active role in guiding and protecting. This passage shifts the focus from human reward to the exaltation of those who carried out divine assignments. The phrase "if they love the word of the name of the Lord of Spirits" introduces another theological shift, aligning with later frameworks that emphasize faith over deeds. The emphasis on speaking "with one voice" appears to reflect an attempt to introduce a doctrinal unity statement, reshaping 1 *Enoch* into a more organized religious ideology. This is evidence that the original text focused on divine justice and exaltation, rather than faith-based devotion.

The magnitude of this event causes all celestial and earthly forces to tremble. The highest angelic ranks, Cherubim, Seraphim, and Ophanim, are explicitly named, alongside all angels of power and dominion. The inclusion of Watchers, along with earthly and water-based forces, indicates a universal reaction extending beyond heaven to affect all of creation. This moment represents an upheaval, where every level of existence is shaken.

The text shows further signs of theological tampering, particularly in the introduction of faith (ሃይማኖት), which is foreign to Enoch's original justice-based system. Nowhere else does 1 *Enoch* require belief. It consistently upholds righteousness through action. The phrase "one voice" stands out as a later theological formula, attempting to reshape the text into a faith-based system. While the core message of blessing and glorifying the Lord of Spirits remains, these alterations shift the focus toward doctrinal alignment not present in the original.

The phrase "Garden of Life" appears to preserve an earlier designation that was later altered. The Greek and Ge'ez texts inconsistently refer to it as the "Garden of the Righteous," while later traditions shift toward "the Garden of Eden." The original text did not use "Eden" as a proper name but described a celestial dwelling of the righteous. This shift in terminology represents an intentional reinterpretation rather than a direct transmission of the original meaning.

The phrase "all flesh" is a later redaction. Nowhere in the Aramaic or Greek does 1 *Enoch* suggest that all of humanity, including those condemned, will bless the divine. This interpolation is confirmed with later theological developments seeking to align the text with doctrines of universal praise. The original 1 *Enoch* does not support the idea that those destined for destruction would engage in worship. The addition distorts the original meaning, imposing an external theological framework onto the text.

The phrase "He is long-suffering in wrath" is another later interpolation. 1 Enoch does not depict divine wrath as delayed. Judgment is immediate and absolute. This phrase reflects a later theological shift that attempts to soften divine retribution, a concept absent in the Aramaic and Greek versions. The original text emphasizes that the Lord of Spirits acts decisively for the righteous and the chosen, not as a patient judge over all humanity.

Chapter 62

Chapter 62 presents a divine command issued to the rulers of the earth, yet signs of theological interpolation are evident. The phrase "the Chosen One" appears inconsistently throughout 1 Enoch, proving a later insertion influenced by messianic traditions. The passage primarily focuses on judgment, describing divine authority over earthly rulers rather than introducing a singular messianic figure.

The Lord of Spirits is depicted seated upon the throne of His glory, consistent with 1 Enoch's portrayal of divine rulership. However, the phrase "the spirit of righteousness was poured out upon Him" raises textual concerns. Nowhere else is the Lord of Spirits described as receiving righteousness externally, as righteousness is inherent to His nature. This phrasing reflects a later theological shift that treats divine attributes as separate forces rather than intrinsic qualities.

The judgment itself is absolute. The phrase "the word from His mouth shall slay all the sinners and all the unrighteous, and from His face they shall perish" aligns with the broader themes of 1 Enoch, where divine decree brings immediate destruction. The emphasis is on the power of command. Those condemned are obliterated by the mere proclamation of judgment. The wording does not necessarily indicate that "the word" itself is an independent force, but rather that the divine utterance enacts judgment instantly.

The passage continues with apocalyptic imagery. The suffering described is universal and inescapable, striking the spirit as well as the body. The condemned are shaken, their faces reveal shame, and sickness overtakes them. The phrase "because of the offspring of the woman who dwells near the throne of glory," a later redaction, reframing the scene toward a messianic or theological direction. The true focus remains on overwhelming dread, inner collapse, and cosmic judgment pressing in on all sides.

The following passages reflect Second Temple-era theological interpolations, introducing messianic themes foreign to earlier Enochian traditions. A stark contrast emerges between those who ruled and the one who was hidden. The kings and mighty ones, who seized the earth through force and injustice, are shown as undeserving of the praise they received. Their power is temporary. In contrast, the "offspring of the woman of life" was hidden from the beginning, protected by the Most High, and appointed for righteousness. This is not a shared destiny, but a dividing line. The rulers are exposed as corrupt, while the preserved one is revealed as chosen. The focus turns from domination to quiet preservation, and from worldly strength to divine intent.

The hidden ones are now revealed, taking their place among the holy and elect. The repetition of "the elect" drives home their importance and separation from the rest of humanity. The phrase "on that day" signifies a predetermined moment of reckoning. This follows the prior revelation that a secret lineage was preserved. Now, they emerge into their rightful role. The passage indicates that the elect have been waiting for this moment, and now they ascend to their destined place.

The collapse of the corrupt rulers is complete. The kings and mighty ones fall, bow, and beg for mercy, but they are handed over to the offspring of the woman of life. Power has permanently shifted. Those who once ruled are now at the mercy of the righteous. Their final humiliation follows as they flee in terror before the Lord of Spirits, only to realize there is no escape. Shame and darkness consume them, marking not just their defeat but their total ruin.

The moment of final judgment arrives. The fallen rulers are delivered into the hands of the angels of punishment, receiving retribution for their oppression of the righteous. Their suffering is not merely a consequence. It is a direct act of divine vengeance. They cry out in agony, but it is too late. The wrath of the Lord of Spirits is fully carried out, their punishment sealed, irreversible, and eternal.

The separation of the righteous and the wicked is final. The elect are delivered, while the sinners are erased from existence. This is not just judgment. It is a complete reset of power. The elect do not merely survive; they ascend, glorified and exalted. The Lord of Spirits dwells among them, solidifying their place in the new order. This marks the ultimate establishment of divine justice. The wicked are erased, and the righteous are raised to eternal honor.

The transformation of the elect is complete. They rise from the earth, free from suffering, clothed in the garments of life, a sign of their eternal state. This marks their true ascension, as the old world fades and the new divine order is fully realized. The garments of life are not just a reward but a fundamental transformation, signifying the permanence of their glorification. Said to never wear out or fade, the clothing itself confirms divine craftsmanship or lost incorruptible technology. Their status is eternal, their presence in the divine realm secure, and their exaltation absolute.

Chapter 63

Chapter 63 begins with the trembling downfall of the kings and mighty ones who possessed the earth. Their terror arises not from divine mystery, but from the direct consequences of their own actions—the "deeds of their hands." The phrase "[they shall fall and worship before the Lord of Spirits and confess their sins before Him]" is a later interpolation designed to shift the narrative from judgment to repentance. This contradicts the core theology of 1 Enoch, where condemnation is final and confession plays no role in the fate of the wicked. The insertion reframes the kings as remorseful, but the original text offers no such redemption. Instead, the authentic voice of Enoch emphasizes cosmic justice: anguish without rest, judgment without appeal. The emotional gravity lies in their helplessness, not in a contrived moment of worship.

The transition from fear to praise indicates interpolation. The condemned rulers, having just been stripped of rest and overwhelmed by anguish, are now shown offering blessings and glorification. This is an abrupt shift that disrupts the surrounding tone. The string of honorific titles resembles post-Enochian liturgical formulas rather than authentic Enochian speech. Terms like "Lord of kings" and "Lord of the rich" appear stylized, confirming the insertion was meant to introduce reverent language from later theological systems. This confession appears forced and theologically motivated, not native to the judgment vision.

This passage, accurately rendered, remains bracketed as a redaction. The glorification and abstract divine attributes reflect a shift from judgment to praise, inconsistent with the tone of surrounding verses. The exalted language emphasizing secrets, eternity, and incomprehensible righteousness betrays the later mystical and liturgical traditions it comes from rather than Enoch's original cosmic justice. Though phrases like "deep are all your secrets," are not inconsistent their placement in a context of divine adoration suggests that the entire verse was inserted to elevate theology over verdict. As such, the passage has been bracketed as an interpolation in full.

The pattern of interpolation continues with a lament of understanding and glorification. The tone of reverent submission is inconsistent with the condemnation already established. In addition, the hierarchical framing is absent from authentic Enochian judgment texts. This verse reflects the inserted theology of divine kingship and imposed devotion. It is bracketed as a continuation of the redaction block introduced earlier.

The text then returns to the authentic tone of 1 Enoch. The condemned no longer offer praise but plead for rest, in desperation rather than reverence. The petition "Who will grant us rest" indicates themes of exhaustion and separation. This part of the passage includes the hope of glorifying and blessing, no longer implying repentance. This verse marks the turning point from artificial liturgy to unfiltered despair, consistent with the pattern found throughout the book.

This verse restores the unaltered voice of 1 Enoch, confirming the finality of judgment. The condemned recognize that rest is no longer possible, and that they have been cast out with no refuge to find. The line "light has vanished from before us" confirms their separation from the divine, while "darkness will be our dwelling forever" anchors the verse within Enoch's broader judgment themes. Unlike earlier interpolations, this passage carries no redirection or theological softening. We see only the irreversible consequences of cosmic justice.

Verse seven contains 1 Enoch's judgment themes but contains phrases that raise red flags. "[We did not believe]" is a theological framework centered on faith, foreign to Enoch's emphasis on justice through deeds. The "Lord of kings" appears only in redacted sections and contrasts with the standard title "Lord of Spirits." The verse preserves the lament and the focus remains on lost hope and the failure of their self-made glory.

This passage maintains 1 *Enoch's* focus on divine justice but includes phrasing that reflects later theological influence. The emphasis on the Lord's faithfulness introduces a tone of divine reliability that may soften the severity of judgment. While the line does not overtly shift the verdict, it subtly reorients the narrative toward a more theological worldview. Still, the verse preserves the core message: no rest is found, no deliverance is given, and the path of judgment remains unbroken. The language of consequence remains intact.

The original voice of Enochian justice continues. The condemned acknowledge their fate is the result of their actions, maintaining the consistent theme that judgment is tied to corruption, not belief. Unlike interpolated passages, there is no mention of faith or redemption. "Our sins are reckoned in righteousness" affirms that justice is measured. This passage is an unaltered expression of accountability.

The condemned are cast into Sheol. The line "our wealth will not save us but descends from us in the flames of heavy Sheol" indicates the futility of their former power. This is absolute separation from the divine presence. Their fate is sealed, their faces are covered in darkness, and the sword of judgment remains ever before His face.

The chapter concludes with the Lord of Spirits issuing a final judgment, the decree, and the fate of the kings and exalted ones who once ruled the earth. The declaration brings closure without appeal or ambiguity. The sentence is final, the authority absolute, and the rulers' dominion permanently erased.

Chapter 64

This verse marks a transition into another vision, as Enoch observes the dwelling place of the righteous. The shift from the previous judgment sequence highlights the contrast between the condemned and those who remain in divine favor.

This passage recalls the corruption brought by the fallen Watchers. The angel describes how these faithless ones (oath-breakers) descended to earth and led humanity astray into transgression. The phrase "into transgression" reflects 1 *Enoch's* cosmic framework, where breaking divine order leads to defilement and disruption, rather than a moralized concept of "sin."

Chapter 65

Chapter 65 introduces Noah as the witness to a great catastrophe. The destruction he sees aligns with 1 *Enoch's* themes of planetary judgment, referencing the consequences of the Watchers' corruption. This passage sets the stage for further revelations about the impending flood and divine intervention.

Noah, in deep distress, calls upon his forefather Enoch for guidance. His journey to the "ends of the earth" symbolizes a search for divine wisdom, and his thrice-repeated plea emphasizes the urgency of his situation. The connection between Noah and Enoch confirms 1 *Enoch's* unique lineage of divine knowledge, which later traditions sought to obscure.

The vision depicts a cataclysmic upheaval, not just destruction but an existential crisis. The earth struggles, labors, and trembles violently (ዖጊ), reacting to an unseen force. Noah's panic, "I am perishing along with it!" This confirms the severity of the event and its unavoidable impact. This is more than an earthquake; the phrase "mighty upheaval" (ሀውክ ዓስይ) describes a world-shaking disruption, aligning with other passages where the earth itself reacts violently.

Enoch arrives directly from his dwelling, confronting Noah over his distress. This confirms that Enoch is still active and aware of events on Earth, a detail erased from later biblical texts. His question emphasizes the magnitude of the catastrophe and Noah's reliance on him for wisdom.

A divine command for destruction is issued against those who dwell in corruption. The Watchers, referred to as "the beloved ones of the angels," passed their forbidden knowledge to humanity, leading to widespread devastation. The text condemns not only the Watchers but also tyrants, satans (adversaries), and their conspirators who perpetuated this corruption. Their influence did not vanish; it was carried forward, ensuring that their legacy of power and deception endured. The flood was not merely an act of punishment but a calculated purge to eradicate this corruption and reset the balance of the world.

The birth of the pure one marks the beginning of the earth's cleansing. Affliction and corruption will no longer rise from the soil. This is not merely symbolic. It begins a shift in the order of creation. With the arrival of the untainted, the old world begins to fall away.

The text describes the destruction of the fallen and corrupted ones. The phrase "those who were not created" indicates unnatural beings, Nephilim or Watcher offspring, who should never have existed. The angel who "did not remain in his place" is a direct reference to the Watchers who abandoned their heavenly station. Their fate is total annihilation.

Noah is physically taken by Enoch and told to flee. The command "Flee!" (ሑC) is an urgent warning, confirming that destruction is not just coming, it is imminent. The phrase "you have seen the Lord of Spirits" indicates that Noah has witnessed something extraordinary, a vision of divine judgment. Unlike *Genesis*, which portrays Noah as merely following instructions, 1 *Enoch* presents him as an informed participant in the unfolding events. A sudden shift in voice briefly occurs, with the verse momentarily framed from Noah's perspective. Enoch remains the primary speaker, but the narrative allows a glimpse into Noah's lived experience, his terror, his calling, and the divine urgency that surrounds him.

Judgment has already been sealed. There is no escape for the rebellious ones. The phrase "because of what they have learned" confirms 1 *Enoch's* consistent warning: forbidden knowledge was the central issue. The destruction of the earth is a direct consequence of their actions. Unlike *Genesis*, which frames the flood as punishment for human sin, 1 *Enoch* makes it clear: the flood is a necessary reset to purge the Watchers' corruption.

Noah's purity is confirmed, not as morality, but as untainted lineage. His genetics remain intact, untouched by the celestial corruption that spread through humanity. He is preserved not for piety, but because his bloodline is stable. Noah is free from the altered seed of the fallen. The phrase "their deeds are not for eternity" affirms that the corrupted will be erased, while Noah endures. Later rewrites portray him as righteous by faith, but 1 *Enoch* is clear: he is chosen because he is pure.

Noah's lineage is divinely preserved. His name is established among the holy ones, setting him apart from corruption. His descendants are set in righteousness "for kings and great glory," pointing to a bloodline meant to rule. The final line, "they will never be removed from the world," contradicts later flood narratives of a total reset. Instead, 1 *Enoch* reveals that a chosen group was always meant to survive and continue.

Chapter 66

This chapter confirms that the Flood was a deliberate act of judgment, not a natural disaster. The angels of punishment actively release the waters from beneath the earth as well as from above, aligning with ancient flood myths that describe both subterranean and celestial waters being unleashed. Unlike later versions that emphasize only rainfall, 1 Enoch presents the event as a controlled and measured act of divine retribution.

The text further establishes that the destruction was regulated. The angels are commanded to halt the waters, ensuring that the judgment does not extend beyond its intended scope. The phrase "overcome by the power of the waters" makes it clear that the Watchers and their corrupted offspring were entirely wiped out by the Flood. This makes clear that the punishment was not chaotic but precisely executed.

The chapter then shifts back to Noah's voice and his departure from Enoch. The phrase "went out from before the presence of Enoch" signals the conclusion of the encounter. This marks a transition from divine instruction to execution. The clarity of the passage indicates that Noah was not a passive recipient of knowledge but was actively engaged in the process, navigating the divine plan that had been set before him.

Chapter 67

This chapter continues Noah's voice and confirms that his destiny was preordained. The phrase "your portion has been set apart" signifies that he was divinely chosen long before the Flood. The repeated emphasis on "portion" confirms that his lineage remained untainted and preserved apart from corruption. Unlike later biblical narratives that focus on moral righteousness, 1 Enoch emphasizes purity in a tangible sense. Noah's selection was not merely a spiritual blessing but a confirmation of his genetic integrity. The final words, "favor and honor," further elevate Noah above the corrupted generations, marking him as the key figure for the preservation of life.

The angels of punishment then take their assigned positions, emphasising their active role in executing divine judgment. The repeated phrase "they stood" accentuates their unwavering presence, ensuring that the judgment unfolds as decreed. The mention of the "seed of life" being scattered upon the earth confirms that the Flood was never intended to wipe out all existence but to cleanse the earth while preserving the untainted. This holds to 1 *Enoch's* consistent theme: judgment is measured, destruction is controlled, and renewal is ensured.

A clear separation is given between Noah and the corrupted generations. The decree ensuring his survival is absolute, "it shall not be overturned." However, the closing phrase "in his name, of the Lord" reveals scribal redaction. The generic term "Lord" appears stripped of its usual attributes, such as "Lord of Spirits," indicating an intentional theological smoothing. The vague phrase "in his name" lacks a clear subject, deviating from Enoch's direct style. These alterations reframe Noah's endurance as divine favor rather than predetermined survival, shifting the narrative toward a later religious perspective.

The angels of punishment proceed with their task, binding the fallen Watchers for those who witnessed their rebellion. This confirms a division in the celestial hierarchy, some angels fell, others remained loyal, and a separate group carried out judgment. The binding takes place in a valley known for its wealth of gold, silver, iron, lead, and tin. Its location in the west near a desert indicates a mining region, further linking this site to a real, geologically significant area. The phrase "if I have seen this before from my lifetime" confirms that Enoch had previously received this vision, which is now relayed to Noah, ensuring continuity in the judgment narrative.

The transformation of the valley is then revealed. As it becomes "great and boiling," its waters violently churn, signifying intense geothermal or volcanic activity. The transition from "if" to "when" confirms that this was not a hypothetical event but something directly witnessed. The description holds that this valley is a real, active location rather than a symbolic construct.

The destruction expands beyond a single valley. Multiple regions burn as a pillar of fire emerges, spreading outward as part of the judgment. The chosen angels tremble at the unfolding events, realizing the full weight of the Watchers' rebellion. Their reaction confirms the lasting division within the celestial order. The fallen ones had sinned not only against humanity but against those who remained aligned with divine law.

The judgment is all-encompassing. The chosen waters bear witness against the mighty ones, kings, and corrupted beings. Their destruction is absolute, affecting both soul and flesh, existence and spirit. The trembling of their flesh signifies not only physical destruction but sheer terror at their fate. Though they saw their doom approaching, they remained in disbelief, refusing to acknowledge the divine authority they had rejected.

The suffering of those judged is final and irreversible. Their bodies are tormented, their spirits bound for eternity. The phrase "the land was not with them" describes total erasure; exile, annihilation, or complete separation from existence itself. This passage marks the absolute finality of judgment, with no possibility of return.

The text then confirms that their disbelief was not passive. They actively spoke against the divine even as destruction consumed them. The title "Lord of Spirits" is notably absent here, replaced by a generic "Lord." This is evidence for intentional scribal redaction to generalize divine authority, stripping away the structured celestial hierarchy found throughout 1 *Enoch*. Traces of the original text indicate that a natural or celestial event led to their destruction, but later scribes altered the passage, inserting theological themes of faith, belief, and blasphemy, concepts foreign to Enoch's original apocalyptic vision. This redaction reframes the event as a moral punishment rather than an act of cosmic restoration.

The passage concludes with the violent transformation of those caught in judgment. The waters twist their bodies, fear spreads, and even the abyss trembles. The imprisoned angels are distorted as the deep waters boil and churn, reinforcing the supernatural nature of their punishment.

Michael then proclaims the final fate of those who fell under judgment. Even the angels of heaven tremble at what has transpired. Yet, instead of repenting, the kings and mighty ones cling to their corruption, sealing their fate. This confirms the division between those judged and those who remain aligned with divine order.

A final scribal alteration is evident in the concluding verse. Originally, the text described the supernatural destruction of the fallen and their offspring as the waters consumed their flesh. However, later scribes inserted a moralized section, introducing faith and testing where none existed. The phrase "so that the faithful waters will test them" does not match the context, revealing a deliberate theological insertion. The true focus remains apocalyptic destruction, not spiritual judgment.

Chapter 68

This chapter confirms that Enoch's revelations were both written and spoken, ensuring their preservation through text and oral tradition. The phrase "he gave to me all of the signs and warnings from Enoch in the book" distinguishes the importance of recording divine knowledge, while the mention of parables indicate symbolic teachings. The line "they taught him to read and to speak the parables in the book" means that Enoch was more than a passive scribe, he was an active recipient of celestial instruction. This also implies that these teachings were meant to be publicly declared, supporting their prophetic nature.

The text bears clear marks of later redaction, particularly in the suppression of key divine elements. The phrase "state of being" strongly suggests life, making it certain that the original text referenced the Tree of Life. Its presence alongside the phrase "upheld yet rejected before her" indicates that a female divine figure, linked to life itself, was deliberately erased. Later scribes removed all references to the tree, exposing a deliberate effort to suppress this knowledge. The shift from direct statements of power and existence to vague theological constructs is a hallmark of scribal tampering. The presence of "before her" further confirms the existence of an erased female divine figure, making this one of the clearest examples of theological interference in 1 Enoch.

A direct statement follows regarding a being who is entirely unmerciful and unchanging, corroborating earlier themes of divine judgment. The phrase "his heart is unyielding concerning her" is unusual and may indicate a deliberate refusal to show compassion toward a specific feminine figure. However, unlike previous passages where a female divine presence was erased, there is no solid evidence of redaction here. The phrase "words of existence" reappears, emphasizing that this judgment is tied to life, being, or creation itself. The final statement confirms that something has already been set in motion regarding these summoned beings, making their fate inevitable.

Clear evidence of Mid-Ge'ez interference appears in the next section. The phrase "for in the likeness of the Lord they shall act" is inconsistent with Old Ge'ez structure and appears to be a later theological insertion. Additionally, the reduction of "Lord of Spirits" to simply "Lord" follows a known pattern of theological redaction seen in Mid-Ge'ez religious texts. The introduction of divine wrath (ተምዐየሙ) is also unusual, as 1 Enoch

211

typically describes cosmic balance rather than emotional reactions. This points to intentional modification to fit later theological frameworks rather than the original Enochian narrative.

The text then emphasizes the inescapable fate of those who have chosen their path. The phrase "existence of those who have chosen" confirms that their destiny was not imposed but willingly accepted. The repeated mention of "eternity of eternities" establishes that this is a permanent state, with no possibility of reversal. The phrase "it shall not be fulfilled, and it shall not be good" teaching that what they sought, whether power, survival, or something else, will never come to pass.

The final passage substantiates this irreversible fate. The phrase "their portion, their faith, their disgrace" is phrased in a way that suggests their faith (or trust) is not what saves them but what condemns them, leading directly to their disgrace and destruction. The concluding statement, "Their existence (remains) as this, for eternity," carries an implied verb. Implied verbs are features sometimes found in Old Ge'ez where verbs are omitted but understood. The added word "(remains)" clarifies the meaning without altering the original intent. This final phrase proves a negative form of existence, destruction or an irreversible transformation.

Chapter 69

This chapter introduces a revelation concerning existence (ħ·1ð), which is both seen and taught. The phrase "they shall make it known and instruct" confirms a deliberate transmission of knowledge. The recipients are "those who dwell in corruption," which refers to the fallen Watchers, their offspring, or another group remaining in defilement. The statement "because these things were seen" indicates that this is a verbal teaching and witnessed firsthand. This marks a shift in perspective, where those in corruption are granted insight into the true nature of existence.

A list of angelic names follows, but the text never explicitly states they are fallen. The Ge'ez text preserves 21 names, while the older Aramaic fragments contain only 13. The additional names suggest either a scribal expansion or an attempt to restore lost names. Some names appear altered or replaced, raising the possibility that the list was redacted to obscure the Watchers' original roles.

The text establishes a hierarchy among the Watchers, assigning command over groups of 100, 50, and 10. The text describes a military-like organization, a potentially bureaucratic system. The distinction between "chiefs" and "heads of angels" implies different levels of authority, putting forth the idea that not all Watchers were equal in power. The passage further identifies a primary figure as "the first" among those who transgressed, while the phrase "lesser holy angels" confirms a celestial order with varying ranks. The statement "they inherited corruption" indicates a fundamental transformation following their rebellion, illustrating the theme of divine beings overstepping established boundaries.

Asb'el is named as a significant figure in the rebellion, providing corrupt counsel that led others into transgression. The text states, "so that they defiled their flesh," confirming that their sin was physical. Gader'el is then identified as a key figure in the deception of Eve and the introduction of warfare. The phrase "all the blows of death" confirming that he taught weapon-making and revealed techniques of war and destruction. His influence extended beyond battle. He is credited with leading Eve astray, directly linking the Watchers to both human conflict and early moral corruption. The text describes something that "went forth from his hands" and was given to the corrupted, marking a moment that would last from that time into eternity. Given Gader'el's prior actions, this likely refers to the moment when he imparted dangerous knowledge to humanity, permanently altering its course.

Penemue is named as the fourth being, responsible for revealing "embittered knowledge" to humanity. His teachings, though presented as wisdom, carried deception and manipulation. This aligns with the broader theme in 1 Enoch, where the Watchers' knowledge brings both advancement and destruction. The text credits him with introducing writing to humanity, though the passage contains clear signs of later interpolation. The use of parchment (kərtas), a Greek-derived word, suggests that the original text referred to an earlier writing medium, such as clay tablets or metal engravings. Similarly, the term for ink (mäyä) may have replaced an older concept related to carving or engraving. The passage portrays writing as a negative revelation, stating that it led many astray, implying that recorded knowledge could be misused and manipulated. This puts forth the idea that the Watchers' teachings were not inherently evil but dangerous when placed in the wrong hands.

The text then directly refutes later theological claims that humanity was originally immortal. It explicitly states that humans were never meant to be like the angels, who are naturally righteous and untouched by death. Instead, mortality was inherent from the beginning. The downfall of humanity is attributed to the mind's capacity for transgression, contrasting later doctrines that blamed "the flesh" or original sin. This passage exposes a deliberate theological distortion, where later traditions rewrote the narrative to fit their doctrines. 1 Enoch preserves the original truth: humans were always mortal, always distinct from angels, and their downfall was an intellectual failure, not a physical corruption.

Kasyadea revealed forbidden knowledge regarding the severing of life, cutting embryos, spirits, and souls. The text hints at abortion, ritual sacrifice, or necromancy by describing the destruction of life in the womb and unlawful cutting with knives. The mention of Taba'eth is unclear but may refer to a hybrid or a figure connected to this knowledge. This passage exposes the Watchers' direct corruption of natural life.

Kesab'el, a high-ranking Watcher, is named the chief of the Oath, revealing its secrets and causing the exalted one to descend. His actions broke a divine boundary, sealing the Watchers' fate. The name Beqa indicates division, confirming that his betrayal created a rift between the fallen and the divine. A Watcher, likely Kesab'el, then delivers knowledge to Michael, revealing "the name of the beloved one" and the sacred Oath. This name held divine authority, meant to be seen, remembered, and feared. Its revelation to "all the children of men" suggests that it had direct consequences for humanity, carrying judgment and enforcement.

The Oath is revealed as more than a pact. It is a cosmic law that upholds creation itself. The heavens are suspended by it, and the world is established through it, proving it existed before time. This divine decree separates the spiritual from the physical, and breaking it had irreversible consequences. The Watchers didn't just rebel. They violated the fundamental order of existence, sealing their fate. The Oath governs the movement of the luminaries, holding the stars, sun, and moon in place. The fixed paths of these celestial bodies confirms that the Oath is a force that even the heavens obey. The Watchers' rebellion was not just disobedience. It was an attempt to overturn the foundations of existence itself.

The Oath also governs spirits, winds, and even the soul of the waters. This makes known that all creation, seen and unseen, has a fixed nature and purpose. Even chaotic forces such as thunder, lightning, hail, frost, mist, and rain are bound by the Oath. These elements do not act randomly but exist within a organized system, confirming that the divine law is absolute. All things bound by the Oath remain strong and unified, aligning their power and purpose in praise of creation's order.

However, this passage contains clear interpolations. The phrase "[for this one, the Son of Man, the Living One]" disrupts the established pattern of the text, attempting to introduce a personal messianic figure where none existed. The forced insertion shifts the focus from cosmic law to a singular theological figure, aligning 1 Enoch with later doctrines. This redaction is especially evident in passages describing an exalted figure sitting on a throne of glory. The original text describes judgment and the removal of sinners, aligning with divine law, but the inserted messianic references distort the passage's intent.

The chapter concludes with the absolute and irreversible judgment of those who defied divine order. The corrupted ones are bound in chains, their gathering is dissolved, and their works are erased from existence. This is not just punishment. It is the complete removal of their influence from the earth. The final verse describes a time when destruction ceases, judgment is enacted, and the wicked are removed. However, the phrase "[the Son of Man]" appears once again as a clear interpolation. The text has been focused on cosmic law and divine judgment, yet this phrase introduces a personal messianic figure, disrupting the passage's established phrasing. This sudden theological shift indicates that later redactors attempted to align 1 Enoch with developing doctrines. The original text appears to describe an impersonal force of judgment rather than a singular figure. The final statement confirms this is part of "the parable that Enoch saw," emphasizing it as a visionary revelation rather than a literal enthronement.

Chapter 70

This chapter describes a figure whose name is exalted before the Lord of Spirits. However, the phrase "[the Son of Man]" is a clear interpolation. The surrounding text refers to "the Living One," which fits the established cosmic framework, but the forced inclusion of a Messianic title disrupts the original meaning. This interpolation attempts to shift the passage toward a singular Messianic figure, aligning it with later theological developments rather than preserving the original apocalyptic vision.

The text then describes a divine ascension via "chariots of spirit," imagery that aligns with other celestial transport narratives, such as Elijah's fiery chariot or Ezekiel's vision of the divine throne. The phrase "his name went forth in their midst" indicates a physical ascension, and one of recognition and power. The language implies a transformation or elevation into a higher celestial state, confirming that Enoch's journey was not just about location but about status and authority within the divine order.

A pivotal transition follows, marking Enoch's departure from the earthly realm into a celestial existence. No longer dwelling among men, he now resides with the spirits and the blessed ones. His ascent before the angelic throne grants him access to hidden knowledge and realms beyond human reach, ensuring his role as one who has transcended mortal understanding. This confirms that his journey is not one of death but of divine translation, setting him apart as an intermediary between heaven and earth.

The final passage describes a direct encounter with the ancients and the righteous who dwell in a specific celestial place. The reference to "the fathers" and "the ancient ones" points to a lineage of wisdom-keepers, possibly Watchers who remained loyal or other figures of great spiritual significance. The phrase "from eternity" confirms that these beings exist beyond time, further proving that Enoch is witnessing those who have fully transcended mortality. This vision lends credence to the existence of a higher order of celestial beings who predate humanity, preserving the original knowledge of creation.

Chapter 71

This chapter marks Enoch's final ascension into the heavens, where he witnesses "the offspring of the holy angels," celestial beings distinct from the Watchers' corrupted offspring. Moving upon blazing fire, clothed in radiant white, and shining like snow, they resemble high-ranking divine entities associated with purity and authority. This establishes a clear distinction between the fallen ones and those who remained loyal to divine law.

Enoch sees two streams of fire and a radiant, illuminating light, manifestations of divine power or celestial energy. The fire bows before him, signaling reverence and confirming his unique status in this vision. Michael, one of the chief angels, personally takes Enoch by the hand and lifts him into a higher realm. This act of direct guidance supports Michael's role as an enforcer of divine order and protector of the righteous. Enoch is brought before "the beloved ones of mercy and righteousness," a distinct group aligning with the earlier mention of "the offspring of the holy angels." This confirms that not all celestial offspring were corrupt and that some maintained an exalted, divine status.

Michael then reveals to Enoch the extremities of heaven, where the beloved ones dwell, and the celestial treasuries of the stars and luminaries. This description aligns with earlier visions of divine storehouses, where cosmic forces are organized and set in motion. The stars and lights have a designated place of origin before the face of the holy ones, maintaining the structured nature of the heavens. The movements of celestial bodies are not random but governed by divine order.

Enoch then witnesses the immovable, central place of divine order, upheld by great pillars. "Tongues of living fire," are either celestial communication or divine energy. The phrase "[And the spirit carried Enoch into the heavens]" is a later insertion and was not part of Enoch's original testimony. This passage further describes a living, molten stream of fire actively flowing around the house. The word "surrounds" indicates movement, not a static barrier. The four pillars may represent a cosmic framework or cardinal points, indicating the divine nature of this place. The fire is alive, consuming, and enclosing. This is no ordinary flame.

Seraphiel, Cherubiel, and Afnin stand as faithful Watchers, guarding the divine throne. Seraphiel, the fiery seraphim, fits the house of fire, while Cherubiel commands the cherubim, keepers of divine mysteries. Afnin represents the Ophanim, the Wheels of the Chariot, though the missing "-iel" suffix through a scribal omission, or later mistranslation. Their role as those "who do not sleep" stresses the exacting celestial hierarchy, where the highest ranks remain ever-vigilant.

Enoch sees countless angels moving in procession, entering and exiting the house of fire in an orchestrated celestial order. At the center stand Michael, Raphael, Gabriel, and Phanuel, surrounded by holy angels who fill the heavens. Their presence marks this as a place of divine authority and active celestial governance. The four archangels and many holy angels then depart from the house of fire. The phrase "those who had not become corrupt" distinguishes these angels from the fallen Watchers, upholding the structured cosmic order.

At this moment, the text abruptly shifts from a group of celestial beings to a single radiant figure. This supreme figure is clothed in brilliant light, his face shining with indescribable splendor. The deliberate shift from plural to singular marks the emergence of an exalted celestial presence. Something irreversible happens, Enoch's body dissolves, his spirit transforms, and he cries out with divine power. This moment marks his final ascension from human to something beyond.

After his transformation, Enoch speaks blessings and glorifications, which are established before the Head of Days. This confirms his presence before the supreme being of celestial time, marking the culmination of his ascension. The Head of Days arrives, accompanied by Michael, Gabriel, Raphael, and Phanuel. This is a moment of immense celestial significance, where divine authority is fully present. The angels in procession confirm the ritualistic nature of the heavens, and those encircling the Head of Days are explicitly identified as angels "who had not become corrupt," distinguishing the loyal from the fallen.

An angel blesses Enoch, declaring him a child of humanity, born for righteousness. This affirms his transformation but does not imply a messianic role. His righteousness remains with him, tied to the Head of Days, marking his place in the celestial hierarchy. The angel further declares peace upon Enoch, extending to the entire world and for all eternity. The phrase "[in his name]" is a later theological addition and is bracketed due to its disruption of the passage's natural flow. This verse emphasizes that this peace was established from the creation of the world, confirming that Enoch's transformation was always part of the divine order.

The chapter concludes by confirming Enoch's transformation into an eternal figure. His destiny is set, and all shall be changed accordingly. Righteousness will never leave him, sealing his place in the celestial hierarchy. The phrase "with you shall be their dwelling place" indicates that Enoch becomes a cornerstone of the righteous, their existence tied to him. The declaration that "his truth shall never be taken away" means that Enoch's name and legacy will endure for eternity.

The final verse establishes a parallel between the peace given to Enoch and the peace granted to the righteous. The phrase "peace, peace for days" points to a lasting and unbroken state of harmony. The term "child of humanity, the one of life" continues to affirm Enoch's transformation, not as a messianic figure but as one whose role extends into eternity. The righteous share in this reward, their portion secured forever under the authority of the Lord of Spirits. The repetition of "for eternity of eternities" confirms the unchanging, absolute nature of this divine order.

Chapter 72

This chapter introduces The Book of the Heavenly Luminaries, a section where Uriel reveals the precise workings of the celestial bodies. The text emphasizes strict divine governance over the luminaries, detailing their names, cycles, and appointed times. The phrase "until a new creation shall be made" indicates a predetermined cosmic order, set to last until a future divine renewal. This aligns with ancient cosmological views of the heavens as a structured and unchanging realm, except when divine intervention reshapes existence itself.

The chapter establishes the divine law governing the luminaries—an unchanging cosmic order. The phrase "gates of El" confirm an association with celestial portals, marking the controlled movement of the heavenly bodies. This aligns with ancient cosmology, where the sun, moon, and stars travel through designated openings in the firmament, emphasizing the structured nature of divine creation.

Uriel reveals the structured celestial pathways of the sun, moon, and stars. The luminaries move through twelve gates—six in the east and six in the west, guided by their governors. The mention of "many windows, arranged in sequence" points to a complex astronomical order, where celestial bodies enter and exit according to predetermined cycles. This structured system reflects an ancient understanding of the heavens as divinely regulated, upholding the cosmic laws that Uriel reveals to Enoch.

The sun is identified as the great luminary, marking its primary role in the celestial order. It goes forth first, assuring a structured system of movement. The phrase "to their left" implies a fixed observational perspective, possibly tied to the eastern gates through which celestial bodies rise and set. The sun's movement is depicted as a chariot burning with fire, illuminating the heavens. This aligns with ancient traditions of the sun as a celestial vehicle, often linked to divine chariots in Mesopotamian and Indo-European mythologies. The "circuit of the heavens" reveals an organized cosmology. The passage also distinguishes between different celestial gates, confirming that the sun follows a precise and preordained path.

The text then describes how the luminaries interact with the waters below. The phrase "the waters shine upon the face" evokes the vision of light reflecting across the surface, like the golden path of the sun upon the ocean at sunrise or sunset. This isn't just about the luminaries themselves. It's about their mirrored interaction with the waters, illustrating the structured harmony between the heavens and the deep.

The sun follows a structured celestial mechanism, moving through twelve open windows within the fourth gate, releasing both light and flames at predetermined times. The sun's emergence through this gate in the first month aligns with an ordered cosmic cycle, emphasizing that the heavens function according to a precise system rather than chaotic movement. The lengthening of daylight and shortening of night as the sun follows its cycle confirms that celestial movements are regulated by divine order.

The phrase "a portion by number" (חלקי מספר) emphasizes that time is divinely calculated and not arbitrary. The mention of eight parts for the day and ten for the night reflects a mathematical division of time, affirming a preordained celestial order. The phrase "returns" (תשוב - tashuv) makes known that this movement is not random but part of an intentional cycle. The eastward shift after a month aligns the gates with measured solar months.

The text describes seasonal shifts as daylight increases and then gradually diminishes. The climax of daylight is marked when the day reaches twelve parts, fully doubling the length of the night. This aligns with structured astronomical laws. The reference to "signs" (האתות - ha-otot) indicates that these transitions are divinely marked, demonstrating that the movement of celestial bodies follows a measured and preordained order.

As the solar cycle reverses, the day shortens as night gains strength. The phrase "rising up to diminish" indicates a calculated celestial adjustment, conveying the structured balance of light and darkness. The sun moves through the measured gates, maintaining its rhythm.

The equilibrium between day and night is reached at specific intervals, confirming the structured, mathematical precision of the solar cycle. The reference to thirty-one days signals the completion of a measured phase, supporting the idea that celestial movements are preordained and predictable.

The chapter continues detailing the gradual seasonal transitions, where daylight and darkness adjust according to a structured cycle. The phrase "because of its signs" (בעבור אותותיו) indicates that these movements follow observable celestial markers. As the solar cycle completes, the sun resets and begins again, ensuring the precise tracking of celestial time.

The text confirms the Enochian solar year of 364 days, a system meticulously structured to track the balance between day and night. The phrase "the day and the night will shorten" again point to a cycle where periods of lengthening and shortening alternate in a predictable rhythm, demonstrating the precise timekeeping encoded in Enoch's astronomical text.

The phrase "by the cycle of the sun" (תקופת החמה) expresses that celestial changes are preordained, predictable, and measurable. The reference to "from day to day" confirms that these shifts occur incrementally, aligning with the structured solar calendar. The text further confirms that the sun's movement is eternal and unchanging in its role. The phrase "for eternity of eternities" (לעולמי עולמים) declares that the sun's cycle is divinely established and will never cease.

The chapter concludes by affirming that the sun follows an unchanging course, never resting, never diminishing, running its path like a chariot. The phrase "that which is so-called" (הנקרא כן) confirms its recognized celestial role, free from later theological distortions. Its light shines sevenfold greater than the moon, yet both are equal in function except in size. This final passage reaffirms the structured balance of the cosmic order, precise, eternal, and unshakable.

Chapter 73

This chapter transitions from the solar to the lunar system as Enoch observes the moon's distinct law. The phrase "small luminary" (המאור הקטן) mirrors "great luminary," echoing the divine pairing between sun and moon. This introduces a parallel system for tracking the moon, confirming that both luminaries follow preordained cycles.

The moon follows a structured, predictable cycle within the circuit of the heavens. The mention of a "chariot" (עגלה) aligns with the ancient understanding of celestial mechanics, where heavenly bodies move along fixed paths. The phrase "is lifted up from" (תנשא מן) suggests a specific point in the lunar cycle when its position shifts, revealing the measured, calculated nature of time in Enoch's system.

Enoch understood that its light was not its own but came from the sun—an ancient truth later forgotten or suppressed. Its phases align with the solar system yet operate independently, establishing a dual celestial order. When the moon reaches full brightness, its light remains one-seventh of the sun's, a cosmic hierarchy between the two luminaries.

A precise celestial moment occurs when the moon and sun align. The moon rises from the east on the thirtieth day, appearing in the same gate the sun previously used. This suggests a pre-calculated cycle, where the lunar and solar paths overlap at designated times, supporting the structured astronomical framework in Enoch's system.

The lunar cycle begins with only one-seventh of the moon's light visible while the rest remains in darkness. The phrase "one-seventh from four" suggests a precise mathematical framework. The bracketed phrase "[from all the light that is hers]" may be a later scribal addition rather than part of the original text.

The moon's movement is not just measured; it is instructed, guided, and regulated. The use of הוֹרֶה (ho-reh, "instructs") suggests that the moon does not move chaotically but follows a governed celestial order. The phrase "receives a seventh and a half" indicates a precise incremental change in its phases, exemplifying the mathematical nature of Enoch's lunar system.

A key lunar shift occurs as the moon's light reaches one-seventh and a half. The moon rises with the sun, affirming their controlled cycle. The phrase "half a portion of light" signals a midpoint in its phase, while "they will be counted" confirms that precise celestial tracking governs its movements.

The chapter concludes with a specific phase in the lunar cycle, showing its consistency. The phrase "it will be seen as the seventh portion exactly" describes the steady growth of light, confirming the way time was tracked in the heavens. The moon's inclination from the sun's setting suggests a closely observed change in its position, matching ancient methods of lunar observation.

Chapter 74

This chapter introduces a new celestial law, separate from the first. The phrase "I saw in it" emphasizes that Enoch is observing an organized, preordained system, not chaos. The statement "it shall be made" (תעשה) indicates a specific celestial process is about to be described, enforcing the precision of Enoch's astronomical revelations.

Uriel, the holy angel, governs the celestial bodies and reveals their cycles to Enoch. The moon's phases and divisions are documented with precision, revealing a regulated system. The phrase "until fifteen days pass" marks a key lunar phase, the midpoint of the month.

The moon operates on a regular, repeating seven-part cycle, confirming its precise motion. The reference to completion of its light in the east denotes a key astronomical moment, the full moon rising in the east. The dual mention of "sevenths" upholds the moon's mathematical precision in its journey.

The waning of the moon marks the completion of its cycle in the west before renewing. The phrase "known months" illustrates an orderly lunar calendar, with predictable changes in its phases. The "special course" confirms that despite these changes, the moon remains bound to a fixed pattern, further proving the precision behind Enoch's celestial observations.

Two specific celestial gates are identified, marking their position within the cosmos. The third and fourth gates correspond to seasonal transitions, marking the measured division of time and aligning with the astronomical system outlined in earlier chapters.

The moon follows a seven-day phase before reaching full illumination at a specific celestial gate. The moon then shifts into the sixth gate for eight days, showing off its measured celestial mechanics. This movement confirms a defined cosmic system based on observation, not later theological interpretation.

The moon tracks seven-day intervals behind the sun, moving from the fourth to the fifth gate before reaching full illumination. It then enters the first gate, following an observed lunar rhythm rooted in astronomical timing, not theology.

The moon's continuous movement follows absolute cycles, with eight-day and seven-day intervals governing its return to the fourth gate. The use of אל (El) as a directional marker (to/toward) tracks celestial pathways, not theology. The cycle is not rudimentary; it is advanced astronomical calculation, not later interpolation.

A system of celestial observation is laid out, tracking the sun's cycles in alignment with lunar months. The phrase תקופה (tqufah – "cycles") refers to astronomical periods, such as solstices or equinoxes. The phrase "measured by a span" (b'zeret) shows that an observational or mathematical system was used to track these cycles, anchoring the precision of the Enochian calendar.

The text lays out a precise five-year celestial cycle, a meticulous system of timekeeping. The mention of thirty days functions as an intentional adjustment mechanism within the calendar—one we still use today. This is direct evidence that Enoch's knowledge of time was based on astronomical law.

The 364-day base year includes a six-day surplus for celestial corrections. A five-year structure methodically adds days to align the sun, stars, and moon. Enochian astronomy that transcends time, even to this day.

The stars and the moon govern time with absolute precision. Their cycles are fixed and unchanging, never exceeding or falling short by a single day. The phrase "only in justice and precision" locks in that cosmic law, not randomness, determines their movements. The reference to "three," to a trifold division of celestial timekeeping (solar, lunar, and stellar cycles), is an esoteric trifecta.

Time is precise; it breaks down years into seasons, then exact day counts. The phrase "their years and days" is a direct correlation between the movements of celestial bodies and the passage of time in perfect observation. Despite later attempts to change its precision and calculations, the world has once again returned to this very timekeeping system.

The eight-year lunar cycle consists of 2,912 days, with a surplus of sixty days and a shortfall of fifty days over five years. The phrase "they will be added for upon its number" confirms a calculated correction system, a full synchronization between lunar and solar measurements.

Over eight years, a shortfall of eighty days accumulates. The phrase "all the days that will be lacking" is an ongoing celestial calculation, evidence of the rigorous timekeeping embedded within Enochian astronomy.

The solar gates regulate movement, marking the sun's entry and exit points. The reference to "thirty days" defines a transitional phase within the celestial order. The final passage leaves no question that Enoch's astronomical system is exact, enduring, and incorruptible.

Chapter 75

This chapter introduces a celestial hierarchy, where appointed leaders govern the forces of creation. The four additional entities remain fixed in a purposeful astronomical role, part of a systematic cosmic vocation.

The text states that four days are cut off from the year's standard count but remain essential in celestial order. The phrase "the people are mistaken" reminds us that calendar distortions happened and require correction. These four gates mark key celestial transitions and anchor seasonal timekeeping.

The sixty-four divisions govern celestial order, overseen by Uriel, who ensures the sun, moon, stars, and constellations maintain cosmic balance. The bracketed phrase "[whom the Lord of Praises]" is marked as a later insertion to align Uriel with a specific divine figure. The sentence reads clearly without it.

The sun moves through twelve fixed gates, not entirely unlike how we think about the months today. These gates regulate both the sun's light and heat in a precise astronomical order. The phrase "chariot of the sun" is a mythological way of saying it moves by a measured cosmic mechanism, not randomly.

The celestial gates open at appointed times, influencing the earth's atmospheric balance. These openings regulate both the winds and the distribution of dew, proving an interconnected cosmic system governing climate and seasons.

Twelve celestial gates are positioned at the edges of the heavens and the earth; they regulate the movements of the sun, moon, and stars. These gates open at specific, preordained times, ensuring cosmic order. The stars move as part of this system, maintaining predictable cycles within the celestial spheres.

The celestial host moves in an east-west alignment. Numerous windows open on either side, allowing controlled energy flow. A single window regulates heat at its appointed time, just as the twelve gates control the stars' paths. The phrase "they shall come according to their number" shows precision, where all celestial movements are accounted for.

The celestial spheres move rapidly through the heavens, above and below. The gates function as entry points controlling these movements, connecting them to the previously described twelve celestial gates. This confirms the nature of the cosmos, where celestial bodies move in designated paths.

The movement of the stars follows the celestial framework. The "one greater than all" refers to the sun, which governs the cycles of light and time. The phrase "encircles the entire world" confirms the sun's role as the primary force regulating the heavens.

Chapter 76

This chapter introduces ten celestial gates at the edges of the earth, a system of cosmic divisions. The mention of "years" links these gates to time cycles, marking a ten-year period in line with the Enochian calendar. Chapters 76 and 77 show that the geography of the Book of Enoch is not based in the ancient Near East, but in North America. The winds, portal directions, and river flows all point to a North American setting.

The division of celestial winds shows an ordered system of atmospheric and seasonal forces. The phrase "three opened opposite the heavens" marks fixed alignments that govern nature's balance. It is the beginning of the trifecta so central to the cosmos.

A triadic division appears in 1 *Enoch*, shaped by three celestial gate groups. The reference to "the left" (mishma'ol) marks a set direction, while the westward term (b'ma'arav) ties the gates to solar movement and horizon tracking. The twelve portals described by Enoch, three in each direction, map onto the cardinal wind corridors across North America.

The twelve winds emerge from fixed gates, four bring peace and blessing, eight bring destruction. Their reach spans land, sea, and all life, acting as cosmic forces shaping the world's balance.

The portals open in fixed order, three each to the east, west, north, and south. This pattern matches seasonal wind behavior and aligns with major wind corridors across North America, including Gulf winds, Pacific systems, polar air, and desert heat.

The Eastern Wind emerges slightly southward, bringing dryness and heat. Cold and dryness appear first, then southern winds, early tracking of direction and effect tied to celestial timing.

Some gates release both blessing and harm. The middle gate brings rain and abundance and is linked to righteousness; the third gate leans north and brings desolation. Each gate holds a dual purpose, protection, and punishment.

A northern gate is paired with "its name is the Sea," suggesting a connection to earthly waters. An eastern gate, angled south, releases both dew and locusts showing layered functions.

Wind, dew, rain, and fragrant air all arrive on schedule, through gates governed by fixed law. This is no chaos; this is deliberate regulation that binds sky and earth to a single order.

The phrase "mountains of the winds" has no ancient Near Eastern match, but fits North America precisely. The Rockies, Sierra Nevada, and Cascade ranges all interact with the jet stream, acting as wind mountains. These terrains align with Enoch's description of atmospheric forces and reinforce the link between geography and celestial mechanics.

The first gate brings only blessings: rain, dew, life, and peace. This establishes a zone of stability. The third western gate, inclined northward, releases both help and harm, articulating the balance.

The western winds emerge from a first gate facing north, bringing dew, rain, frost, cold, snow, and chill, marking it as a distinct source of winter conditions. These three celestial gates are distinguished by function:

One releases cold-weather forces (dew, rain, frost, cold, snow, and chill). Another, positioned within, brings only blessings (dew, rain, peace, and prosperity).

The final southern gate produces harsh conditions (dryness, destruction, blight, and annihilation). In this contrast are laid out the characteristics of cosmic order, where moisture and aridity are governed by distinct celestial mechanics.

The South Wind is where the Most High descends, marking the southern direction as a point of divine entry. It is associated with lasting blessing, favor, and abundance. The Sea Wind follows, identified as the West Wind, continuing the classification of directional winds.

Each celestial gate aligns with specific meteorological effects, from dew and rain to desolation and dryness. The southern portals are linked to divine descent and correspond with regions like New Mexico and Nevada, including Roswell, Area 51, Sedona, and others in the south west.

The final revelation of the twelve celestial gates confirms their fixed laws, governing both blessings and destruction. The last gate represents absolute devastation: blight, ruin, and annihilation.

Enoch affirms to Methuselah that he has now revealed the full celestial order, establishing his vision. Although Enoch calls Methuselah "my son," Methuselah is actually his grandson. This reveals the ancient cultural practice where male descendants were called "sons" when receiving lineage knowledge. This formal transmission confirms Methuselah as the chosen heir to Enoch's revelations.

Chapter 77

This chapter establishes the East Wind as the first and ancient wind, confirming its primordial role in Enoch's celestial system. The structured naming of winds reinforces an ordered meteorological framework, where each wind has a specific function within the cosmic order.

The West Wind is designated as the wind of cosmic descent, aligning it with the setting of celestial lights.

The North Wind is unique, divided into three domains: one governs human habitation, one oversees waters, and one rules the Garden of Righteousness. This reflects a deliberate cosmic order, where each wind has a defined jurisdiction.

Enoch sees seven towering mountains, greater than any on earth, from which snow emerges. Their presence signifies a connection to timekeeping and celestial order, reinforcing their role in regulating days and appointed times. The seven great mountains align with known ranges: Rockies, Appalachians, Sierra Nevada, Cascades, Coast, Wasatch, and Brooks.

Enoch sees seven immense rivers, greater than all others, forming a global hydrological system. One flows from the west, suggesting a directional order linked to celestial or seasonal cycles. This vision expands Enoch's cosmic structure to include the earth's great waters. Enoch names rivers flowing east to west, a rare pattern only found in North America. The Columbia, Snake, F raser, Skagit, Stikine, Kootenay, and Deschutes rivers perfectly match this direction and geography.

The structured hydrological vision continues, describing major rivers flowing into vast bodies of water. Two rivers flow from the north into the sea, reinforcing the directional order in the earth's waters. The seventh river empties into the Shihor in the east, further expanding the cosmic geography. No major rivers in the ancient Near East flow this way, ruling out the traditional setting.

Enoch's hydrological order is reinforced, with the Shihor in the east as a key drainage point. The four northern rivers divide—two into the Shihor, two into the Great Sea, maintaining a structured water system. The vision then shifts to seven islands, some on land, some in the sea, with the Greek fragment linking them to the Red Sea and ancient waterways.

These features confirm that Enoch's vision is grounded in the geography of North America, not myth or allegory.

Chapter 78

This chapter opens with the naming of the sun, Oriras (אור, "light") links to solar radiance, while Tamash (אש, "fire") confirms its solar nature. The Greek fragment is incomplete, but "καλε" verifies the presence of celestial naming traditions.

The next passage repeats 78:1 but names four lunar entities. Uriya (אוּרִיָה) contains "Or" (light), indicating its connection to the moon's radiance. The other names: Ashoniya, Avala, and Benaashi but they lack clear Hebrew roots, pointing to foreign origins or lost designations. This structured enumeration of names confirms that 1 *Enoch* maintains a deliberate cosmology.

The sun and moon are then described as the two great lights, moving in distinct, cycles. The moon receives one-seventh of the sun's light, confirming its derived illumination. The phrase "sphere of the sun" indicates an early understanding of celestial bodies as round, while "in measure" indicates a regulated lunar cycle.

The moon's movement follows a specific pattern, passing through celestial "gates," an ancient model of astronomical order. The northward turn reflects observed lunar motion, while the entry and exit through gates confirm a regulated cosmic cycle. The phrase "upon the face of the heavens" emphasizes the predictability of its path.

The moon's waxing cycle is described in detail, beginning with its first appearance and increasing until full brightness on the fourteenth day. The structured increase in illumination follows an ordered mathematical pattern. The text then details the waning cycle, confirming that each phase follows a fixed schedule.

The standard lunar month is recorded as twenty-nine days, though some months have only twenty-eight. This acknowledges the ~29.5-day lunar cycle, requiring adjustments in ancient calendars. The mention of a 28-day month points to the specific calendrical correction required.

Uriel reveals a second cosmic law, explaining when and where the moon receives light from the sun. This confirms that pre-Flood knowledge understood the moon's light as reflected, a fact later lost and found, and misunderstood.

The New Moon is identified as "Molad," a term still used in lunar calendars. The waxing, full, and waning phases are described in their precise structure, with each phase following a fixed schedule. The same fixed schedule we know today. The full moon rises as the sun sets, shining all night until fading at sunrise. This confirms an early understanding of lunar-solar opposition, an astronomical fact, also, later lost to many medieval thinkers.

The moon's cycle is laid out with months alternating between 30 and 29 days. The 170-day period marks a key division in Enoch's astronomical system, illustrating a measured cosmic order. The moon's changing appearance is noted, with its markings resembling a face at night, while by day it appears faint and sky-like. The phrase "nothing else is in it, only its light" reveals that the moon has no inherent radiance but reflects the external light of the sun.

Chapter 79

Enoch addresses Methuselah, summarizing his teachings on celestial laws. The phrase "all the laws of the stars of the heavens" reveals the divine rhythm that governs the universe.

The text details the fixed laws regulating days, months, weeks, and years. The phrase "their goings forth" refers to the movements of celestial bodies, all operating under divine ordinance.

The moon's waning phase is described, marking the loss of all light in the sixth gate, signifying the New Moon and the beginning of the month. The fixed celestial order ensures the lunar cycle follows a measured pattern.

The moon's waning follows a measured cycle of one hundred and seventy-seven days, divided into twenty-five weeks and two extra days. This precise tracking of time confirms the Enochian lunar calendar and its alignment with the greater celestial order.

The text explains a five-day adjustment in the lunar cycle to align with the solar year. The phrase "it departs from this place and shall be seen" refers to a definite astronomical shift, marking a key moment in the celestial system.

Uriel is confirmed as the celestial overseer of the luminaries. He reveals the appearance and form of all heavenly lights, ensuring that Enoch fully understands their fixed order. The title "prince of the luminaries" establishes Uriel's authority over the celestial system.

Chapter 80

Uriel confirms that Enoch has received a full revelation of the celestial order. The sun, moon, and stars operate under divine laws, following fixed courses, cycles, and appointed times. The leaders of the stars enforce the governance of the heavens, ensuring that all celestial bodies follow an unchanging order.

The text describes a time of disruption when the natural order collapses due to corruption. Time itself will shrink, agriculture will fail, and the entire system of existence will change. The phrase "the heavens will be stopped" refers to nothing less than a global cessation or divine intervention, placing Enoch's vision of celestial laws governing earthly events firmly in the realm of prophecy.

A total collapse of agriculture is described. Crops and trees will fail. The phrase "it will not sprout in its time" is repeated, emphasizing that this is not a delay, it is a complete disruption of nature's cycles. This directly responds to the previous verse, where rain ceases and the heavens are restrained, cutting off life from above.

A major disruption in the moon's cycles follows. The phrase "it will not be seen in its time" prophesies that its phases and visibility will no longer follow predictable patterns. This continues the previous signs of celestial breakdown, revealing that heavenly laws are unraveling in response to earthly corruption.

The text then describes a celestial crisis affecting the western sky. The phrase "the ends of the chariots" refers to constellations or celestial mechanisms altering their positions. The increase in brightness marks an unusual astronomical event, proving the progressive breakdown of universal order.

A celestial rebellion or disruption is described. The "appointed ones of the stars" (פְּקִידֵי הַכּוֹכָבִים) refers to ruling planetary forces that maintain order, yet they will deviate from their paths. Celestial bodies will fail to appear at their designated times, prophesying the collapse of the divine system.

As the movement of the stars ceases, people will misinterpret these events, abandon their paths, and turn to idolatry. They will worship the stars as gods. This parallels historical star-worship practices, particularly among the Greeks, whose cultures ignored Enoch's warning that such disorder leads to spiritual corruption, yet preserved his words.

The chapter concludes with the final reckoning for those who corrupted the heavens and the earth. The phrase "many evils will multiply" confirms escalating disasters as a consequence: celestial, terrestrial, and geological. Judgment is inevitable, leading to total destruction.

Chapter 81

Chapter 81 presents Enoch's access to celestial records and his role as a scribe of divine law. He is granted the ability to read the Book of the Tablets of the Heavens, a record of celestial order and eternal law. This proves the concept that all human actions are documented, ensuring that nothing is lost or forgotten. The mention of both tablets and a book brings to light multiple formats of preserved knowledge, illustrating the meticulous nature of divine record-keeping.

Enoch confirms that every action of humanity is recorded on tablets and in books, spanning beyond history into eternal generations. This proclaims that divine law governs all existence, and nothing escapes heavenly scrutiny. However, one passage in this chapter exhibits clear signs of scribal tampering. The phrase "the Lord, the King, the praised one forever" mirrors later Jewish liturgical formulas rather than the astronomical focus of 1 Enoch. Additionally, "for His patience" (ארך אפו) is inconsistent with Enoch's portrayal of divine figures as enforcers of order rather than moralistic or merciful beings. Another suspicious phrase, "in the name of all the sons of the earth," resembles priestly blessing formulas rather than Enoch's usual first-person declarations. The combined weight of these alterations confirms that this verse was corrupted before the original translator received it. Since no alternative manuscript is available, the entire passage is bracketed rather than reconstructed.

The text flows naturally, proving the previous verse was a later addition. Written later in the style of Hebrew wisdom literature, this section contrasts the fates of the righteous and the wicked. The phrase "Blessed is the man" follows traditional wisdom formulations.

Enoch is then returned to earth and commanded to reveal everything to Methuselah. The phrase "no flesh shall be justified" indicates judgment, requiring proof of the purity of the DNA, or judgment would come. He is given one year to recover and instruct his sons before being taken away permanently in the second year. This brings home the importance of writing and testifying, and the central theme of preserving hidden knowledge for future generations.

Before his departure, Enoch is reassured that the righteous will endure, depicted as a self-sustaining community where wisdom and justice are continuously revealed and celebrated. The chapter reveals a heavenly balance. The righteous uplift and bless each other, while the wicked destroy one another. This confirms the principle that divine justice is self-executing: sin leads to self-destruction, and transgression causes one to sink, whether metaphorically or literally.

The suffering of the righteous due to human corruption is acknowledged, but so is their removal from the presence of wickedness. This marks the conclusion of Enoch's divine instruction. After fulfilling his role, he is allowed to return home, where he blesses the Lord of Eternity.

Chapter 82

Chapter 82 focuses on the transmission of celestial knowledge and the structured order of time. Enoch formally delivers his wisdom to Methuselah, both orally and in writing, commanding him to safeguard these records for future generations. This ensures that Enochic preserves the wisdom, so that this very divine knowledge is never lost. The transmission extends beyond Methuselah to his descendants, down through the ages, establishing the lineage of knowledge that will guide future generations in understanding these laws.

The chapter emphasizes the supremacy of wisdom over material sustenance, presenting it as more satisfying than physical nourishment. Those who truly grasp divine knowledge will dedicate themselves entirely to it. The contrast between wisdom and ignorance continues as the text describes astrological movements of celestial bodies, which dictate the seasons and establish universal order. The mention of four key figures, indeed, angels, who mark the seasonal divisions brings home the deep connection between divine regulation of the seasons, and the natural cycle of time.

The text tells of humanity's widespread confusion regarding celestial events, emphasizing that most fail to recognize their significance within the greater universal structure. Enoch details the precise measurement of time, stating that the year consists of 364 days, a fundamental component of the Enochian solar calendar. The phrase "for me, the lord of all creation" is identified as a later interpolation, influenced by later theological revisions, and is bracketed accordingly. Similarly, the term "feasts" appears anachronistic, potentially reflecting a later attempt to align Enoch's calendar with ritual observances. If authentic, Enoch is referring to the Equinoxes and Solstices as Holy Feast Days.

The chapter continues with an account of how the movements of the sun, moon, and stars follow a predictable pattern. The phrase "revolve in their circuits" explains the concept of celestial precision, with each body maintaining its designated path. This theme extends into a discussion of celestial governance, where specific rulers oversee the timing and movement of astronomical events. These appointed figures ensure the proper alignment of time, detailing the idea that the heavens operate under strict supervision.

A full description of the celestial calendar follows, revealing a hierarchy where four leaders govern the seasonal divisions, twelve overseers for the months and additional figures who regulate the four extra days are required to maintain the solar cycle. The text establishes a clear chain of command, bolstering the idea that time is maintained through a strict and orderly system. The role of a chief positioned between the leader and the follower further brings home the nature of celestial governance.

The chapter lists the names of the four celestial leaders responsible for the seasonal divisions, linking them to divine rulership and order. Their presence maintains the proper separation of time and balance. Malkiel is identified as the ruler of the first division, marking the transition in the solar cycle. The name Teimani indicates a directional reference (south), a specific designation within the solar framework. The text confirms that each season lasts ninety-one days, preserving the Enochian 364-day calendar.

The environmental conditions corresponding to each celestial ruler's period are described, bringing in the theme of seasonal balance. The text depicts a time of intense heat, where fruit-bearing trees flourish while winter trees wither. The mention of sweat, heat, and distress warn of extreme seasonal changes, reflecting a broader planetary climatic pattern. This cyclical nature of flourishing and decay proves the seasonal controlled transitions within the celestial calendar.

A further hierarchy of subordinate celestial rulers is listed. Barqel and Zalbasha'el follow the traditional angelic naming pattern, but Elisaf (אל׳סף) stands out as an anomaly, not ending in "-el." The phrase "one who is added" indicates that he was not originally part of the primary celestial hierarchy. This gives the idea that the celestial order was at some point adjusted or expanded.

The second celestial leader, Elimelech, is introduced, governing another seasonal transition. His title, "Shining Sun," directly associates him with solar regulation, aligning with timekeeping. Again, the ninety-one-day period is confirmed, preserving the quarter-year division within the 364-day calendar.

The seasonal conditions under Elimelech's rule describe both abundance and hardship, with fruit-bearing trees coexisting with drying vegetation and harvests occurring alongside extreme heat and drought. The mention of full wine presses indicates a time of transformation and renewal, again illustrating the cyclical pattern of life, decay, death, and rebirth within the Enochian calendar.

The text concludes with additional celestial rulers overseeing the proper division of time. Aspa'el is described as "one who is added," similar to Elisaf, further indicating modifications or expansions within the celestial order. The structured completion of these rulership cycles reaffirms the precise and measured nature of time in the Enochian system.

See Appendix C for more on Angels and their specifics.

Chapter 83

Chapter 83 marks a transition into a new section where Enoch begins revealing his recorded visions to Methuselah. The phrase "all the visions that I have seen" confirms that what follows is a direct transmission of prophetic experiences and validates Enoch's role as both a seer and a celestial scribe. The intentional act of passing down divine knowledge ensures its preservation across generations.

The text contains evidence of scribal tampering. The bracketed "[I saw]" was identified as being inserted by Goldschmidt to "fix" a missing word. Additionally, the phrase "[I prayed before the Lord]" does not align with Enoch's usual terminology. Enoch consistently refers to divine authority as "Head of Days," making "the Lord" a term that originates from later theological interpolation. The verse remains coherent without this phrase, providing evidence of a later addition to mimic biblical phrasing.

The vision Enoch describes unfolds while he is resting in the house of his grandfather, Mahalal'el. He witnesses an upheaval. The heavens are falling and crashing down upon the earth. The phrase "inclining to fall" is a deliberate, impending collapse rather than a sudden impact, clearly indicating the described nature of this event as something coming down from the heavens. This vision foretells a predetermined global shift, manifesting that the universe follows a defined pattern of destruction and renewal.

The collapse intensifies as the earth itself begins to break apart. Entire mountains and trees are uprooted and submerged into a vast abyss. The phrase "mountains hovered over mountains" brings to mind extreme geological or continental upheavals, tectonic shifts, or violent atmospheric disturbances such as volcanic and seismic activity. The imagery of descending layers—earth, mountains, hills, and trees, all being swallowed by the abyss is a complete breakdown of the established order.

Enoch reacts in shock and despair, realizing the full magnitude of the catastrophe. The phrase "a word fell into my mouth" means an involuntary, driven response to the vision. His exclamation, "Woe! The earth is perishing!" confirms that he comprehends the totality of the destruction. His reaction is a human response to the overwhelming nature of the vision and the absolute certainty of its fulfillment.

Mahalal'el wakes Enoch from his vision and responds to his cries. His immediate questioning and the intensity of Enoch's distress mark it as an audible and physical reaction. It bridges the visionary and waking worlds.

Enoch recounts his vision to Mahalal'el, who recognizes its gravity. He acknowledges that the vision reveals hidden knowledge concerning the sins of the earth, which will lead to its eventual destruction. His statement confirms that the earth's corruption will result in its submersion into the abyss, signifying a total reset. This proves that the vision is a direct warning of impending judgment.

Mahalal'el urges Enoch to pray in response to this catastrophic revelation. The phrase "Lord of Praises" (אדון התשבחות) appears elsewhere in 1 *Enoch*, indicating a distinct celestial designation of Enoch's grandfather and a reference to his divine authority, along with evidence that Mahalal'el is of divine origin. The plea focuses not on stopping the destruction but on the survival of a remnant. This codifies the idea that Mahalal'el understands this judgment is inevitable but selective.

Mahalal'el warns Enoch that the catastrophe he has witnessed will descend from the heavens and bring destruction upon the earth. The context strongly hints at the Flood but remains open to other large-scale disasters. The wording authenticates that this is not merely a human event but one initiated from above, confirming divine orchestration of the coming judgment.

Enoch not only experiences the vision but immediately records it as a permanent document for future generations. This demonstrates that his role extends beyond witnessing. He is a scribe tasked with preserving knowledge. His promise to show everything to Methuselah confirms that this legacy of wisdom was meant to be passed down and possibly survived into later traditions.

A final instance of scribal tampering appears in the phrase "[the Lord of Judgment]" (אדון המשפט). Enoch does not use this title elsewhere, and its placement disrupts the natural flow of the passage.

This chapter ties Enoch's bloodline to divinity through his grandfather, Mahalal'el is listed as son of Kenan, Mahalal'el married Dinah, and is the father of Jared, Enoch's father. Mahalal'el is known to have lived 895 years and continues his legacy through Enoch's son Seth who births Noah.

Chapter 84

Chapter 84 opens with a later scribal insertion, following a known pattern of corruption. The bracketed section introduces theological rhetoric that reframes the chapter to align with later doctrine. The use of "*Elohim*" is particularly suspect, as Enoch does not use this term anywhere else in the text. The wording is unnatural compared to the rest of his speeches, making this a clear case of theological tampering.

However, the following verse preserves a key phrase: "*Elohei kol ha-Elahin*" (God of all the gods). This directly acknowledges multiple divine beings, contradicting later monotheistic redactions. The survival of this phrase proves that elements of the original divine hierarchy remained intact despite later doctrinal modifications. This confirms that early traditions recognized a heavenly hierarchy rather than a singular, absolute deity.

Another addition appears in the phrase "[you have made everything, and]" as the sentence remains coherent without it. Additionally, the final section "[And you know, and see, and hear everything. And nothing is hidden from you, for you see everything.]" conflicts with earlier passages in 1 Enoch. The original text consistently portrays knowledge as something presented before the Head of Days rather than inherently possessed. This follows a scribal pattern of attempting to reinforce divine omniscience, aligning the text with later theological developments instead of remaining true to the original framework.

The text maintains a central theme of 1 Enoch: celestial beings were responsible for human corruption. The phrase "the angels of the heavens have acted wickedly" confirms that divine rebellion, not human sin, was the root cause of suffering. The reference to "human flesh" indicates that divine punishment is not immediate but rather an ongoing consequence until an appointed time of judgment.

A further scribal interpolation appears in this chapter, where the text shifts from plural to singular, mirroring a known pattern of tampering in early chapter insertions. Once removed, the passage flows naturally, proving that this was a later attempt to reshape the text within evolving theological frameworks.

The term "*Adonai*" appears here but does not occur anywhere else in 1 *Enoch*. The Aramaic composition of Enoch did not traditionally use "*Adonai*" as a divine title. This term became a substitute for the Tetragrammaton (YHWH יהוה) during the Second Temple period, when the pronunciation of YHWH became restricted. Its appearance in this passage is overwhelming evidence of a later editorial addition rather than an original element of Enoch's writings.

Despite these insertions, the core message remains intact: Enoch pleads for the survival of the righteous. The phrase "raise up to plant seed forever" indicates a divinely sanctioned continuation of the just, reaffirming the theme of separating the wicked from the righteous in preparation for the final judgment.

Chapter 85

Chapter 85 begins with a scribal insertion meant to artificially suture the transition between verses. The bracketed section in 85:1 ("and visions were shown to me. My son, all of it.") was added to smooth the shift into 85:2. Likewise, the opening of 85:2 ("And Enoch answered and said to Methuselah his son,") follows the known pattern of scribes inserting transitions where none were originally needed. The reference to "my son" flows naturally within 85:2, making these additions unnecessary.

The vision begins with a bull emerging from the earth, followed by a cow that gives birth to two bulls: one black, one red. This imagery indicates a foundational figure, a maternal lineage, and two opposing forces. The black bull overpowers the red bull and chases it across the earth, but the red bull ultimately vanishes completely. This signifies defeat, exile, or destruction, alluding to a permanent separation between the two.

As the black bull rises to power, he is joined by a female, leading to the birth of many offspring in his image. These bulls follow him, founding a dominant ruling lineage. Meanwhile, the first cow departs from the first bull and searches for the red bull, but he is nowhere to be found. Her loud cries and persistent search convey a deep sense of loss, distress, and a severed connection.

The first bull finds the cow and silences her cries. His presence ends her lament, marking a shift in the vision. She then gives birth to another white bull, followed by many bulls and black cows. This vision depicts an expanding lineage with a distinction between white and black offspring.

As the white bull matures, he transforms into a massive ox-bull, symbolizing power and dominion. From him arises a new generation of white bulls. This lineage demonstrates the expansion of the bloodline. The white bulls continue multiplying, each resembling the one before, moving in a disciplined manner. Their movement confirms an expanding lineage governed by a divine or celestial plan.

Chapter 86

Chapter 86 opens with a celestial event that changes everything. A star falls from the heavens, mourns, and joins the bulls, symbolizing a fallen angel, as confirmed in the Book of Luminaries. This marks a descent from a higher realm, whether divine plane, state of being, or sky itself. The mourning reflects both exile and transformation through the fall.

As the vision goes on, the great bulls change their places and pastures, and their offspring change as well. This shift is accompanied by moaning, indicating turmoil, disruption, or distress. More stars fall and join the first fallen star among the bulls, fully integrating into the earthly world.

The fallen ones take earthly mates, openly displaying their transgression. Their offspring are unnatural hybrids. These are symbols of a corrupted creation and a violation of cosmic law. The bulls, terrified by these beings, flee in fear but soon resist, engaging in a violent battle. Using their horns to bite and gore the invaders, they fight back against those who disrupted the natural order.

Despite their resistance, the bulls begin to be devoured, leading to widespread fear and panic among the sons of the earth. The chapter ends in chaos, as humanity flees in terror from the consequences of this unnatural incursion.

Chapter 87

Chapter 87 continues the chaotic aftermath of the fallen ones' transgression. The bulls turn on each other, attacking and devouring one another, escalating the violence. The earth itself cries out in response, reflecting the magnitude of the destruction.

Enoch then witnesses a new vision in which an entity is created. Suddenly, "many" white beings descend from the heavens, *appearing in human form*. One of these moves forward, while three remain stationary. Again, the four archangels but the text does not name them.

The three celestial beings who had stayed behind now take hold of Enoch and lift him from the earth. They bring him to a high place, revealing a towering structure on the mountains, while the surrounding hills appear diminished. This perspective gives Enoch a bird's-eye view without involvement.

Enoch is politely instructed to sit and observe what is about to take place. The phrase "Sit, please" (שב נא shev na) confirms that he is a witness to unfolding events, particularly concerning the elephants, camels, donkeys, rams, and bulls.

Chapter 88

Chapter 88 describes the beginning of the Watchers' imprisonment and the escalation of celestial judgment. One of the original four celestial beings captures the first fallen star, binds its hands and feet, and casts it into a deep, dreadful valley. This act marks the initial phase of divine retribution against the rebellious Watchers.

A dramatic shift follows as one, who we are not certain, draws a sword and hands it to the hybrid creatures. Then those beings started to fight among themselves. This action ignites a massive conflict among them, plunging the earth into chaos. The battle is so violent that the entire earth trembles, reinforcing the catastrophic consequences of the Watchers' actions.

Enoch watches as one of the four cast [...] down from the heavens. There is no evidence what [...] is and we assume nothing into the text where it does not have a specific answer. That same one of the four gathered all the "wandering stars" and bound them and cast them into the abyss.

Chapter 89

Chapter 89 continues the vision of the bulls, unfolding the events of the Great Flood, the survival of a select lineage, and the unfolding history of their descendants. The text presents a universal scale upheaval, a division of peoples, and conflicts that arise from their divergence.

The vision begins with one of the four revealing a secret to a "raised one", who trembles in fear. The words "raised one" alone bring questions as this individual undergoes transformation, first appearing as a bull before becoming a man. He constructs a *tevah* (box/structure) and enters it. Three bulls are also present, but the text then shifts abruptly to an act of aggression. "He attacked them" remains ambiguous. The floodwaters rise, and darkness and vapor obscure the vision.

Outside the tevah, in the courtyard, the bulls, rams, and other creatures gather as the waters surge upward, swallowing everything in their path. The force of the waters carries the bodies away, ensuring that nothing remains. This passage confirms the Nephilim (hybrid offspring of the Watchers) were not in the tevah but perished in the floodwaters. The reference to Tehom (תהום, the Abyss) is significant, linking this directly to the Sumerian Flood story, where divine judgment resets both humanity and the watchers.

As the waters recede, the vessel comes to rest, not on a mountain, but upon land. The darkness dissipates, and light returns, signaling the restoration of order. A white bull, representing Adam, exits first. Following this, three bulls arise: one white, one red like blood, and one black. They symbolize a division among them. Their separation marks the establishment of a new order.

From these bulls, diverse creatures emerge, including both land beasts and birds, symbolizing the spread of distinct groups across the earth. The lineage of the white bull produces a wild donkey, which multiplies rapidly, while another white bull maintains the original line. These divisions foreshadow future conflicts.

The lineage splits again, one producing a black wild boar and a white lamb, from which twelve sheep arise. The twelve are entrusted to the donkeys, but one is mistakenly given to the wolves. This error leads to oppression, as the wolves persecute the sheep, even drowning their children. The sheep cry out in distress, prompting the master of the sheep to descend from his elevated position.

The master appoints a single sheep as a messenger to the wolves, warning them not to harm the flock. Another sheep joins the mission, and together, they confront the wolves. However, the oppression intensifies, and the wolves use all their strength against the sheep. In response, the master intervenes, striking the wolves down and reversing the balance of power. The surviving sheep escape, but the wolves, blinded and desperate, pursue them.

At a river crossing, the master of the sheep parts the stream, allowing the sheep to pass safely. The pursuing wolves, seeing their doom, attempt to flee, but the waters return, consuming them completely. This marks the final destruction of the oppressors.

The sheep emerge into the wilderness, and their eyes are opened. The master provides for them, ensuring their survival. A single sheep ascends a high rock, separating from the others before being sent back to lead them. This moment signifies divine appointment.

A shift occurs as the sheep tremble before the overwhelming presence of the master, their fear preventing them from even looking upon him. When the leading lamb ascends, the flock becomes blinded, straying from the path. The master, consumed by wrath, returns to confront them. In a decisive act, he gathers those who remained, but violently strikes down those who had strayed. This marks a transition from passive leadership to enforcement through power.

The lamb, having become a man, constructs a house for the master of the sheep, bringing the flock into it. A great transformation follows, as the generational leadership shifts. The previous lamb dies, leaving only the smaller sheep, who move toward a new pasture. Their mourning is short-lived, as they cross another stream, arriving in a pleasant land where their house remains.

Their vision wavers and sometimes they see, sometimes they are blind. Until another lamb arises, restoring them. However, new threats emerge, as dogs, foxes, and wild boars begin to devour the sheep. The oppression continues until a ram rises up, wielding his horns against the foxes and boars, wiping them out completely. Yet, even he strays, trampling the very flock he was meant to protect.

To correct this, the master selects another lamb, secretly appointing him as the new ram. Despite this change, the oppression of the sheep does not cease. The previous ram pursues the newly appointed leader but falls before the beasts. The new ram, however, establishes order, leading the sheep to growth and prosperity.

The house is lowered as a tower rises above it, marking a shift in hierarchy. The master of the sheep now dwells in the tower, where a table is set before him.

A crisis unfolds as the sheep abandon the house, wandering many paths. The master appoints leaders from among them, but instead of guiding the flock, they turn against their own, slaughtering them. A single survivor escapes, crying out for help. The master intervenes, rescuing her and bringing her back into his presence. He then sends additional ewes, but they are rejected, left only to bear witness to the suffering of the flock.

The abandonment worsens as the sheep are handed over to wild predators: lions, leopards, wolves, jackals, and foxes, who tear them apart. The house and the tower are forsaken, sealing their fate. Seeing this, Enoch himself cries out to the master of the sheep, demanding justice.

The shocking response: silence. Instead of rescuing them, the master rejoices in their destruction, leaving them to be swallowed and devoured. He expels the flock, delivering them into the hands of seventy shepherds, each given specific orders. However, the shepherds go beyond their commands, slaughtering the sheep far beyond what was decreed.

A second observer is called to record their actions in secret, ensuring that judgment will eventually be rendered. Every excess slaughter, every deviation from command is documented. The destruction escalates, the stronghold burns, and the sheep disappear, never returning home.

A single scribe records every act of destruction, delivering the final account to the master of the sheep. The book is sealed, ensuring nothing can be altered.

Despite the destruction, three sheep return and rebuild, marking the first sign of renewal. The tower is restored, renamed "The High Tower," yet the bread upon the table remained impure.

The sheep and their shepherds remain blinded, unable to recognize the reality of their condition. Many are delivered over for slaughter, but no intervention comes. The scribe presents the book, reading it aloud before departing. Judgment is left in the hands of the master.

Chapter 90

Chapter 90 continues the vision of the shepherds, revealing the final reckoning for both the flock and its corrupt leaders. The passage confirms a structured cycle of leadership, where groups of shepherds rule for appointed periods, each repeating the mistakes of the last. The arrival of predatory birds: eagles, kites, herons, and ravens, signals the beginning of the flock's destruction. These birds systematically peck out the sheep's eyes and consume their flesh, demonstrating a deliberate, organized attack rather than mere chaos. The shepherds' failure is absolute; they have not just neglected the flock but have actively led them to destruction.

As the vision unfolds, the flock is nearly annihilated, reduced to bones scattered across the earth. A new group of shepherds takes over, completing a cycle of fifty-eight appointed periods, providing a strict timeline of rulership. A shift occurs when new lambs are born, and unlike their predecessors, they open their eyes and cry out in a moment of awakening. Yet the older sheep remain blind and deaf, unable to recognize what is happening.

The ravens emerge as enforcers, seizing the lambs and systematically cutting off their horns to suppress them. However, one lamb grows a large horn, which triggers an awakening among the others. The newly aware lambs resist the ongoing destruction, while their leader stands firm. Despite their efforts, the powerful predators: eagles, lions, and ravens, launch a coordinated attack, overwhelming the flock in one final assault.

At the height of the crisis, the scribe appears, revealing the extent of the destruction and bringing forth the record of the shepherds' deeds. The last twelve shepherds have committed even greater slaughter than their predecessors. The records are presented before the Lord of the Sheep, signaling the moment of judgment.

Judgment begins with the staff of wrath, an instrument of divine reckoning. The oppressors are cast into the earth, fully erased. The remaining sheep are given a great sword, and in a dramatic reversal, they rise up against their former oppressors, subduing them completely. A throne is set up in the chosen land, where the Lord of the Sheep takes his seat and opens the sealed books, initiating the final trial.

The seven white ones (archangels) are summoned. They gather the fallen stars who were the first to rebel and fall. The seventy shepherds, who were entrusted with leadership but exceeded their orders, are also restrained and placed before the throne. Judgment is swift: the stars are sentenced first, cast into a valley of fire and pillars of flame. The seventy shepherds follow, meeting the same fate.

A second valley of fire opens, where the blind sheep, those who had gone astray, are brought forward for judgment. They, too, are cast into the flames, marking the end of their corruption. The old house is dismantled, its beams, pillars, and ornaments removed and placed in a designated area on the right side of the land.

From the ruins, a new house is raised, greater and taller than the first house. This marks the full restoration of the flock. The remaining sheep enter the new house, while the beasts of the mountains and the fallen birds bow before them. Those who once ruled now plead for mercy.

A final transformation occurs: every sheep becomes a white bull, fully restored in purity and stature. A new leader arises among them, his great horns distinguishing his authority. Even the once-powerful beasts now fear him and seek his favor.

As Enoch awakens from his vision, he realizes the full weight of what he has seen, the complete revelation of humanity's deeds, their destruction, and their renewal. Overcome with emotion, he weeps, knowing that everything he has witnessed will come to pass.

Chapter 91

Chapter 91 contains Enoch's final words of prophecy, marking a solemn farewell and an eschatological revelation of the end. He summons Methuselah and commands him to gather all his kin, declaring that the spirit has been poured upon him. This establishes divine authority for the vision that follows.

Methuselah obeys, and Enoch addresses his assembled family, offering a testimony intended to bind them to justice and truth. His tone is direct and prophetic. Certain bracketed sections interrupt this flow with theological and stylistic elements foreign to Enoch's voice, providing supporting evidence of later insertions designed to bring in the legalistic or doctrinal interpretations.

Enoch warns against aligning with deceit or approaching righteousness insincerely. He affirms that true righteousness leads to guidance along just paths, while the corrupted will perish. One verse is marked as a later insertion due to its unnatural sentence flow and singular to plural inconsistencies.

The prophecy then describes a sweeping judgment in which corruption is punished and completely eradicated. The phrase "all its uprising shall be changed" is evidence of transformation rather than annihilation. This is followed by an acknowledgment that corruption is cyclical; after one judgment, evil returns, necessitating renewed justice.

A later addition reframes divine justice in terms of vengeance, invoking the title "Holy Lord," a term Enoch does not use. However, the original voice of the text returns with the declaration that oppression and deceit will be uprooted from beneath the heavens, again proving the universal nature of the cleansing.

False power structures are dismantled. Idols, images, and towers of authority are cast into She'ol of fire. She'ol is left untranslated due to its debated nature, but the judgment described is final and permanent.

A heavily interpolated verse attempts to introduce personal resurrection theology by altering wisdom from a force to be pursued into one passively "given," further distorting Enoch's original cosmology. This shift is rejected in favor of Enoch's authentic themes.

Violence, referred to explicitly using the Hebrew word ḥamas (חמס), is named as the root of destruction. Unlike earlier judgments of fire, this judgment is described as being carried out by the sword, an earthly reckoning.

The eighth week begins a new era in which the righteous execute justice with that sword. This inverts power as sinners are handed over into their hands. This marks a transition from divine intervention to righteous agency.

In the ninth week, a final restoration unfolds. The righteous inherit the earth, the House of God is rebuilt in splendor, and a new divine rule is established. This is eternal. The house will never fall again.

The tenth week brings complete and irreversible judgment. The Watchers who abandoned their place are condemned forever. This verdict extends beyond earth, affecting the heavens themselves.

The universe is remade. The old heavens pass away, and new ones shine sevenfold in perfection. This represents eternal light, order, and restoration.

The closing verse describes the eternal state. Time continues unbroken in righteousness. Sin is defeated and erased from all memory. This is the final fulfillment of universal justice.

Enoch ends his message with a clear and urgent call. Two paths lie ahead: righteousness and violence. He affirms that he has revealed all that will come. Those who choose righteousness will live; those who follow hamas will be destroyed without trace.

Chapter 92

Chapter 92 opens with a scribal preface, which was later added to justify the text. The phrase "Praised in the mouth of all men" is inconsistent with Enoch's voice and serves as an external validation rather than an authentic introduction. The true message begins when Enoch directly addresses the final generations, emphasizing wisdom as the guiding force for the righteous.

Enoch reassures the righteous not to be troubled by the passage of time. The appointed times of judgment and restoration are fixed, they do not unfold randomly. Time itself has been measured and assigned by the Holy and Great One as part of the divine order.

A full interpolation appears next, attempting to introduce resurrection theology into Enoch's text. The phrase "The righteous one shall rise" does not exist in Enoch's framework and was added by later scribes. The sentence collapses without it, proving that this phrase was inserted as a separate unit. This follows a known scribal pattern of adding theological constructs between authentic passages.

Another full interpolation follows. The term "The righteous one" does not match Enoch's language, and the phrase "dominion forever" aligns with messianic theology, which is foreign to Enoch's cosmology.

Likewise, "walking in eternal light" reflects later religious imagery rather than the established pattern of justice of Enoch's vision. This verse was modified using the same scribal pattern as the previous interpolation, adding evidence of deliberate insertions.

The final authentic verse describes sin's complete and permanent eradication. It vanishes into darkness and never returns. Unlike the previous interpolations, this passage is consistent with Enoch's theme of justice and restoration, evidence of its legitimacy within the original vision.

Chapter 93

Chapter 93 continues Enoch's apocalyptic chronology, outlining the great epochs of human and cosmic history. However, the chapter opens with a later scribal addition, marked by a third-person reference inconsistent with Enoch's voice. This framing device was inserted to introduce the section artificially, separating it from the core vision. This however relays the idea that there were multiple books that Enoch recounted from.

Another bracketed section follows, also a scribal insertion third person, someone else is telling the story instead of Enoch. Where Enoch is said to introduce his words in a formal style that does not match his typical speech. His true voice begins with the direct phrase: "Behold, I speak with you." From this point, the content returns to authentic revelation, focused on the message rather than the audience.

Enoch identifies himself as the seventh in the lineage from Adam, grounding his place in sacred chronology. The reference to "the books" proves that his vision draws from divine encounter, oral tradition, and recorded knowledge, written traditions existed even in the antediluvian era.

The prophetic timeline begins with the second epoch, when wickedness and deceit spread. The arrival of "they" marks the descent of the Watchers, a turning point in history. The "first end" signals the first great judgment, and violence increases afterward. A single man is saved (Noah), who becomes the bearer of divine law for a new age.

The third epoch centers on the selection of a man who upholds justice and righteousness. His influence endures, embedding righteousness as a permanent force in the world.

By the end of the fourth epoch, visions of the holy and righteous ones appear, indicating an age of divine revelation. A lasting covenant is established, and inheritance is granted across generations.

The fifth epoch culminates in the construction of a house of glory and kingship. A stable institution of divine order and rulership.

During the sixth epoch, the people awaken, but they reject wisdom. Though a man arises to lead, the period ends in destruction: the house of kingship is consumed by fire, and the chosen lineage is broken.

The seventh epoch is one of complete and absolute societal collapse. Every system, belief, and structure is overturned. Corruption is total. The world is not simply unstable; it is fully inverted! Nothing remaining of what came before.

Despite this, the epoch concludes with a reward for the righteous. Those who endured and remained committed are described as divinely cultivated. For this their reward is eternal and incorruptible. The "sevenfold law of all creation" does not point to commandments but to the foundation of reality itself, the hidden architecture of divine wisdom and existence.

The next four verses (93:11-14) are confirmed interpolations, inserted to undermine and suppress Enoch's revelation of knowledge. They are written in a rhetorical style foreign to Enoch and repeatedly deny human access to the very truths Enoch spent his life receiving. The phrases question whether humanity can understand heaven, light, the stars, or the cosmic order, despite the fact that Enoch was entrusted with this knowledge directly.

Each of these interpolated verses is bracketed. Their style, message, and tone contradict both the immediate context and the overarching message of Enoch's writings. They were introduced to diminish the power of what Enoch revealed, replacing revelation with theological ignorance.

Chapter 94

Chapter 94 continues Enoch's condemnation of corruption, explicitly identifying ḥamas (חמס) as the force of destruction. While the structure of certain verses may reflect later editing, the core message remains intact; violence, oppression, and injustice will lead to downfall.

Appendix A: Ch 94

The divide between the righteous and the wicked is sharply drawn. Those who reject violence and corruption will walk in righteousness, while those who embrace destruction are doomed. The righteous are not only warned against following these paths. They are commanded to completely separate from them. The warning is absolute: even coming near wickedness brings destruction.

Enoch urges the righteous to pursue justice, live well, and walk in peace, for their reward will be joy and life. This reflects the cosmic law of balance, those who align with righteousness will endure, while the wicked will perish.

A direct warning follows: sinners will corrupt wisdom. The phrase "erasing from the heart" does not mean simple forgetfulness, it alludes to a deliberate suppression of true knowledge. Wisdom itself is not lost; rather, truth is distorted, and understanding is manipulated. This going right along with Enoch's repeated theme that deception, not ignorance, leads humanity astray.

The builders of violence (hamas) establish power through oppression, injustice, and deception. Their downfall will be sudden and final. They will not find peace. Their houses, built without justice, will collapse. They will be uprooted, slain by the sword, and stripped of their wealth.

One verse is bracketed due to scribal tampering. Its phrasing is overly smooth and moralistic, aligning with later theological themes rather than Enoch's raw apocalyptic style. The use of "The Most High" (Elyon, עליון) is a Second Temple-era term, and the theme of trusting in riches appears to have been reworded to fit post-exilic moral narratives.

The wicked have sealed their own fate. Their deeds of destruction (niklah) and violence (hamas) ensure their judgment. They are set apart for bloodshed, darkness, and destruction.

Their creator himself will destroy them, and no falsehood will bring them mercy. Even those who once followed them will rejoice in their downfall.

The chapter concludes with a grim reality: in the days of corruption, the righteous will be mocked and persecuted by the wicked. Justice will be overturned, and moral distortion will replace truth.

Chapter 95

Chapter 95 opens with a lament framed by a rhetorical question, accompanied by imagery of overflowing tears. The bracketed phrases are unnecessary and reflect later scribal embellishment intended to add emotional weight. Enoch's original voice is sharper, more focused without ornamental grief.

The chapter proceeds with a direct condemnation of those who spread hatred and commit evil. Justice is not optional. it is inevitable and will come for them in full.

A reassurance is given to the righteous: judgment will come, and their suffering will not go unanswered. However, this verse also contains a theological interpolation. The use of the name YHWH, which Enoch never used. This divine title was inserted by a J-source scribe. The same redactor responsible for reshaping Torah texts to emphasize YHWH as the singular deity. Its appearance here is a clear later addition intended to retrofit Enoch into post-Mosaic theology. It has no place in the original Enochian cosmology. Yet this proves that they had access to these scrolls as well as the Torah.

The next verse condemns those who unite in evil. Their alliance does not protect them, healing will never come, and their sin remains with them.

Enoch then issues a warning to those who harm their own kin. Their betrayal will bring about their own downfall. Justice is not abstract; it is causal and exact.

False witnesses and deceivers are singled out next. Their judgment will come quickly, and they will be destroyed. Yet, the phrasings here obvious later scribal influence, from the Second Temple period, where moralistic and judicial themes were smoothed and expanded.

The final verse condemns sinners who persecute the righteous, warning that their violence will not be forgotten. The term "men of violence (literally, "ḥamas: חמס)" is again central those who pursue the innocent will be overtaken by darkness, losing their place and their power. Like the previous verses, the language here carries signs of later stylization, it has theological consistency but dilutes Enoch's raw tone.

Chapter 96

Chapter 96 delivers a call to the righteous, urging them to rise up without fear. The sinners will be cut off, and the righteous will ultimately rule over the wicked, this is a reversal that has already been desired.

The righteous are depicted as ascending, while the wicked are cast down in suffering and fear. The use of eagle and nest imagery evokes safety and elevation, while the rabbits seeking refuge symbolize vulnerability. The wicked, by contrast, are reduced to groaning like goats, stripped of power and dignity.

Enoch reassures the righteous not to fear during times of chaos and distress. Healing is promised, and a bright light will shine over them. They will hear the sound of rest from the heavens, marking their place of peace in contrast to the groaning of the wicked.

The chapter turns to wealthy sinners who mimic righteousness. Those who speak and appear holy, but whose hearts are corrupt. Their deception is exposed, their guilt inescapable. Enoch reaffirms that their wickedness will not be forgotten, echoing the central theme of accountability and judgment.

Those who consume abundance while trampling the poor are condemned. Their luxury comes at the cost of justice, and their oppression is noted. They rule not by merit but by exploitation.

The text warns that abundance taken for granted will not endure. These sinners drink freely without recognizing the source, but the waters will dry up, and they will be left to burn. This echoes earlier imagery of divine withdrawal, where blessing is removed as judgment falls.

Rulers who lead through violence and deceit are warned. Their legacy will testify against them and they will not be remembered with honor. Even their memory will become a judgment, ensuring that their wickedness is never erased from the record.

The chapter ends with a clear contrast: the oppressors' downfall is sealed despite their power, while the righteous will inherit long and good days, affirming the order of justice.

Chapter 97

With Chapter 97 we return to the bold and italicized text indicating that older manuscript sources are available: Chapter 97 – Syncellus (Byzantine Chronicle), Chapters 97–107 Codex Bodleianus 185 in fragmentary form. The chapter opens with the image of a cursed mountain a place marked by oaths and judgment. It will remain buried under cold, snow, and frost, a symbol of divine rejection, until the great day of judgment, when the sinners who swore upon it will be disgraced and destroyed.

The mountain, once covered, will then be burned, brought low, and melt like wax, showing that even the strongest structures of defiance will not endure. This transformation marks the final reckoning. A lasting blot against the land itself. The wrath of heaven turns upon the sons of men. A notable shift from Enoch's usual phrase "sons of Adam." This linguistic change may indicate a broader scope of judgment, extending beyond a specific lineage. The judgment will not cease until the appointed time of their complete destruction.

The chapter establishes the 120-year lifespan limit, a clear divine restriction placed upon humanity after judgment. This aligns with the law that imposes temporal boundaries on mortal life. No one will live beyond this limit, and no one will escape the wrath that has been kindled by the King of all ages. Judgment is unrelenting, and every individual must face it, there is no way out.

A divine courtroom scene follows, where the words of lawlessness are read aloud before the Great Holy One. The sinners are confronted with their own deeds, and everything done in secret or in defiance of the law is laid bare. Judgment falls upon sinners on land and sea, no one escapes. Their sins are remembered and recorded, and nothing is overlooked. This affirms that justice is not random, it is exact and all-encompassing.

Those who accumulate wealth unjustly are called out. They boast in their security, convinced their riches make them untouchable. But their pride reveals their ignorance: judgment will reach them, and their wealth will not save them.

The chapter ends by exposing the wicked's arrogance. Trusting in silver and luxury as protection, unaware their destruction is already decreed.

Chapter 98

Chapter 98 begins with a solemn oath to the wise, warning them of the lawlessness that will unfold on the earth. A sharp distinction is drawn between the wise and the foolish, that only those with true understanding will recognize the scale of corruption and judgment to come.

The next passage describes the ruling elite, drowning in luxury, vanity, and decadence. The imagery is striking: men adorning themselves more than virgins, gold and silver flooding their homes like water. This is a society consumed by excess, blind to its impending collapse.

The text then delivers a devastating verdict: the wicked, devoid of wisdom, will perish along with their wealth and honor. Their downfall is destruction of body and spirit, without redemption or remembrance.

Enoch makes a theological correction: sin was not sent from heaven. It was not divinely ordained or imposed by the "Most High." While the Watchers introduced forbidden knowledge, humans chose to embrace and propagate it. Sin is a human choice, and those who commit it bring a curse upon themselves.

This principle continues: slavery, lawlessness, and barrenness were not divinely decreed. Women were not created to be slaves, nor was fruitlessness meant to be a punishment. These were consequences of human injustice and systemic corruption, not divine will.

Judgment is all-encompassing. Every act of wickedness is seen and known. No injustice is hidden; no sin is overlooked. The heavens themselves are witnesses, and nothing is forgotten. This surveillance system ensures total accountability.

A strong warning follows: do not deceive yourselves. The "Most High" sees everything. While the Ge'ez version uses the term "Elohim" (Gods) instead of "Most High," this shift reflects a known pattern of scribal tampering meant to reshape the divine hierarchy.

Every injustice is recorded daily, none are forgotten. Judgment is delayed only by the divine order of reckoning.

The foolish will perish because of their own ignorance. They reject the wisdom that could save them, and as a result, goodness will never reach them. Though part of this verse is missing, the meaning is clear: there is no reward for those who despise truth.

The wicked are warned again: atonement is no longer possible. The day of judgment is coming, and for them it will bring only distress and disgrace. Those who commit cruelty and defilement will be left without sustenance or peace. They will be cut off from all goodness, their very presence erased from the covenantal order.

They will be handed over to the righteous for judgment. Their false hopes of escape or mercy are crushed, and the warning is firm: no deliverance will come.

A particularly intense condemnation is delivered to those who rejoice in the misfortunes of the righteous. The phrase "your pit shall not be dug" implies they will be left without burial—forgotten even in death.

The chapter then addresses those who attempt to silence or discredit the righteous, declaring that they have no hope of salvation. Their words are void, and their judgment is certain.

This theme reaches its peak with a direct condemnation of those who create and spread false writings. They are accused of leading others astray and are held fully responsible for the corruption they unleash. This verse directly targets scribes and theologians who alter sacred truth for control or gain.

The chapter concludes by declaring that the wicked are deceived and joyless, and their destruction will come swiftly. There is no escape, no mercy, and no restoration for them.

Chapter 99

Chapter 99 is primarily the Codex Bodleianus (Koine Greek) and it is fragmented for this chapter. Gaps are filled using Goldschmidt's 1892 Hebrew reconstruction, as evidenced by the unbolded italics. This chapter resumes the apocalyptic judgment themes with strong condemnation of deception, falsehood, and idolatry.

The opening curse targets those who gain honor through deceit, declaring their destruction to be complete and their salvation denied. This sets the tone: judgment here is absolute, with no room for redemption once the line has been crossed.

The next judgment falls upon those who corrupt the truth and twist the eternal covenant. The warning is sharp. Those who imagine themselves as sinless or immune will be swallowed by the earth. This is a clear reference to final and total annihilation.

The righteous are then instructed to bring their petitions before the celestial messengers, who serve as witnesses. These petitions act as eternal records, ensuring that the wicked are held accountable before the Most High. The passage sticks to Enoch's legal framework, where all deeds are entered into a divine archive, classic "P" scribal legalistic language. The wicked are warned that the Day of Destruction will shake them to their core. Their downfall is not a possibility, it is inevitable, brought about by their own wickedness.

A scene of complete societal breakdown is described. Even maternal bonds collapse, symbolizing the dissolution of all human connection in the face of coming judgment. The repetition of this image shows the total unraveling of the human order. Idolatry is condemned in clear terms. Those who worship demons and spirits, or who craft idols from precious materials, are portrayed as deceived and doomed. These practices offer no real help, and the false entities invoked cannot save their followers from destruction.

The theme of spiritual deception continues with a warning about false dreams and visions, which mislead the foolish. These are not divine revelations but products of internal confusion, another common theme in apocalyptic literature.

Those who commit corruption, false works, and spiritual manipulation are declared unredeemable. Their own actions will bring about their downfall, with no possibility of escape or mercy.

The chapter affirms that those who follow wisdom and the Most High's commandments are blessed, avoiding deception and finding salvation.

Spreading discord, evil, and sin is once again condemned. The text affirms that such individuals will perish in Sheol, emphasizing not only physical destruction but spiritual erasure.

Another verse accuses the wicked of bringing bitterness to the earth, emphasizing that their influence poisons the world. Their destruction will be total.

Those who build grand structures through exploitation, without honest labor, are exposed. Their achievements are hollow, lacking any divine legitimacy.

A final condemnation is delivered to those who reject their true inheritance, turning away from what was divinely given. As a result, they will be hunted by deception and forever lack peace.

The judgment concludes by targeting not only the wicked but also their enablers, those who support oppression, murder, and injustice. All are held accountable.

The chapter ends with a sweeping declaration of final judgment. False glory will be erased, wrath will rise, and the wicked will fall by the sword. The righteous will remember their evil, ensuring their legacy is one of infamy and destruction.

Chapter 100

Chapter 100 unleashes a prophetic vision of mass slaughter and judgment. The opening verses describe a gruesome battlefield, where fathers and sons die together in one place. The Greek confirms the phrase "in one place," while the Hebrew sentence structure affirms that this is a unified prophetic scene, not a series of disconnected images.

The judgment escalates as human bonds collapse entirely. Loved ones turn against each other, and the distinction between sinner and honorable vanishes. This is not a moment of violence, it is a sustained, all-day massacre, with no survivors spared.

The bloodshed becomes stark: a horse stands chest-deep in blood, a chariot submerged to its axles. This is no metaphor; "the blood of the sinners" confirms divine judgment, so complete, the wicked flood the battlefield with their own blood.

Appendix A: Ch 100

The text then shifts from human judgment to angelic accountability. The angels who assisted in injustice are cast into hidden places. They are gathered together for sentencing and banished or imprisoned, aligning with earlier references to fallen angels bound in darkness. This is a pivotal moment: the Most High rises, and the final Day of Judgment begins.

A moment of restoration follows. The righteous and holy ones are protected by holy angels, described as being preserved like the pupil of an eye, a phrase denoting tenderness, value, and protection. Once sin and evil are removed, the righteous will dwell in peace and rest, free from fear.

The chapter then presents a scene of human realization. The wise will understand, and people will recognize the truth too late. Wealth, once powerful, becomes worthless in the collapse of injustice. The writing, once ignored, is finally understood, but not by those who need it most.

Condemnation returns for those who oppressed the righteous during times of distress. They are imprisoned in fire, and what they did to others is done to them. This is a clear statement of measured judgment, where all deeds are repaid in kind.

Next comes a portrayal of the wicked as always awake and scheming, consumed by their own malice. Despite their power, they are surrounded by fear, with no one to help them. Their isolation confirms that they are abandoned and devoured by their own wickedness.

The text then condemns both speech and action. The wicked once knew righteousness, but turned from it. Though the verse breaks off, the judgment remains clear and they are lost entirely.

A vision of divine investigation follows. The angels examine the deeds of the wicked, and even the sun, moon, and stars serve as witnesses. These celestial bodies record the crimes committed against the righteous, confirming the magnitude of the testimony. The final phrase may be a fragment or corruption, but the meaning holds.

The focus briefly turns to divine control over the weather. References to rain, dew, clouds, and mist appear, possibly connected to offerings for rainfall. The phrase "write in gold" may allude to divine inscription. A judgment that cannot be altered by wealth or pleading.

The chapter concludes by affirming that nature itself becomes a weapon of judgment. Snow, frost, and ice are described not as mere weather, but as plagues. The phrase "you will not be able to withstand" confirms total helplessness before these afflictions. In the end, even the elements rise against the wicked.

Chapter 101

Chapter 101 issues a call to humanity: recognize the works of the Most High and fear to do evil. The phrase "fear to do evil" establishes moral accountability as the natural outcome of understanding divine power. This is not abstract reverence; it is a direct warning.

A rhetorical question follows, addressing divine consequences in the natural world. If the heavens are shut and there is no rain or dew, it is because of human sin. This aligns with earlier warnings: nature will rise against the wicked. The closing phrase, "what will you do?" is rhetorically challenging. It denies any escape.

The next passage contrasts present arrogance with future desperation. The wicked speak "great and harsh words" now, defying divine authority. But when judgment comes, they will plead for mercy. The question posed exposes their hypocrisy: pride in peace, begging in wrath.

Attention then shifts to the sailors at sea, a metaphor for humanity's fragility. Their ships are tossed by waves, shaken under the surge, unable to withstand the force of nature. This sticks to the theme: those who defy divine order are not secure.

As the storm worsens, the sailors throw their possessions into the sea, desperate to survive. The phrase "the sea will swallow them" reveals their fear, and the fate of all who resist divine authority. When judgment comes, possessions are worthless, and escape is impossible.

The sea itself is declared to be under divine control. The phrase "He bound it" confirms that even chaos has boundaries. The sand is its limit, echoing ancient cosmology in which divine command restrains the sea's destructive force.

The power of divine rebuke is then described. At His word, the waters dry up and the fish tremble. Though the sentence breaks off, the message is clear: nothing resists divine judgment, life itself responds to His voice.

The chapter closes with a question: "Who gave knowledge?" This affirms that wisdom is a divine gift. Sailors tremble before the sea, yet sinners do not tremble before the One who made it. The contrast is striking. Those who fear nature but not its Creator are the most blind of all.

Chapter 102

Chapter 102 opens with a vivid depiction of inescapable fiery judgment. The phrase "surge of fire" conveys an overwhelming force, and the rhetorical question that follows leaves no doubt, no place is safe. The final line introduces the direct voice of divine judgment, prophesying the certainty of what is to come.

Terror overtakes the world. A great sound causes fear, and the entire earth shakes, trembles, and is violently disturbed. This is not localized, it is global, total.

The scene expands to the heavens. Angels enforce divine judgment as commanded. Even the celestial bodies tremble, emphasizing the scale of what unfolds. All humanity witnesses it, but the sinners receive a direct curse, with no possibility of joy or escape.

In contrast, the righteous are reassured. The phrase "take courage" confirms that their fate is secure. Both the righteous and the pious are acknowledged, affirming that divine justice will not forget them.

Despite this promise, the next verses acknowledge the sorrow of the righteous in death. They did not receive their reward in life. Their time on earth was spent under the rule of sinners, which explains the injustice they endured. But that injustice has been recorded, and it will not stand.

The sinners' voices now take center stage, filled with mockery and contempt. They see no benefit in righteousness, no reward in holiness. The phrase "died according to fate" expresses their cynical view that the righteous died just as they did, making no distinction between holiness and sin.

Their taunts continue. The phrase "they died just like us" denies divine protection or any afterlife reward. The mention of sorrow and darkness intensifies their mockery, insinuating that suffering is all the righteous gain.

They scorn the idea of resurrection entirely. "Let them rise," they say, mocking the dead. They live in luxury and joy, while the righteous remain forgotten in the grave. This is a reversal of values, where corruption appears triumphant.

The sinners justify their actions. Seizing, sinning, and stealing are, in their eyes, the path to prosperity. Their words make it clear: they have rejected righteousness entirely in favor of material gain.

But the final verses reverse the illusion. Those who claimed to be righteous are exposed. The question "what became of their destruction?" confirms they did not escape judgment. No righteousness was found in them, and their ruin was complete.

The chapter ends with the total erasure of the wicked. They vanish from memory, as though they never existed. Their souls descend into Hades in suffering, and though the final line is damaged or incomplete, the meaning is unambiguous: this is final judgment, and it is irreversible.

Chapter 103

Chapter 103 is corroborated by a multitude of manuscripts, including 7QEnoch from the DSS in Koine Greek and the Codex Bodleianus (CB). Opening with a solemn oath, invoking the greatness of divine splendor to emphasize the authority behind the message. The repetition of "I swear to you" signals that what follows is unquestionably true and binding.

Enoch affirms his access to the tablets of heaven, where divine decrees are recorded. These are not mere writings, they are permanent, engraved records of events that cannot be changed. The decree of reward for the dead is part of this celestial archive, already prepared and recorded. The Greek (CB 185) adds the word "righteous", but the Dead Sea Scrolls (7QEnoch) confirm only "of the dead," proving that the original was more inclusive and later scribes narrowed its meaning.

The righteous are promised eternal endurance. Their spirits will not perish, and their remembrance is preserved forever before the Great One. This legacy spans all generations of the ages, confirming a continuous divine memory. The command "do not fear" rebukes any belief that the wicked can erase or override what is divinely upheld.

The wicked, meanwhile, speak in delusion. They boast, saying "Blessed are the sinners," believing that earthly pleasure and success prove favor. But their boast is hollow. Their focus is entirely temporal, ignoring the judgment that awaits them.

Enoch confirms that the wicked died without facing judgment in life. The delay in their punishment is not an oversight, rather, it is a divine plan. Their reckoning will come, but not when they expected.

A direct warning follows: the wicked know their fate. They are not ignorant; they persist in defiance. The reference to Hades confirms that their souls are destined for eternal descent, a descent they cannot escape.

The text describes their final fate in vivid terms: distress, darkness, and fire. Their torment is eternal, not symbolic or temporary. The phrase "your souls in all the generations of eternity" confirms the permanence of their sentence. The closing "woe to you" seals their fate—there will be no joy for them again.

The voice then shifts to the righteous, warning them not to say their suffering was in vain. Their exhaustion, pain, and lack of justice are real, but they must not lose hope.

Enoch acknowledges the depth of the righteous suffering. They felt crushed, abandoned, and unheard, yet he affirms that their cries have not gone unnoticed.

The righteous were consumed by sinners, oppressed without reward, and treated unjustly at every turn. They were pierced, surrounded, desperate, and their search for salvation went unanswered.

Even their pleas were ignored. The wicked refused to listen, rejected their cries, and hardened their hearts.

The final condemnation is reserved for those who sided with the oppressors. The righteous were murdered and forgotten, while the sins of the wicked remained unpunished and unchallenged.

Chapter 104

Chapter 104 opens with a promise to the righteous: they are not forgotten. The angels remember them before the Great One, ensuring their names remain in divine memory and judgment will favor them.

The righteous are urged to endure, even amid suffering. A time will come when they will shine like the lights of heaven, and divine favor will be revealed. This passage confirms that their affliction is not eternal, but their reward will be.

Their cries will be heard, and justice will follow. The oppression they endured will not go unanswered. Judgment is assured against those who wronged them.

A command for perseverance follows. The righteous are told they will share in the joy of celestial beings, "like the joy of the angels of the heavens." This image makes clear their integration into the divine order, and the phrase "do not abandon your hope" confirms that steadfastness is the key to enduring trials.

A division is then made clear: the righteous will not be judged with the sinners. The word "plundered" speaks to the devastation awaiting the wicked, while "eternal judgment," proves this separation is final.

The righteous are warned not to be discouraged by the temporary success of sinners. The command "do not become their associates" is a rejection of compromise. Instead, they must keep far from injustice, no matter how appealing sin may appear.

Sinners are warned that their sins will be sought out. Time will not erase wrongdoing. Nothing is forgotten.

A galactic system of accountability is introduced: light and darkness, day and night, observe all sin. These are perpetual witnesses, ensuring that no evil escapes the divine record.

The chapter condemns deceit, falsehood, and distortion of truth. "Do not alter the words of truth" rebukes those who manipulate divine teachings, while "do not deny the words of the holy one" foretells the warning. A fragmented scroll with interpolation includes idolatry or lying.

A sharper warning follows: some have rewritten the truth, leading many astray. The verse condemns those who "fabricate great falsehoods" and "inscribe the writings upon their own names." This is a clear denunciation of those who falsely claim authorship over sacred texts, replacing Enoch's voice with their own.

A plea is then made to preserve the truth. The instruction "neither remove nor alter these words" is absolute. The command to "write all in truth" confirms the sacred responsibility of transmission.

The chapter concludes with a second mystery: Enoch's writings are meant for the righteous, the holy, and the wise. The phrase "for the joy of truth" shows that these books are intended to restore understanding, especially after so much distortion.

The righteous will receive these books and believe them. They will rejoice and exult, not only in the recovery of truth but also in the wisdom and clarity these writings bring. The final purpose is established: "to learn from them all the ways of truth."

Chapter 105

Chapter 105 is brief but definitive. It commands the righteous to call all humanity to truth and to act as witnesses of divine knowledge. The phrase, "*you are their guides*" declares they are not just observers but appointed *guides*, responsible for helping others walk in wisdom.

Enoch uses, "Children of Adam," a true Enochian term for humanity. The phrase 'The Lord' appears here, but the sentence retains its integrity without it, further confirming it as a later insertion.

The reward for this role is spiritual and it is "great upon the earth." The promise is given that those who lead in truth and righteousness will receive both truth and peace: in the *valley of righteousness*. A significant location that has ties to the *Garden of Eden*.

Chapter 106

Chapter 106 marks a dramatic shift, introducing a child of extraordinary, non-human origin, born during a time when righteousness was greatly diminished. The lineage from Methuselah to Lamech is established, grounding this event in history, while also signaling a disruption in the natural order.

The child's appearance is unlike anything human: his skin is white and red, his hair is wool-like and curly, and his eyes shine like the sun. This radiance is not metaphorical, signaling celestial or hybrid origin. His ability to speak and bless immediately after birth proves that this being is not mortal.

Though the phrase "blessing the Lord of the Ages" appears, it reflects later theological interpolation. The behavior and appearance described are not human, and the narrative confirms this.

Lamech is horrified by his son's nature. His terror and retreat confirm that this child is perceived as a divine anomaly or a potential threat. He flees to Methuselah, convinced the child is not his and may be angelic.

Lamech declares the child must be from the angels, articulating that the celestial features are undeniable. He expresses fear for what this child might bring into the world and urgently demands an answer. He begs Methuselah to find Enoch and ask for divine guidance.

Methuselah travels to the ends of the earth and pleads with Enoch to return with him. Enoch greets him warmly, confirming the bond between them. Enoch acknowledges the urgency and listens to Methuselah's request.

Enoch affirms that the child is not ordinary, but that he has seen another like him before. He connects this birth to a renewal of divine ordinance, referencing the generation of Jared, when the Watchers broke the heavenly covenant by taking human wives.

The offspring of the Watchers were fully flesh, not spirits. This child fits that same pattern: born of woman, but marked by divine radiance, linking him to the legacy of the Watchers' defiance.

Enoch reveals that a great flood is coming, a year-long destruction brought by divine wrath to purge the corruption of the earth. However, this child and three of his sons will survive while the rest of humanity perishes.

This child is not only a survivor, he is the instrument of peace. He will be the one through whom the earth is cleansed. Enoch instructs Lamech to accept the child and recognize his righteousness. Though the name "Noah" appears, it may be a later addition; other cultures record different names for the survivor of the Flood.

The chapter concludes with Enoch reading from the tablets of heaven, confirming that this revelation is not speculative. It is part of the divine archive. Enoch's role as the scribe of judgment and restoration is reaffirmed.

Chapter 107

Chapter 107 concludes the birth narrative introduced in Chapter 106, anchoring the child's identity within a prophetic framework. It opens with a sweeping statement: each generation will grow more wicked, until a righteous generation finally arises. When that moment comes, wickedness will be destroyed, sin will be removed, and goodness will return to the earth. This is not a new revelation. It was already written in the prophetic records, stating the inevitability of this transformation.

Lamech receives reassurance: the child is truly his, despite his supernatural appearance. The urgency of the message confirms the importance of accepting the child's role in the coming restoration.

Enoch gives Methuselah a secret revelation, identifying the child as Noah, naming him as the one through whom joy will come to the earth in the midst of its destruction. His name becomes synonymous with restoration and survival, closing the vision with hope beyond the judgment.

Chapter 108

Chapter 108 opens as a second book of Enoch, written for Methuselah and future generations. However, the introductory framing is a later interpolation, attempting to insert legalistic structure and a new literary division. Enoch resumes speaking in the first person, continuing his prophetic voice uninterrupted.

The guilty are warned to wait for their appointed judgment. All evildoers will be destroyed, and the strength of the wicked will be taken away, confirming that justice is not delayed, it is fixed on a divine timeline.

The wicked are erased from the records of the holy ones. Their lineage is cut off, and their souls are destined for destruction. Their end is in fire and desolation, not only physical but eternal.

Enoch describes a deep place of burning fire, surrounded by bright, moving mountains, certainly not the heavens. Instead, it is a location of intense suffering, filled with cries, weeping, and torment.

A holy angel explains that this is where the souls of sinners, criminals, and deceivers will be sent. Among them are those who deliberately alter the words of the prophets, a direct condemnation of scribal corruption. This brings home the earlier warnings about those who forge or distort sacred writings.

The next verses are interpolations, easily identified by theological shifts in language and focus. The use of "Elohim," a plural term foreign to Enoch's vocabulary, reflecting post-Enochian theological insertions. Enoch consistently refers to titles like "Head of Days" or "Ancient of Days," never "Elohim" or "the Lord" in this form.

The inserted verses emphasize martyrdom, asceticism, and rejection of wealth, themes absent from the original Enochic tradition. Phrases like "giving their flesh to be trampled" and "rejoicing in suffering" align with Second Temple and early Christian concepts, not with Enoch's galactic vision of justice.

Dualistic imagery begins to dominate: "dwelling of light" vs. darkness, and language about shining forever. These are lifted from *Daniel* 12:3 and later mystical traditions, not the apocalyptic warnings of Enoch's earlier messages.

The focus shifts from justice to worship, another break from Enoch's themes. Statements like "those who love my holy name" introduce devotional language that contrasts with the original emphasis on obedience, judgment, and truth.

Phrases like "he will give faith to the faithful" and "according to their faith" contradict Enoch's view of righteousness, rooted in justice and order not belief or devotion. The chapter ends with a mystical vision of light, thrones, and inscriptions. The elements that are foreign to early Enoch and drawn from later apocalyptic rewrites.

Appendix B
Overview of the Source Manuscripts

This translation is based on a strict hierarchy of manuscript authority: Aramaic Dead Sea Scrolls (DSS), then Greek, then Ge'ez (Ethiopic), and finally Latin—used only for limited comparison. This structure ensures that the earliest and most authentic readings are prioritized, and all later distortions are exposed.

Aramaic Dead Sea Scrolls (Qumran, Cave 4 and Cave 2)
The Aramaic fragments represent the oldest surviving versions of the Book of Enoch, dating between 150–300 BCE. These include:
 - 4Q201–4Q212, 4Q247 (Cave 4)
 - Unpublished Cave 2 fragments, accessed via www.deadseascrolls.org.il

These sources form the absolute foundation of the restored text. Where Aramaic survives, it is used without alteration or assumption. These sections are marked in bold italics, indicating their priority as original language fragments.

Greek Fragments – Confirmatory and Supplementary
Greek sources are used only when Aramaic is missing. Though fragmentary, the Greek texts are centuries older than the Ge'ez and often preserve phrasing that predates theological tampering. These include:

 - Gizeh 1 (Codex Panopolitanus) – Chapters up to 72, with overlaps in Chapter 77
 - Gizeh 2 – Chapters 19–21
 - POxy 2069 (Oxyrhynchus Papyrus) – Chapters 77, 85–87
 - Vaticanus 1809 (V1809) – Chapter 89:42–49
 - Syncellus (Byzantine Chronicle) – Chapter 97
 - CB 185 (Codex Bodleianus 185) – Chapters 97–107
 - 7QEnoch (Cave 7, DSS) – Chapter 103

Greek sections are marked in bold when they stand alone. When a Greek phrase aligns with Aramaic or reconstructed Hebrew, it appears in bold italics. Greek is never bracketed unless it is clearly a later addition or does not match the surrounding text.

Ge'ez (Ethiopic P, Rylands 23) – Used Only When Nothing Else Exists

The Ge'ez manuscripts, while the most complete, are also the latest and most redacted (~1400 CE). They are used only when no Aramaic or Greek source survives. All Ge'ez-derived sections are left unbolded to reflect their lower authority.

When Ge'ez aligns with Greek, it is marked in bold. When Ge'ez aligns with Hebrew–Greek reconstructions, it appears in bold italics.

Goldschmidt's 1892 Hebrew Edition

The reconstructed Hebrew edition by Lazarus Goldschmidt is used for Chapters 72–108, but only where no Aramaic, Greek, or reliable Ge'ez survives. These sections appear in unbolded italics, maintaining a clear visual distinction from all other sources.

Latin Fragments – Untrusted and Used for Exposure Only

The Latin (BL) fragments, such as those appearing in Chapters 99 and 106, are used only to identify distortions introduced by later theological editors. They are never used for restoration unless the corruption itself needs to be documented. These sources are not marked in the body of the text but are referenced in the appendix where relevant.

Formatting Notes

(Parentheses) indicate minor additions.

Greyed text throughout the translation indicates author reconstructions where clarity was needed but no manuscript survives.

All scribal interpolations are clearly marked in [brackets] to distinguish them from the original text.

Bold italics mark Aramaic DSS.

Bold marks Greek and Ge'ez comparisons, and Greek alone.

Ge'ez alone remains unbolded.

Goldschmidt's 1892 Hebrew is in unbolded italics.

Bold italics are also used for Hebrew–Greek comparisons.

Appendix B: Source Manuscripts

Historical Origins, Contents, and Current Locations

What follows is a catalogue of the manuscripts, scrolls, and codices that brought this edition of the Book of Enoch to life. Each entry outlines its origin, contents, location, and the role it played in uncovering the original voice of Enoch that was buried beneath centuries of distortion.

Aramaic Dead Sea Scrolls (Qumran, Cave 4 and Cave 2)
Date: ~150–300 BCE
Language: Aramaic
Scrolls: 4Q201–4Q212, 4Q247 (Cave 4); unpublished Cave 2 fragments
Discovered: 1947–1956, Qumran Caves near the Dead Sea
Current Location: Shrine of the Book (Israel Museum, Jerusalem); additional fragments remain unpublished in institutional archives.
Contents:
- The Book of the Watchers (Chapters 1–36)
- The Astronomical Book (Chapters 72–82)
- The Book of Dream Visions (Chapters 83–90)
- The Epistle of Enoch (Chapters 91–105)

Notes:
These are the earliest and most reliable sources for reconstructing Enoch. They preserve the original Aramaic language and reflect a pre-theological, pre-sectarian version of the text.

Gizeh Codices (Codex Panopolitanus: Gizeh 1 and Gizeh 2)
Date: ~300 CE
Language: Greek
Manuscripts: Codex Panopolitanus (Gizeh 1), Gizeh 2
Discovered: Akhmim (ancient Panopolis), Egypt in the late 19th century
Current Location: Cairo Museum
Contents:
- The Book of the Watchers
- The Book of Parables (partial)
- The Epistle of Enoch (partial)
- Chapters 19–21
- Part of Chapter 77

Notes:
These Greek manuscripts predate the Ge'ez and help restore lost or softened passages. Gizeh 2 preserves Chapters 19–21, detailing the heavenly prison and fiery judgment, scenes heavily redacted in later versions. Together, they retain harsher judgments, cosmic geography, and direct language aligned with the Aramaic worldview.

POxy 2069 (Oxyrhynchus Papyrus)

Date: ~200 CE
Language: Greek
Manuscript: Papyrus Oxyrhynchus 2069
Discovered: Oxyrhynchus, Egypt (late 19th century)
Current Location: Sackler Library, Oxford
Contents:
- Chapter 77
- Chapters 85, 86, 87

Notes:
Preserves key material from the Dream Vision section. POxy retains symbolic imagery and raw descriptions that Geʿez tends to smooth or omit.

CB 185 (Codex Bodleianus 185)

Date: ~6th–9th century CE
Language: Greek
Manuscript: Codex Bodleianus 185
Discovered: Unknown origin
Current Location: Bodleian Library, Oxford University
Contents:
- Chapters 97–107
- Overlaps with Chapter 99 and 106
- Partial alignment with Chapter 103 (7QEnoch)

Notes:
Preserves original phrasing and prophecies lost in Geʿez. Includes the "King of all ages" and 120-year lifespan passages, evidence of pre-canonical doctrine.

Syncellus (Byzantine Chronicle)

Date: ~800 CE (compiled)
Language: Greek
Author: George Syncellus
Current Location: Preserved in Byzantine monastic and academic archives
Contents:
- Fragments from Chapters 1–16
- Direct commentary on Chapter 97

Notes:
Syncellus preserves quotations from older Greek manuscripts now lost. Useful for confirming or challenging Geʿez text where no Aramaic remains.

Appendix B: Source Manuscripts

Vaticanus 1809 (V1809)

Date: ~9th–11th century CE
Language: Greek
Manuscript: Codex Vaticanus Graecus 1809
Discovered: Vatican Library holdings
Current Location: Vatican Library, Rome
Contents:
- Chapter 89: verses 42–49

Notes:
Preserves a controversial block of Dream Vision content. Shows divergence from Ethiopic tradition and helps identify post-Enochic insertions.

7QEnoch (Cave 7, Dead Sea Scrolls)

Date: ~1st century BCE
Language: Greek
Manuscript: 7QEnoch (also labeled 7QEnoch 1)
Discovered: Cave 7, Qumran site, Dead Sea Scrolls
Current Location: Israel Antiquities Authority, with fragments curated by the Israel Museum
Contents:
- Fragment of Chapter 103

Notes:
This rare Greek fragment from Qumran is significant because it confirms the transmission of 1 Enoch in both Aramaic and Greek during the Second Temple period. Its presence supports the authenticity of Chapter 103 and ties it directly to pre-Christian Jewish traditions.

Ge'ez (Ethiopic P, Rylands 23)

Date: ~1400 CE (manuscript), based on older translations from 4th–6th century CE
Language: Ge'ez (Classical Ethiopic)
Manuscript: Ethiopic P, Rylands 23
Discovered: Preserved in the Ethiopian Orthodox Church; Rylands 23 is one of the earliest collected copies
Current Location: John Rylands Library, University of Manchester
Contents:
- The only complete version of the Book of Enoch (Chapters 1–108)

Notes:
Though it preserves the full text, Ge'ez is theologically redacted and includes later doctrinal insertions. It is only used in this translation when no Aramaic or Greek survives.

Goldschmidt's 1892 Hebrew Edition

Date: 1892 CE
Language: Hebrew (reconstructed)
Editor: Lazarus Goldschmidt
Current Location: Widely available in print and digital academic collections
Contents:

* Chapters 72–108

Notes:

Goldschmidt's edition is used only where no Aramaic, Greek, or reliable Geʻez source survives. Unlike many of his contemporaries, he approached the text as a scholar, not a theologian. His translation from Geʻez into Hebrew was independent, avoiding the biases and smoothing tendencies found in the works of Charles and Dillmann. While he acknowledged their contributions, he neither relied on nor incorporated their interpretations. Instead, he preserved the raw structure and linguistic character of the text, resisting the urge to harmonize difficult passages.

Latin (British Library Fragment)

Date: ~8th–9th century CE
Language: Latin
Manuscript: Latin BL Fragment (British Library)
Discovered: Part of a late transmission tradition in Western Europe
Current Location: British Library, London
Contents:

* Fragmentary material from Chapters 99 and 106

Notes:

The Latin fragment of 1 Enoch appears in British Library MS Royal 5 E XIII, a 9th-century Breton manuscript rediscovered by M. R. James in 1893. He found it misfiled among Christian writings, listed only as a vague "Prophecy of Enoch concerning the Flood." It preserves part of Chapter 106, where Enoch confirms Noah's destiny and foretells the coming Flood. This is the only known Latin manuscript containing a full narrative section of Enoch, offering rare evidence of its presence in the Latin West.

Based on Greek, the Latin is abbreviated, paraphrased, and shaped by Christian theology. Key scenes are condensed, and details found in Greek and Ethiopic are missing. The text likely served as moral instruction, framed to support themes of divine punishment and repentance. While not used for restoration, it stands as proof of how Enoch's voice was preserved, altered, and nearly forgotten in medieval Europe.

Appendix B: Source Manuscripts

Manuscript Differences & Translation Choices

The Book of Enoch is a survivor. Its path through history is littered with broken fragments, buried scrolls, theological edits, and mistranslations so severe they obscure the original voice entirely. This edition restores that voice by prioritizing the oldest and most reliable witnesses: the Aramaic Dead Sea Scrolls, followed by Greek fragments, then Ge'ez (Ethiopic P, Rylands 23), and lastly the Latin fragment—used only to expose corruption, never for reconstruction. Every choice in this restoration is deliberate. There are no assumptions, no smoothing, and no theological reinterpretation. Where the text is missing, it remains missing. Where interpolations have occurred, they are exposed and bracketed. This is not a rewrite—it is a restoration.

The most catastrophic damage to Enoch's legacy came not from age or decay, but from translators like R. H. Charles, whose widely circulated English edition of 1 Enoch continues to distort public understanding of the text. Charles restructured chapters, inserted theological language, and "harmonized" difficult passages—flattening the apocalyptic power of Enoch's voice into a tidy framework that fit 19th-century Anglican expectations. He worked without access to the Codex Bodleianus 185, which is his only defense, but his decision to rearrange entire sections of the book, alter phrasing to match canonical sensibilities, and smooth over divine names is a grave violation of the text's integrity. His errors misled not just readers but generations of scholars. The ripple effects of his tampering still poison commentary and doctrine to this day.

Dillmann, while more careful, still fell prey to theological bias, relying heavily on the Ge'ez and treating it as fixed, despite its known redactions. His work laid the groundwork for later scholars to treat Ge'ez as "complete," despite clear evidence of alteration. Ge'ez was translated from Greek, which in turn came from Aramaic—and each step in that chain filtered Enoch through theological lenses that reflected the agendas of their age. Key phrases were deleted, replaced, or overwritten. Divine titles were normalized. Apocalyptic warnings were softened or rephrased into moral exhortations. Even the Zadokite community (Damascus Document)—which revered Enoch and preserved echoes of his words—was buried under centuries of canonical suppression. The rediscovery of Enoch fragments among the Dead Sea Scrolls confirmed what had long been suspected: Enoch was not a theological curiosity; he was the foundation of a rival tradition deliberately erased from history.

Lazarus Goldschmidt (1871-1950) was a German scholar and linguist, best known for his first complete German translation of the Babylonian Talmud. Unlike Charles or Dillmann, he worked independently, refusing to smooth or rewrite difficult passages. His 1892 Hebrew edition of 1 *Enoch* preserved the text without theological bias, treating the Ge'ez with caution rather than authority. His commitment to accuracy is why his work is used only when Aramaic and Greek are lost. Every restored line in this edition stands as a rebuke to distortion, and every bracket is a scar left by centuries of tampering.

Scribes, Redactors, and the Hands That Rewrote Enoch

Biblical scholars have long known the Torah was composed by multiple sources—J (Jahwist), E (Elohist), D (Deuteronomist), and P (Priestly)—each with its own style, theology, and agenda. But what few acknowledge is this: their red pens reached far beyond *Genesis*, *Exodus*, and *Deuteronomy*. They reached into *Enoch*. They cut. They rearranged. They overwrote the voice of the antediluvian prophet. And in doing so, they exposed themselves.

The J scribe (c. 950-850 BCE) wrote vivid stories with personal, walking gods—intimate, earthy, southern. The E source (850-750 BCE) echoed northern kingdoms, dreamers, angels, and celestial messengers. D (650-500 BCE) was a firebrand—the preacher of covenant punishment and legal reform. P (600-500 BCE) was the ultimate systematizer, obsessed with order, rituals, cosmic frameworks, and divine transcendence. These were not mere recorders of tradition. They were architects of theology, bending ancient voices to fit new paradigms.

And their fingerprints are all over Enoch.

In the process of restoration, these cracks revealed themselves. Chapter 93 was gutted and replaced with orderly chronology. Chapter 97 was recast as moral lament instead of prophetic curse. Chapter 98 imposed a cosmic ledger, reducing divine mystery to courtroom determinism. These were not accidents. These were redactions.

Worse still, the interpolators that followed—labeled here as "xyz"—left pious debris across the text: theological buzzwords, singular gods where there had been many, and phrases like "Lord of all creation" and "Adonai" that do not belong to Enoch's world.

Appendix C: Angelic Names

The early chapters are especially targeted, softened, corrupted—only to leave the middle mostly intact, then return at the end with heavy theological insertions to force closure. And yet, somehow, the original voice still rises between the lines. A whisper behind the veil. A name that cannot be unspoken.

This is not merely about phrasing or word choice. It is about timelines. It is about power. The Book of Enoch operates from a 364-day solar calendar—precise, cosmic, anchored in creation itself. This calendar, known from Enoch and the Qumran scrolls, was still in use during the First Temple period. But it was overthrown during the Second Temple era, replaced by the lunar calendar of the priestly elite. The shift was not practical—it was political. A conquest of time. And with it, the *Book of Enoch* was pushed into silence.

But in the silence, the truth remained. The solar calendar that Enoch preserved—rejected by the redactors and branded heretical by later scribes—outlived them all. Our modern reckoning of time, structured in solar years, hews closer to Enoch's vision than to theirs. The very rhythm of the world bears his signature.

They tried to erase him. They replaced his gods, rewrote his visions, and overturned his calendar. But Enoch endured. And time itself remembers him.

Appendix C
Angelic Names & the Ones Who Walk Among Us

The Book of Enoch is a record of names—radiant, ruinous, and remembered. These aren't mere titles. Each name carries a role, a mission, a betrayal, or a secret—and many were altered, erased, or hidden over time. This index gathers the complete registry of celestial beings found in the oldest manuscripts, from the loyal archangels to the corrupted Watchers, their oaths, and their lasting impact on the world of men.

The Unnamed 180

Verses 47–226 describe 200 descended angels. Only a few are named. The remaining 180 were erased, hidden, or lost. They are the fathers of the Nephilim and builders of early civilization. This is not mythology. This is a ledger of real beings, the record proves:

They walked among us.

278

The seven holy archangels (Enoch 20)

Michael (מיכאל) "*Who is like God?*" – Archangel of war and righteousness. Oversees the best part of humanity. Never takes human form but appears as a prince in Daniel. The great celestial warrior, Azazel's mirror opposite.

Raphael (רפאל) "*God heals*" – Healer, binder of Azazel, protector of the Tree of Life. In Tobit, disguises himself as a man named Azariah, proving angels walk among humans.

Gabriel (גבריאל) "*Strength of God*" – Oversees Paradise, serpents, and cherubim. Bringer of visions and enforcer of justice. Later sanitized into a herald. Originally a being of thunder and terror.

Uriel (אוריאל) "*Light of God*" – Reveals secrets of heaven and hell, stars, and underworld. Cartographer of the celestial realms. Can be identified as the most active angel in earthly affairs.

Raguel (ראגואל / רגואל) "*Friend of God*" – Takes vengeance on celestial disorder. Can be identified as the same Raguel who appears as Sarah's father in Tobit, confirming a Watcher who walked among men.

Sariel / Saraqael / Suriel (שריאל) "*Command of God*" – Oversees judgment of fallen spirits. Fragmented identity: some versions call him holy, others fallen. This is one being rewritten into two. (Also appears in the fallen registry, confirming redaction or a divided legacy.)

Remiel (רעמיאל) "*Thunder/mercy of God*" – Oversees resurrection and souls of the dead. Can be identified as a bridge between this world and the next. Later erased due to dangerous associations.

Angels of the stars and seasons (Enoch 82)

Adnarel (אדנראל) / Adnar'el (אדנאראל) "*Fire of God*" – Watches stars and seasons. Can be identified as having been altered into Adonai. Represents an early celestial power stripped of identity.

Yehoshua'el (יהושואל) "*God saves*" – Listed in 82:14. Name predates Joshua and Jesus, confirming retroactive appropriation by later traditions.

Yehuda'el (יהודאל) – *"Praise of God"* Appears in 82:13. One of three who lead the days and guard the four seasons. Name reflects divine praise and celestial order.

Yofiel (יופיאל) – *"Beauty of God"* Appears in 82:13. Appears in 82:13. One of the three "who lead the days." Represents celestial harmony, aesthetic order, and guardianship of appointed times.

Barqel (ברקאל) Beraqī'ēl *"Lightning of God"* –Appears in 82:17 and Enoch 6:7. One of the 20 chiefs of the Watchers. Taught astrology. Was worshipped as a sky-god in antediluvian societies.

Elimelech (אלימלך) *"My God is king"* – Human figure in Ruth, but his sudden placement in a royal bloodline confirms a celestial interloper.

Mahalal'el (מהללאל) *"Praise of God"* – Enoch's grandfather. Was a celestial being who took human form to pass down light through genealogy.

Elisaf / Elisael (אליסף) *"God has added"* – Appears in 82:17. Was added after the celestial hierarchy was formed. A second-generation Watcher.

The twenty chief Watchers (Enoch 6–7, 69)

Shemihazah / Semjaza (שמחזא) – *"Renowned name."* Leader of the rebellion. Made the pact on Mount Hermon. Was deified by early humans.

Azazel (עזאזל) – *"Scapegoat of God."* Taught warfare, cosmetics, sorcery. Bound in Dudael. Became source of destruction. Later distorted into a desert demon. alternate spelling Azāz'ēl appears in 69:2.

Armaros (ארמרוס) – *"Cursed one."* Bound one. Name confirms he was doomed from the start. **Armen** – Variant of Armaros. Armrəs in 69:2.

Batar'el (בתראל) – *"Rain of God."* Governed agricultural calendars and climate rituals. Also spelled Baṭaryāl.

Turel / Tur'el (טוראל) – *"Mountain of God."* Symbol of anchored knowledge. A pillar or foundation deity in ancient myth. Ṭurya'ēl also. Ṭuma'ēl, Ṭar'ēl.

Chazaqiel (חזקיאל) "*Cloud of God*" – Taught meteorology and signs of the skies. Connected to storm-watching and weather magic.

Kokabiel (כוכביאל) – "Star of God." Taught astrology. Distorted heavenly knowledge into corrupted celestial worship.

Shamsiel (שמשיאל) – "Sun of God." Taught signs of the sun. Linked to ancient solar priesthoods. Also spelled Simaṭīsē'ēl.

Sariel (שריאל) – (See above)

Daniel (דניאל) – "God is my judge." Taught laws and judgments. Origin of ancestor cults. Also appears as Dāni'ēl in 69:2. Variant form may distinguish him from the prophet of canon.

Arakiel / Arakiba (ערכיאל) – "Earth of God." Taught geomancy. Involved in construction of megalithic structures.

Amezarak (אמצראק) – "Strong earthbound one." Taught magic, root-cutting, spells. Source of pharmakeia and enchantment.

Penemue (פנמוא) – "Inner knowledge." Taught writing and deception. Dual role: wisdom and lies.

Asael (עשאל) – "Created by God." Often confused with Azazel. Taught metallurgy and adornment.

Tamiel (תמיאל) – "Perfection of God." Taught astronomy and signs. Split into two identities.

Rameel / Ramiel (רעמיאל) – Same name as holy Remiel. Recontextualized or split after the fall.

Kesabel – Chief of the Oath. Led the pact of descent. A celestial contract-holder. Almost totally erased from later texts.

Additional named Watchers (Enoch 69 + variants)

Arstikifa – Chief of oathbreakers. Role unclear. Replaced by Kesabel in later texts.

Lekaḇa'ēl – "Taken of God." Was bound early.

Baṭaryāl – *"Divider of God" or "God's cleaver."* Fractured the firmament or wielded storm power.

Basas'ēl – *"Trampler of God" or "Defiler."* Name confirms ritual violation or corruption of the sacred.

Anan'ēl – *"Cloud of God."* A meteorological being or veil-caster.

Simaṭīsē'ēl – *"Sign of God" or "Destiny of God."* Taught hidden forces or manipulated fate.

Nuqa'ēl – *"Silent of God."* Role erased. Remained hidden.

Yitər'ēl – *"Excellence of God."* Vied for leadership. Believed himself superior.

Ṭuma'ēl – *"Impurity of God."* Defiled Enoch's record or corrupted knowledge meant for the righteous.

Ṭar'ēl – *"Search of God."* A spy, scout, or rogue wanderer among the fallen.

Ruma'ēl – *"Highness of God."* Viewed himself above the others. Refused to submit.

Rumyāl – "Exalted of God" or "Cast Out."

Izēzē'ēl – *Echo of Azazel.* A twin figure, shadow fragment, or splintered identity.

THE FIVE WHO TAUGHT FORBIDDEN KNOWLEDGE

Asb'el – Corrupted the lesser angels. Gave evil counsel and led them into defilement with the daughters of men.

Gader'el – Led Eve astray. Taught warfare, weaponry, and death to humanity. Direct parallel to the serpent figure.

Kasdeja (Kasyadea) – Revealed abortion, soul-cutting, and womb rituals. Possibly birthed from a hybrid entity named Taba'eth.

Penemue (פְּנֵמוּאֵל) – Revealed bitter knowledge, writing, ink, and parchment. Caused humanity to stray by deception and learning. Dual-natured: wisdom and ruin in one.

Shemihazah (relisted here) – Chief of the Watchers. His transgression is retold in this section to emphasize that he was first, and his influence caused all others to follow.

Other figures & possible hybrids

Beqa (בקע) – *"Cleft / divide."* Symbolic name for the rift caused by the rebellion.

Remashel (רמשאל) – *"Thunderclap of God."* Appears in rare versions.

Samsapeel (שמשפאל) – "Brightness of God." Solar-associated being.

Hilujaseph (חילוגסף) – *Unknown origin.* A Nephilim hybrid or post-rebellion fusion.

Appendix D
The ark: tevah or coracle?

The traditional image of Noah's ark, a long wooden boat with a house on top, is a product of Renaissance imagination, not ancient texts. The Book of Enoch, when examined alongside Sumerian and Akkadian flood records, tells a different story. The word tevah (תֵּבָה) used in Hebrew does not mean "boat" or "ship." It means box, container, or vessel, a sealed structure designed to float, not sail.

The Hebrew word tevah appears only twice in scripture: once to describe Noah's ark, and once for the basket that carried the infant Moses through the Nile. Both were vessels of destiny, not ships but sealed cocoons of survival, drifting through flood and empire alike. The message is clear: a tevah is not meant to steer, it is meant to preserve what must endure.

In the Sumerian flood account, the ark of Ziusudra (or Utnapishtim) is described as a perfect cube, equal in height, width, and length. Babylonian records recovered and translated by Dr. Irving Finkle confirm that this vessel was essentially a giant coracle: a round, tub-like boat used in ancient Mesopotamia, made of reeds and waterproofed with bitumen. The idea was simple: survive, not navigate. The flood wasn't a journey, it was a planetary reset.

In Chapter 89, Noah is described as crafting a "great box" and sitting inside it with three others. This vessel floats during the flood and later rests upon the land. There are no sails, no steering, only protection and preservation. The imagery aligns closely with the Mesopotamian tradition of the cube-like coracle, and the Hebrew tevah, meaning box or enclosure, not ship.

This challenges not only popular biblical art, but theological interpretations that assume Noah captained a boat. The ark is not a ship, it is a survival chamber. A celestial "black box" dropped into chaos. The fact that Mesopotamian records describe it the same way, and long before *Genesis* was compiled, indicates that the Enochian tradition preserves the older, more accurate memory.

In other words: Noah didn't sail. He drifted, sealed inside something not unlike a capsule. And that changes everything.

Appendix E
Ancient Aliens, Genetic Tampering, and the Technologies of the Watchers

Enoch says he was taken to a place where there was no firmament above him, a void where sky should be, and where fire moved in impossible patterns. The building he enters is unlike anything on Earth: walls of fire, flooring of crystal, portals of flame, and energy that moves but does not descend. This is not heaven in any traditional sense. Nowhere in the text does Enoch call it "heaven." It is a construct, a place built by those with unimaginable technology.

This is not a vision of the afterlife. It is an orbiting or dimensional structure. Enoch lacked the language for metal alloys, translucent flooring, plasma shielding, and energy fields. His descriptions match modern science! Depictions of deep space facilities, holographic, teleportation, and interdimensional gateways. This chamber of fire and crystal aligns with what Erik von Däniken described as "the throne room of the gods," a place where the divine were not ethereal spirits but beings who controlled technology Enoch could only perceive as fire and light.

In *Chariots of the Gods?*, von Däniken laid the groundwork asking whether the throne visions of Ezekiel and Enoch were actually descriptions of command modules, orbital stations, or otherworldly transport crafts. In later interviews, von Däniken compared Enoch's descriptions of "no sky" to leaving Earth's atmosphere, a recognition of being in space, weightless, with no horizon above.

And in the Ancient Aliens series, Giorgio A. Tsoukalos expanded on this, calling the fire that does not burn a possible "contained plasma field or artificial gravity chamber," a technology the Ancient Aliens may have mastered.

This building, surrounded by fire, light, crystal, and blinding energy, is not divine metaphor, it is engineered. And it may not be the only one. If these beings had the power to descend and alter Earth, they also had the power to establish base stations above or beyond it.

Desolate Realms, Dimensional Gates, and the Watchers' Infrastructure

In 1 Enoch 18:10–12, Enoch is taken to the far reaches of the world, where he witnesses a realm utterly alien to any known terrestrial experience. He writes: "*¹⁰ It is a place at the end of the great earth. There the heavens shall be completed. ¹¹ And I saw a great chasm into which columns of fire descended, and there was no measure, neither in height nor in depth. ¹² And beyond this chasm, I saw a place where there was no firmament of heaven above, nor was the earth established below, nor was there water beneath it, nor any bird. It was a desolate and terrifying place.*" This place is not symbolic. It is defined by what it lacks: no sky, no land, no water, no life. It is, by every description, a dimensional vacuum, a space between realms where natural laws do not operate. The "columns of fire" descending into an immeasurable abyss hint at physical forces or energy flows, possibly gravitational fields or plasma conduits, descending into a containment zone.

The account continues in 18:13–14: "*¹³ There I saw seven stars, like great burning mountains, that do not move. And when I inquired about them, they did not answer me. ¹⁴ The messenger said, 'This is the place at the end of heaven and earth. It has become a prison for the stars and the forces of heaven.'*" These "stars" are not celestial decorations they are living entities, locked in stasis, "like great burning mountains" that do not move. This place, defined by its artificial boundaries and its isolation, is not punishment in the traditional sense, it is containment. As the messenger says, this has become a prison, a controlled environment engineered to hold transgressing beings. Ancient Alien theorists such as Giorgio Tsoukalos have long proposed that the stars and "heavenly beings" in such texts are not metaphors, but literal extraterrestrial entities, whose confinement in off-world or extradimensional facilities matches what Enoch describes here.

In 18:15–16, the timeline becomes explicit: "*¹⁵ And the stars that roll in the fire—these are the ones who transgressed the command at the beginning of their rising. A place outside heaven is empty, for they did not appear at their appointed times. ¹⁶ And he was enraged with them and bound them until the time of the completion of their sins, for thousands of years.*" These beings disobeyed their instructions and violated the parameters of their appearance. Their punishment was not erasure but binding, held in a location "outside heaven," which implies a place detached from the designed celestial grid. The punishment is for "thousands of years," again implying measured containment rather than eternal condemnation. This is a system of quarantine, possibly to prevent further interference with Earth or the human genome.

Then in 1 Enoch 19:1, the messenger identifies who inhabits this place: "*¹ And Uriel said to me, 'Here the angels who mingled with women will stand, and their spirits, becoming diverse, will corrupt humans and lead them astray, urging them toward demons until the great judgment, in which they will be judged for destruction.'*" These are the same Watchers who descended to Earth and initiated the genetic corruption of humanity. Their spirits are "becoming diverse," implying either unstable manifestations or adaptive forms. This supports the idea that these beings have the ability to shift form, possess bodies, or manifest in ways that disrupt human order. And the line begins with "Here," marking this as a specific location, not a spiritual abstraction. Enoch is not receiving a parable. He is being taken on a physical reconnaissance of engineered prison zones.

Enoch continues his account in Chapter 33, where his journey brings him to the edge of the world. What he sees is not symbolic, but observational. He writes: "*¹ And from there I went to the boundary of the earth, and I saw there great beasts that were different from all others, and birds whose appearances, sizes, and voices were different from all. ² And beyond them, for all the beasts, I saw the boundary of the earth, where the sky ended and stretched over the vast expanse. ³ And I saw how the stars of heaven emerge and are divided according to their paths, and they move accordingly. And I wrote down all their exits, their names, their ranks, their positions, their times, and their cycles, as the angel Uriel explained them to me. ⁴ And everything was shown to me on the tablet, and I wrote and arranged their names, which were recorded on the tablet, along with their commands and their deeds.*" These verses do not describe religious prophecy or mystical language, they describe record-keeping. Enoch observes the sky ending over a vast expanse, then documents the exits and paths of the stars themselves. He is handed a tablet, implying physical storage, a data system, or viewing interface, and he is shown their positions, functions, and timing. This is a celestial map with engineering-level precision, not a symbolic vision, it describes a primitive astrolabe or star-chart.

In Chapter 34, Enoch's journey takes him further west. He writes: "[1] *And from there I went west, to the boundary of the earth, and there I saw a great and mighty assembly, which surrounded the entire boundary of the earth.* [2] *And there I saw the sky, with openings in the heavens, three from each direction, through which the winds emerge. From the direction of the west, they blow forth cold, hail, frost, heat, mist, and rain.* [3] *And from one cavern in the heavens, it will blow. And therefore, in all of them, they shall breathe. With power and great strength, it shall be established upon the earth. And with might, it will blow.*" These "openings in the heavens" are described as directional wind gates, each assigned function and output. The specificity of three gates per direction is consistent with engineered grid logic, not poetic symbolism. What Enoch calls "winds" may very well be elemental forces or energy flows managed through a planetary atmospheric control system. Ancient Alien theorists have long speculated that such repeated, directional weather systems, complete with assigned caverns and cycles; insinuates deliberate manipulation of climate or energy transfer.

Then, in Chapter 36:3–4, we are shown what may be the core power source beneath it all. Enoch writes: "[3] *From one direction, powerful winds pass through the stars of the heavens and disturb the west with force, whenever they appear.* [4] *And therefore, I saw them bless, and at all times I blessed the Lord of glory, who has made great wonders. And we praised him, because he reveals his glorious works to his angels and the souls of men, so that they may praise his deeds. And all his works shall be seen, so that they may glorify his mighty power and bless his great work forever.*" These "powerful winds" that pass through the stars and disturb the west do not behave like natural currents. They resemble high-energy fields, radiation bands, or electromagnetic streams that pass through star systems and ripple across the Earth. They are timed, directional, and have impact on global conditions. Enoch calls them "great wonders," but he also states they are to be seen, revealed, and praised, meaning they are observable phenomena, not hidden mysteries.

What Enoch describes is not a set of scattered visions, but a guided tour of infrastructure, from the void beyond the chasm to celestial prisons, star gates, elemental flows, and planetary wind systems. His use of terms like boundaries, caverns, exits, and gates point to systems of control, not chaos. Far from mystical heaven, this is engineered design. The Ancient Aliens hypothesis finds real footing here: Enoch saw structures, not symbols.

Appendix E: Ancient Aliens

The True Afnin [Ophanim]: Gimbal-Mounted Guardians of the Throne

In mainstream theology, the "ophanim" are best known from the Book of Ezekiel, where they are described as "wheels within wheels" covered in "eyes all around." This vision has been treated as mystical or symbolic, but it's a corrupted echo of a much older and clearer source found in Enoch's original account.

In this restored translation of 1 Enoch 71:5–8, there are no wheels and no riddles. The entities guarding the throne of glory are named directly: *Seraphiel, Cherubiel, and [Afnin]* "the faithful ones, those who do not sleep." These are not poetic images. They are functional sentries. Ezekiel may have witnessed the same structures, but misunderstood what he was looking at. If he saw "eyes," but didn't have the words to articulate "camera lenses" with multi-directional sensors built to observe and track. What he took for divine vision may have been an intelligent surveillance array, pivoting in all directions at once.

The Afnin's sleeplessness implies automation—not spiritual endurance, but mechanical precision. In modern terms, they resemble multi-axis gimbal-mounted sensor rigs: devices used on drones, spacecraft, and orbital defense platforms to maintain continuous visual and data input. These systems don't rest. They don't blink. They rotate and recalibrate in real time to track movement across every field of view.

A gimbal is a stabilizing device used to rotate and position mounted cameras or sensors across multiple axes. It keeps its mounted "eye" trained on its subject, even while the host system moves. It's the backbone of military tracking systems, drone optics, and autonomous visual AI. In that light, the Afnin appear less like angels, and more like sentient surveillance sentinels, placed to guard the threshold of divine power and ensure nothing enters, or escapes, undetected.

Where Ezekiel mystified, Enoch clarified. His throne room is not a place of worship, it's a command center. The Afnin are not worshipers. They are guardians of a protected zone, intelligent monitors built to detect, document, and secure. Not myth. Not metaphor. Mechanism.

The Afnin are not wheels.
They are the Watchers' Eyes—and they never stop watching.

Engineered Bloodlines and the Fall of the Long-Lived Kings

The ancient world did not evolve. It was triggered.

For hundreds of thousands of years, humans lived in biological stasis gathering, hunting, and surviving in tribal bands. Then, in a sudden flash approximately 10,000 to 12,000 years ago, everything changed. Agriculture emerged. Cities were built. Writing, astronomy, law codes, metallurgy, and complex calendars appeared nearly overnight. This was not the gradual curve of evolution. This was the result of intervention.

According to the Sumerian King List, the first rulers before the Flood reigned not for decades—but for tens of thousands of years each. Alulim of Eridu ruled for 28,800 years. En-men-lu-ana ruled for 43,200 years. Dumuzid reigned for 36,000. These lifespans are not myth—they are biological anomalies. They are the early results of the Watchers' genetic tampering, the same program mirrored in the Book of Enoch, where the patriarchs, from Adam to Methuselah, live between 895 and 969 years. These were not symbolic numbers. These were enhanced hybrids.

But the program failed. The hybrid offspring, violent, unstable, and insatiable, began to corrupt the earth. And so, a reset was initiated. In Enoch 97:4, the decree is given: "And their days shall be one hundred and twenty years." A lifespan limit. A genetic cap. The Watchers' engineering had gone too far, and it was now being forcibly shut down.

Noah's birth marks the end of the hybrid line and the beginning of the new one. In Enoch 106, his father Lamech becomes disturbed by the child's appearance. "And I suspect that he is not from me, but from an angel. And I fear him, lest something happens in his days on the earth." (106:6). Lamech isn't just afraid of the child, he's afraid of what the child signifies. Even he recognizes Noah's genetic code is unnatural, and that something catastrophic is coming. That catastrophe would be the Flood.

Noah's body shone. His eyes lit up the house. His appearance resembled the "sons of the angels." And yet, he was chosen to survive. This wasn't because he was normal. It was because he was the final experiment, the one hybrid that worked. In Enoch 107:3, the divine messenger confirms: "And this son who has been born to you, he will remain on the earth, and his three sons will be saved with him." Noah becomes the vessel through which the bloodline continues—but now, under control.

Appendix E: Ancient Aliens

This pattern of insemination, erased mothers, and the birth of hybrid saviors repeats throughout sacred history. Sarah, wife of Abraham, conceives long after her biological window has closed, following a visitation by heavenly beings. Mary, the mother of Jesus, is overshadowed by a "spirit," with no earthly father involved. Both children become "chosen ones," both are said to be gifts from God, and both are attached to massive spiritual movements that reshape the world. But if Noah's mother was artificially inseminated, and every detail in the text indicates that she was, then these other stories must be re-evaluated through the same lens. They are not miracles. They are programmed genetic interventions, designed to preserve and activate a very specific bloodline.

The Watchers did not just fall, they planted. They seeded a lineage. They elevated human biology, then destroyed what went wrong. But they preserved the one line that mattered. And that line survived the Flood.

Noah wasn't chosen because he was righteous.
He was chosen because he was built to survive.

They altered the human genome once, what's to stop them from doing it again? The Watchers may have been cast out, imprisoned, or removed from view, but there's nothing in the text that confirms they were destroyed. They left our skies... but did they ever truly leave? Or did they retreat behind dimensional veils, waiting? Every generation looks to the heavens for the return of something divine, but what if the so-called "second coming" isn't spiritual at all? What if the return of the Son of Man is the return of the bloodline, a reactivation of the Watchers' hybrid program? What if "Messiah" is not a theological event... but a biological one?

If they seeded us once, they can trigger the next phase at any time.
And when they return, they won't come with halos.
They'll come with data, DNA, and a new directive.

Appendix F
The Firebomb — The Prophecies

This is not metaphor. This is not allegory. This is prophecy written for a generation that would need it, not to hope, but to witness. In Enoch's words, the ancient term "ḥamas" appears plainly. The same Hebrew word used today to name a modern organization of terror, war, and violence was already recorded in the earliest prophecy of judgment. It does not refer to abstract sin. It refers to the builders of destruction, those who structure their world upon violence itself.

In 1 Enoch 94:6, the judgment is clear: "*Woe to them, the builders of violence (hamas) and wickedness, who set deception as their foundation. For suddenly they shall be cut off, and there is no peace for them.*" This is not the language of consequence; it is the language of annihilation. Those who build on violence will not fall gradually. They will be cut off suddenly, and there will be no peace, not in life and not in death.

But the prophecy does not stop with destruction. In 94:9, it names both the action and the outcome: "*And you commit destruction (niklah) and violence (hamas). Therefore, you have consecrated yourselves for the day of bloodshed, the day of darkness, and the day of great judgment.*" To consecrate something is to make it sacred. These men are not accidentally violent. They have made destruction holy. They are devoted to bloodshed and prepared for darkness.

Then Enoch delivers a line so dangerous that even the most devout theologians avoid it: "*For your creator will destroy you.*" (94:10). Not God. Not angels. Not nations. Their creator. This is not a spiritual judgment, it is a betrayal. Whoever gave rise to them, trained them, armed them, funded them, or birthed them, whether earthly or celestial, will be the one to end them. The destruction will not come from the outside. It will come from the hand that formed them.

In 1 Enoch 96:7, the message continues: "*Woe to you, sinners, who persecute the righteous, for you will be repaid. And you men of violence (hamas), you will continue to pursue, but darkness will fall upon you.*" There is no redemption here. There is only the certainty that their pursuit will end, not in victory, but in shadow. In silence. In absolute removal from the realm of the living.

Appendix F: The Firebomb

And finally, in 92:19, the verdict is sealed: "*For all who walk in the ways of violence (hamas) shall be cut off forever.*" Not punished. Not chastised. Cut off. And not for a time, but forever. No restoration. No second chance. The path of ḥamas leads to final and total severance.

There is no doubt. The violence we see in our time was already named in Enoch's. The word is the same. The outcome is the same. But what the world does not yet see is that their destruction will come from their own creator. Whether it is Iran, the Muslim Brotherhood, the ancient Watchers themselves, or the unseen forces who birthed them into being, this prophecy says clearly: their undoing has already been written.

And if they were created once, they can be created again. If they fall, another may rise. But the seed of violence carries the code of its own extinction. They were not consecrated for life. They were consecrated for blood.

This is the prophecy the world is not ready for.
But now, it can never be taken back.

Many of the prophecies in Enoch have already been fulfilled. But some are still active, burning beneath the surface of the present, and others have yet to arrive. In 1 Enoch 80:2–3, the timeline fractures: "*In the days of the sinners, the years will be shortened... the rain will not fall, and the heavens will be stopped.*" Time collapses. Nature breaks. Crops fail. Rain doesn't come. These are not metaphors; they are ecological warnings written in the language of judgment.

Then, in the very same passage, the prophecy expands: "*All existence that is upon the earth will be altered.*" (80:2). Not just famine, but transformation. This sounds like DNA modification, bioengineering, species distortion, what modern science would call extinction-level interference. Creation itself is being rewritten. The planet is no longer natural.

The judgment is not only upon Earth. In 1 Enoch 91:15, tied to the 10th and final week of the vision, Enoch writes, "*There shall be an eternal judgment upon the great Watchers... and upon the heavens forever.*" This has not happened. It is still coming. The ones who seeded corruption have not yet been erased. But their judgment is already inscribed.

In 91:11, we are told that *"the roots of violence (hamas) shall be uprooted... and the blasphemers shall die by the sword."* This is the final strike against the systems of bloodshed. Not just the men, but the roots, the entire structure of their existence, will be pulled from under heaven. Their end is coming fast.

In 1 Enoch 51:4, the earth itself rises in protest: *"The deserts shall burn like a furnace... and the abyss shall be torn open."* This is more than metaphor, it is geological. Something beneath the surface will erupt. Whether tectonic, volcanic, or dimensional, the prophecy is clear: the abyss will not stay sealed.

Yet even in this fire, there is a seed of survival. In 1 Enoch 107:1, we are told: *"A generation of righteousness will arise, and wickedness will be destroyed."* That generation has not yet fully come. But the shaking indicates it is already being born.

And finally, in Chapter 93, Enoch describes the unfolding of human history as a series of "weeks." Each week is a generation of transformation, of ascent or collapse. In these visions, he describes a future "generation of upheavals," and a time when "sin shall no longer be remembered for eternity." Based on the conditions now, we are somewhere between the seventh and tenth week. Multiple global events are still waiting. They will not be stopped.

These are not vague dreams. These are coordinates.
And the map is unfolding beneath our feet.

In the scroll of prophecy, Enoch saw not only the fall of kings and the destruction of the violent, but also the unraveling of motherhood itself. In 1 Enoch 99:5, the vision is merciless and precise: *"In that [time], those who give birth shall cast out and suffer greatly, and they shall abandon [the infant] child. And those who are pregnant [shall miscarry], and those who nurse [shall cast away their children], and they shall not [turn back] to their infants, nor upon those who nurse, nor shall they have pity..."* This is not war. This is not famine. This is a spiritual collapse so deep that it severs the most sacred human instinct: the bond between mother and child. It is already happening. We see it now in border zones, in hospitals, in modern wildernesses where human life is traded like cargo. And Enoch told us, plainly, that they would not turn back.

Appendix F: The Firebomb

The Final Warning

Enoch did not write these things for scholars. He did not speak for theologians or priests. He wrote for the last generation. The one that would live to see the blood on the ground and know that it had been written already. The one that would look into the skies and remember that the heavens had been warned. These are not ancient hopes. These are living prophecies. Some have begun. Some are still waiting. But every one of them was carved into stone for the moment the world forgot who made it.

There is no more mystery. There is only witness. The pillars will fall. The roots of violence will be torn out. The false kings will eat their own children. The mothers will not look back. The skies will go dark, and the order of the stars will shift. The abyss will boil, and the righteous will rise. This is not the end of the world. It is the end of the illusion.

Enoch's words were not sealed.
And now, neither are yours.

Appendix G
The Names of God in the Book of Enoch
Index

ELOHIM 84:2, 84:5
ADONAI 65:6
EL 72:2, 82:13, 82:17, 82:18
GOD 9:4, 10:1, 16:3, 18:8, 20:7, 25:3, 26:5, 27:7, 84:3, 91:13, 99:3, 103:13
MOST HIGH 10:2, 10:9, 10:11, 12:3, 13:10, 48:7, 60:1, 61:7, 77:1, 94:8, 95:7, 99:3, 99:10, 100:4, 103:1, 103:6, 103:8
HOLY ONE 1:3, 10:1, 25:3, 84:1, 105:11, 108:6
GREAT ONE 1:3, 1:4, 13:2, 14:5, 84:1, 93:2, 97:4, 103:1

RARE & COMPOUND DIVINE NAMES
YHWH 89:26
Kyriō 9:4
Holy One of Glory 25:3
Great Holy One 108:6
The Exalted, the Great, and the Holy One 10:1
Lord of Lords, King of Kings, God of Gods 9:4, 84:3
Light of God 10:1

Epilogue

There were nights I stared into the void of translations, of these ancient scrolls and felt them staring back—alive, waiting, relentless. This was never just a project. It was a reckoning. Enoch didn't whisper. He roared. He tore through centuries of silence and said, Write me the way I wrote it and meant for it to be written. And I fought the translation and interpolation nightmares of centuries.

There were days I wanted to quit. Days the weight of it bent me at the soul. Translating these words wasn't just language, it was memory. It was blood. It was betrayal. And still, Enoch's voice echoed through it all, fierce, raw, urgent. This is his testimony, but it became mine too. And if you felt it, if it gripped you like it gripped me, then you are part of this now. This scroll chose you, too.

This was never meant to be safe. Not for me. Not for you. It was never meant to be clean, or pretty, or polite. It was meant to burn. To leave a mark. And if you're holding this book in your hands, if you've reached this page, then you've already felt the heat. That is no accident. That is recognition.

I didn't write this for religion. I wrote it for the ones who know there's more. For the ones who see through the veils, who remember things they've never been taught. For the ones who carry truth in their marrow and prophecy in their breath. For the ones who are done waiting for permission to awaken.

This is the first of The Forgotten Scrolls. There is more to come. I don't need to tell you what it is. You'll feel it when it calls to you. Some scrolls are found in caves. Others are found in fire. And fire always returns.

To those who made it this far, thank you. You are the ones this was written for. You are the reason it survived. You are the reason Enoch still speaks. May your hands stay steady. May your sight stay sharp. May your spirit never kneel to the architects of forgetting.

I send this book into the world with fire and blessing. May the liars tremble. May the seekers rise. May your lineage remember you as the one who dared to remember what others were told to forget.

Rev. Mother Mary Kateryn, H.P., D.D.